AFRICA
after
APARTHEID

South Africa, Race, and Nation in Tanzania

RICHARD A. SCHROEDER

INDIANA UNIVERSITY PRESS
Bloomington and Indianapolis

This book is a publication of

Indiana University Press
601 North Morton Street
Bloomington, Indiana 47404-3797 USA

iupress.indiana.edu

Telephone orders   800-842-6796
Fax orders   812-855-7931

Manufactured in the United States of America

Library of Congress Cataloging-in-Publication Data

Schroeder, Richard A.
    Africa after apartheid : South Africa, race, and nation in Tanzania / Richard A. Schroeder.
    p. cm.
    Includes bibliographical references and index.
    ISBN 978-0-253-00599-1 (cloth : alk. paper) — ISBN 978-0-253-00600-4 (pbk. : alk. paper) — ISBN 978-0-253-00850-3 (e-book) 1. South Africans—Tanzania. 2. Whites—Tanzania. 3. Tanzania—Race relations. 4. Tanzania—Social conditions. I. Title.
    DT443.3.S77S36 2012
    305.8968—dc23
                                                        2012008657

1 2 3 4 5   17 16 15 14 13 12

Dedicated to the memory of
Toby Schroeder
(2001–2005)

Contents

Preface

During my first trip to northern Tanzania in December 1995, my wife and I were invited to a dinner party at the home of some friends. The day of the party was crystal clear, the majestic peaks of Mount Meru and Mount Kilimanjaro emerging from the clouds to provide a spectacular backdrop. We arrived early and sat outside in a small circle of chairs, drinking beer and enjoying the pleasant weather. Meal preparations went on around us, and several neighbors dropped by to exchange greetings. Most of the guests were, like us, white expatriates, but they included at least one mixed European/Tanzanian couple. It was a lazy, laid-back affair.

After an hour or so, a white South African who worked for a safari company based in the nearby city of Arusha dropped in uninvited and joined us for a drink. The subject of the ensuing conversation escapes me now, but I do remember how this man repeatedly and unselfconsciously used the racial slur "kaffir" in reference to Tanzanians.[1] While this term was widely used in South Africa to refer to blacks during the apartheid years, I was shocked to hear it used in Arusha. This was not because this particular *individual* used it—he fit my stereotype of a racist South African white, so his use of racial slurs was somehow to be expected—but because he seemed to feel so comfortable using it in *Tanzania*, a country that was one of the staunchest opponents to apartheid. The implication was that in polite, white expatriate gatherings in northern Tanzania, calling locals "kaffirs" was an acceptable form of speech.

Since I was new to the area, I wondered how widespread this practice was. Was I correct in thinking that it was out of place in Tanzania? Were others at the party similarly offended by this man? What would Tanzanians make of this situation? I was aware that this safari operator was one of thousands of white South Africans who relocated to Tanzania and other parts of the continent in pursuit of new business opportunities after the democratic elections that brought Nelson Mandela to power in Pretoria in 1994, but I was unclear whether his behavior was an exception or the rule. The historic post-apartheid encounter between South Africans and the rest of the continent certainly bore watching.

As it turns out, I may have gotten my story about the dinner party wrong: my wife also vividly recalls the conversation I described above, but she places it at the home of another couple entirely; I may have conflated the memories of two different parties in my reconstruction of the event. This disparity might not be worth mentioning, except that it led me, years later, to ask both couples if they could identify the South African in question. While none of the four hosts specifically remembered the conversation that day, each couple readily named an individual who they thought might have been responsible for the racist comments. This was striking in its own right. Another long-time resident of northern Tanzania reinforced the notion that South Africans had brought about a change in social mores in Tanzania when I showed her a draft of this preface during a brief visit to Arusha in 2011. After reading the first few paragraphs, she turned to me and said, "This is not about my house, is it?" When I assured her that it was not, she continued, "Because it could be. We all know someone like that. The only question, I suppose, is whether we are all talking about the same person." Clearly the dinner party guest's behavior in 1995 was not an isolated event. The social landscape in northern Tanzania had undergone a troubling transformation.

A second footnote to this story was added in an exchange I had with one of my students. I frequently use the dinner party anecdote to explain how I got involved in the research that led to this book. After repeating the boorish dinner guest's comments, I describe how I exchanged looks of incredulity with my wife and then, on impulse, made myself as unobtrusive as possible to better observe the ensuing social interactions. My academic colleagues recognize this well-worn tactic of participant observation. One of my undergraduate research assistants, however, responded in a very different way. Engrossed in my story, she impatiently asked, "So what did you *do*?" When I answered that instead of challenging the speaker or walking out on him I watched and listened to see what I could learn, I could tell that my student thought this was not a satisfactory reply, so I tried to explain myself further.

I pointed out that ethnography often requires a careful negotiation between the desire to directly confront objectionable behavior and the need to maintain a sometimes uncomfortable silence in order to effectively observe, record, and ultimately understand it.[2] I explained how, as the project took shape and I gained the confidence of research subjects, I often found myself in positions where I observed insensitive behavior or overheard offensive speech. As an example, I told her how I once saw a South African gemstone dealer pull out a taser gun and playfully threaten a Tanzanian subordinate with it (see chapter 5), and suggested that I would never have been in a position to witness this insensitive display if I had been more confrontational in my approach to South African research subjects from the beginning.

I was nonetheless forced to acknowledge that my failure to directly confront the rude dinner guest left me at least somewhat complicit in his behavior (cf. Sanders 2002). The issue of complicity is one that my South African research subjects understood all too well: in the eyes of the world, the enactment of apartheid attached a powerful stigma to South African national identity. Nelson Mandela himself invoked this fact in his inaugural speech when he noted that South Africa under apartheid had become "the skunk of the world" (Mandela 1994). In one way or another, all of the South Africans who settled in Tanzania after 1994 were forced to contend with this national stereotype as both they and the rest of the continent struggled to parse the meaning of apartheid for subsequent generations.

Africa after Apartheid

As a research problem, the notion of studying "Africa after apartheid" implies the use of a particular sort of cognitive map. The goal of tracing apartheid's legacy in "Africa" begins with the premise of South African exceptionalism. Drawing on popular imaginaries that circulate widely in South Africa, it constructs a boundary between South Africa and the rest of the region, locating "Africa" somewhere beyond South Africa's national borders. Historically, this way of seeing, and being, on the continent directly informed the apartheid government's creation of fictive "homelands" to house its unwanted "African" populations (Butler et al. 1977). It is also discernible in the recurrent notion that South Africa is a "first world" island surrounded by a sea of black African poverty. This idea featured prominently in the rationale former South African president Thabo Mbeki used to promote his regional economic development plan known as the "New Economic Partnership for African Development" or NEPAD (see chapter 2). The implicit recognition of a dividing line between South Africa and the rest of Africa also underpins the notion of difference that has so tragically inspired recent outbursts of "negrophobic" violence directed at foreign (that is, "African") migrant workers in South Africa (Gqola 2008; see chapter 1).

My own purpose in drawing out the distinction between South Africa and "Africa" in this book is straightforward: I am interested in focusing attention on a neglected aspect of the post-apartheid story, namely the way the post-apartheid transition has played out in the rest of the region. I accordingly mark this difference with my own set of references to South African firms moving "onto the continent" or investing "in Africa." The point is to underscore the historic significance of the encounter. It is, after all, primarily white South Africans who are now effectively colonizing areas they were never even allowed to visit a scant two decades ago, showing up like so many uninvited dinner party guests in diverse national settings stretching from Mozambique to Nigeria and beyond. This group inevitably carries the baggage of apartheid wherever they go. Anecdotes like the one I shared above have led locals in countries that are hosting new arrivals to conclude that apartheid-like social relations are being reproduced in their midst. The process of "ending" apartheid, including the painful work of repairing damaged race relations, has thus been displaced in time and space to other parts of the region. The outcome of this process in the incipient white enclaves popping up across the continent remains as uncertain as it is within South Africa itself.

Acknowledgments

The core of the research presented here was carried out during a year-long intensive ethnographic study from July 2005 to June 2006. I also made shorter trips to Tanzania in 1995, 2000, 2004, 2007, and 2011. The benefit of following a particular story line for a decade and a half is that one can track the narrative as it develops and can definitively assess whether its significance has withstood the test of time, as this story has. The downside, if one can call it that, is that one ends up with a lot of people to thank.

To begin with, I would like to acknowledge generous research funding received from the Fulbright Faculty Research Abroad Program, the Rutgers University Research Council, the Rutgers School of Arts and Sciences dean's office, and the Rutgers Department of Geography. I am also grateful to the Tanzanian Commission on Science and Technology for providing research clearance. Professor George Jambiya of the University of Dar es Salaam has served as my official Tanzanian research contact since the beginning of the project. George has always shown a keen interest in my work and has gone out of his way on more than one occasion to offer advice and administrative support, for which I am very grateful.

Several short sections of the book have been published previously. Sections of chapters 1, 2, 3, and the conclusion first appeared in modified form in "South African Capital in the Land of *Ujamaa*: Contested Terrain in Tanzania," AfricaFiles *At Issue Ezine* 8, no. 5 (May/June 2008); that e-article was then published as "South African Capital in the Land of *Ujamaa*: Contested Terrain in Tanzania," *African Sociological Review* 12, no. 1: 20–34. Portions of chapter 4 first appeared in: "Tanzanite as Conflict Gem: Certifying a Secure Commodity Chain in Tanzania," *Geoforum* 41, no. 1: 56–65. I would like to thank the editors and publishers of these publications for granting permission to incorporate revised versions in this book.

Tanzania has an extraordinarily talented group of political cartoonists, and they have had a field day in covering the rapid growth of South African investment in Tanzania. Two of these cartoons appear in the book, one drawn by Samuel Mwamkinga (Sammi Jo'une) and the other by King Kinya. Both cartoons first appeared in the Tanzanian daily newspaper, *The Citizen* (see the editions published on 16 February 2006, and 1 April 2006), and are reprinted here with the permission of the original artists and Mwananchi Communications, publishers of *The Citizen, Mwananchi* and *Mwanaspoti* newspapers in Tanzania. Mwananchi Communications also graciously provided permission to reprint a photograph from its 11 May 2006 edition. Finally, I would like to thank Angelo D'Silva, who generously shared key documents pertaining to his father Manuel D'Silva's original discovery of tanzanite, the iconic gemstone featured in chapter 4.

Portions of the book have been presented at meetings of the African Studies Association, the Association of American Geographers, and the New York Area Africanist Historians working group. At Rutgers, I have discussed my findings at events sponsored by the Department of Geography, the Center for African Studies, the Center for Race and Ethnicity, the Institute for Research on Women and the Post-colonial Studies Group. I have also given guest lectures or participated in workshops devoted in part to my work at the University of Dar es Salaam, Florida International University, Kansas University, the University of Kentucky, the University of Maine-Farmington, the University of North Carolina, Penn State University, Temple University, Virginia Tech University, West Virginia University, and Yale University. I am grateful to my hosts and the audiences at all of these institutions for their willingness to engage with the ideas and empirical concerns reflected in this project.

I have benefited enormously from countless discussions with friends and colleagues engaged in different aspects of this research. Among the Tanzanianists who shared their thoughts and insights are Kelly Askew, Paul Bjerk, Ian Bryceson, Ben Gardner, Rebecca Ghanadan, Bruce Heilman, Dorothy Hodgson, Jim Igoe, Joe Lugalla, Greg Maddox, Lawrence Mbogoni, Sheryl McCurdy, Garth Myers, Roderick Neumann, Stefano Ponte, Lisa Anne Richey, Tom Spear, Philip Stigger, Aili Tripp, Martin Walsh, and Brad Weiss. Rod Neumann in particular has been steadfast in his friendship and intellectual engagement since our years together in graduate school at Berkeley. Both he and my wife, Dorothy Hodgson, read earlier versions of the manuscript and offered valuable advice and timely encouragement. Other Africanist colleagues who share my interest in the theory and politics of South Africa's economic expansion in Africa and the implications of this development for race relations in the broader regional context include Padraig Carmody, Judy Carney, Clifton Crais, John Daniel, Belinda Dodson, James Ferguson, Amanda Hammar, Gillian Hart, Kimberly DaCosta Holton, Janet McIntosh, Darlene Miller, Martin Murray, Olajide Oloyode, Anne Pitcher, P. S. Polanah, Richard Saunders, Pamela Scully, Brett Shadle, and Roger Southall. Darlene Miller was especially helpful in connecting me to other scholars studying "South Africa in Africa."

I have been privileged to work with Dee Mortensen at Indiana University Press, whose editorial guidance has been unfailingly insightful from the very beginning. Ann Youmans applied expert copy-editing skills to the manuscript, and Angela Burton, Peter Froehlich, Sarah Jacobi, and June Silay were helpful in sorting out various technical issues related to publication. Gill Hart and a second anonymous reviewer for IUP were painstaking in their reviews of my manuscript, offering both detailed comments and supportive general advice on how to move this project forward. I could not have asked for a more conscientious or constructive engagement with reviewers.

Over the life of this project, I have worked with a number of research assistants, each seemingly more dedicated and talented than the last: Marion Clement, Edith Hannigan, Shuhan Hu, Tayo Jolaosho, Latoya Jones, Kyle Loewen, Nimu Njoya, and Preethi Ramaprasad. I owe thanks, too, to Jackson Njau and Hemed Almasi for their translation skills. Mike Siegel from the Rutgers Geography Department Cartography Lab displayed his usual care and precision in the production of two historical maps for chapter 1. Michelle Martel provided key technical and graphic design assistance, and Theresa Kirby and Betty Ann Abbatemarco provided administrative and logistical support.

I have been very fortunate over nearly twenty years now to work in the company of an extraordinary group of scholars and friends at Rutgers University. In the Department of Geography, Trevor Birkenholtz, Robin Leichenko, Tania Lopez, Ken Mitchell, Joanna Regulska, Asa Rennermalm, Dave Robinson, Laura Schneider, and Kevin St. Martin have been great colleagues. Kevin in particular has buoyed my spirits on an almost daily basis with his sense of humor, his warmth, and his generosity. At the Rutgers Center for African Studies, Akin Akinlabi, Ousseina Alidou, Carolyn Brown, Abena Busia, Gabriela Carolini, Barbara Cooper, Renee Delancey, Jack Harris, Angelique Haugerude, Dorothy Hodgson, Al Howard, David Hughes, Walton Johnson, Renee Larrier, Barbara Lewis, Julie Livingston, Susan Martin-Marquez, Alamin Mazrui, Edward Ramsamy, Richard Serrano, Jim Simon, Genese Sodikoff, and Meredeth Turshen have provided consistent and vital intellectual engagement over the course of countless collaborative projects since we established CAS back in 1999. In this group, I owe a special intellectual debt to David Hughes, whose work on whiteness in Zimbabwe provided a critical basis of comparison for my own study, and who collaborated with me in organizing a conference at Rutgers in 2008 on the theme: "The Future of White Africa: Reproducing Privilege on a Changing Social Landscape." Other Rutgers faculty members who have been especially supportive friends and colleagues include Daniel Goldstein, Laura Ahearn, Keith Wailoo, and Lisa Miller. Finally, I have had the pleasure of working with a very talented group of graduate students, including Lincoln Addison, Margo Andrews, Za Barron, Lindsay Campbell, Stella Capoccia, Luke Drake, Amelia Duffy-Tumasz, Nate Gabriel, Saemi Ledermann, Jessica Kelly, Raysa Martinez-Kruger, Ben Neimark, Rich Nisa, Jack Norton, Eric Sarmiento, Debby Scott, Abidah Setyowati, Sean Tanner, Kim Thomas, and Bradley Wilson.

A number of other close, if occasionally far-flung, friends have provided crucial support along the way, including Louise Fortmann, Gail Hollander, Cindi Katz, Paul Lopes, Katharyne Mitchell, Scott and Deb Sussman, and Michael Watts. Finally, my extended family, including Tim and Jan Schroeder, Laurie and Kirk Velett, and Tom Schroeder and Jenny Kelley, have kept me grounded with their unwavering love and care.

In Tanzania, I owe special thanks to Tinus Aucamp and Lesley de Kock, who introduced me to several prominent members of the South African community. Jo Driessen, Judith Jackson, Alais Morindat, and Leo Fortes were vitally important in helping me get situated in Arusha. Marjorie and Simon Mbilinyi, Chris Maina Peter, George Jambiya, Diane Carvalho, and Sheryl McCurdy did the same for me in Dar es Salaam. Robin and Thad Peterson, Dave and Trude Peterson, Mike and Lisa Peterson, Paul and Fini Strebel, Rod and Barbara Stutzman, Trish McCauley and Kees Terhel, and Pat Patten all welcomed us with open arms when we moved to Arusha in 2005. They also held my family close when we needed it most. For that, I owe them a debt of gratitude that I will certainly never be able to repay.

My wife, Dorothy, is an anthropologist who has worked in Tanzanian Maasailand as a development worker and researcher since the early 1980s. When we were first married, we faced a dilemma. My prior research and professional experience, including three and a half years in The Gambia and two years in Sierra Leone, had all been in West Africa, whereas her work was based almost exclusively in Tanzania. If we were going to be able to be together during research stints, one of us was going to have to cross the continent and begin a new project. When I eventually opted to begin working in Tanzania, this meant starting all over again: learning to speak Kiswahili, immersing myself in Tanzania's historical and ethnographic records, establishing a network of personal and professional contacts. Fortunately, Do was with me every step of the way. Not only was she a model of scholarly excellence—having the opportunity to watch her carry out her own research projects in and around Arusha was a privilege unto itself—but she was a trusted confidante and best friend, offering critical support and encouragement. For all of that and much more, my love and my thanks.

Our oldest son, Luke, basically grew up over the course of this project, and he seemed as happy as I was when I completed the first draft of the manuscript several months ago. He has matured into an extraordinarily smart, talented, funny, and sensitive young man, and Do and I are immensely proud of him.

Our youngest son, Toby, traveled with us to Tanzania when we moved there for a year of research in 2005. To the extent that a four-year-old can have a dream and imagine the experience of a lifetime, going to Africa was it for Toby. He flung himself into that adventure in much the same way as he used to fling himself into our waiting arms for one of his famous "Toby hugs": with fierce love, joy, and total abandon. It still seems incredible to say it, but we lost our beautiful, sweet Toby to pneumonia during that trip. It is hard not to be centered on him as this project comes to its conclusion. This book is dedicated to his memory.

HIGHLAND PARK, NEW JERSEY, 12 DECEMBER 2011

Acronyms

ABSA	Amalgamated Banks of South Africa
ACOA	American Committee on Africa
AFGEM	African Gemstones Ltd.
AIDS	acquired immunodeficiency syndrome
ANC	African National Congress
ASM	Artisanal and Small-scale Mining
ATCL	Air Tanzania Corporation Ltd
BBC	British Broadcasting Corporation
BEE	Black Economic Empowerment
BoT	Bank of Tanzania
CCA	ConsCorps Africa
CCM	Chama Cha Mapinduzi (Party of the Revolution; Tanzania's ruling party)
CEO	Chief Executive Officer
COMESA	Common Market for Eastern and Southern Africa
COSTECH	Commission on Science and Technology
DRC	Democratic Republic of Congo
EAB	East African Breweries
EAC	East African Community
FDI	Foreign Direct Investment
Frelimo	*Frente de Libertação de Moçambique* (Mozambican Liberation Front)
FLS	Frontline States
GDP	gross domestic product
HIPC	heavily indebted poor countries
HIV	human immunodeficiency virus
HSRC	Human Sciences Research Council
IMF	International Monetary Fund
JKT	Jeshi la Kujenga Taifa (National Service Corps)
LC	Liberation Committee
MDG	Millennium Development Goals
MPLA	Movimento Popular de Libertação de Angola (Popular Liberation Movement of Angola)
NBC	National Bank of Commerce
NEDLAC	National Economic Development and Labour Council

NEPAD	New Economic Partnership for African Development
NGO	nongovernmental organization
NIMR	National Institute for Medical Research
NMB	National Microfinance Bank
OAU	Organization of African Unity
PAC	Pan Africanist Congress of Azania
PRC	Parastatal Reform Commission
PSRC	Parastatal Sector Reform Commission
RENAMO	Resistência Nacional Moçambicana (Mozambican National Resistance)
RTD	Radio Tanzania Dar es Salaam
SA	South Africa
SAA	South African Airways
SAB	South African Breweries
SABF	South African Business Forum
SADC	Southern African Development Community
SADET	South African Democracy Education Trust
SAHC	South African High Commission
SARPN	Southern African Regional Poverty Network
SMS	Short Message Service (cellular telephone texting)
SOMAFCO	Solomon Mahlangu Freedom College
STAMICO	State Mining Corporation (Tanzania)
SWAPO	Southwest African People's Organization
TANESCO	Tanzania Electric Supply Company
TANU	Tanganyika/Tanzania African National Union
TAZAMA	Tanzania Zambia Mafuta (oil pipeline)
TAZARA	Tanzania Zambia Railway Authority
TBL	Tanzania Breweries Ltd
TGI	Tanzania Gemstone Industries
TIC	Tanzania Investment Centre
TRA	Tanzania Revenue Authority
TRC	Tanzania Railways Corporation
UDI	Universal Declaration of Independence
UN	United Nations
UNCTAD	United Nations Conference on Trade and Development
URT	United Republic of Tanzania
ZANLA	Zimbabwe African National Liberation Army
ZANU	Zimbabwe African National Union
ZAPU	Zimbabwe African People's Union
ZIPRA	Zimbabwe People's Revolutionary Army

AFRICA
after
APARTHEID

Introduction

The rise and fall of South Africa's system of racial oppression known as apartheid marked one of the most infamous chapters in modern world history. The effects of apartheid on the 40 million South Africans who witnessed the inauguration of Nelson Mandela as their country's first democratically elected president in 1994 are indelible. Indeed, they continue to profoundly shape social interactions in that country nearly two decades later. The violence enacted by the hated apartheid regime and the long battle for emancipation by the South African majority also had a significant impact in other countries. The struggle to end apartheid riveted the world's attention and was closely monitored by millions who supported the anti-apartheid movement, arguably the world's first truly global political action campaign (Thörn 2006, 2009).

While both the ongoing national struggle for racial reconciliation in South Africa and the inspirational example of the transnational anti-apartheid movement have been extensively discussed and debated in the popular and scholarly literature devoted to apartheid and its aftermath, the rest of the African continent has been relatively neglected in the telling of this history. This is a significant gap. From the perspective of observers situated elsewhere in Africa, it is clear that the phenomenon that was apartheid was never confined to South Africa's borders. To the contrary, its influence was, and is, felt across the region. Historically, the apartheid economic system relied heavily on access to surplus labor from perhaps a dozen countries in southern Africa. Apartheid South Africa's national security and defense forces were directly involved in attempts to undermine liberation struggles in Mozambique, Angola, Zimbabwe, and Namibia. This, in turn, led to the formation of strategic alliances among the newly independent African governments geared toward ending colonial rule and white domination everywhere in Africa.

Similarly, important elements of the post-apartheid transition—the dismantling of racially skewed social systems, the launching of efforts to reconcile historical animosities, the rebuilding of political and economic relationships—have also had far-reaching consequences for Africans living beyond South Africa's national borders. The end of the economic boycott against South Africa by international anti-apartheid campaigners was an important turning point in this history. Under the boycott, the combination of bilateral trade restrictions, the withdrawal of public and private investment capital, and consumer actions to avoid purchasing South African goods and services had the dual effect of isolating South African capital and insulating the rest of the continent from direct competition with South African businesses.

When the boycott was suspended in the early 1990s, hundreds of South African firms set their sights on regional investment targets. While the threat of economic competition from powerful South African corporations generated anxiety in many receiving nations, the fact that most of these initiatives were led by white investors was perhaps even more disconcerting (Swarns 2002). This aggressive presence was not what most Africans expected from their first encounter with the "new" South Africa after apartheid.

This book analyzes the social, cultural, and political-economic dynamics that were set in motion after 1994 when thousands of white South African investors fanned out across the continent in search of new economic opportunities. Its focus is the East African nation of Tanzania, once one of Pretoria's staunchest political opponents, but it could just as easily have been written about Zambia, Mozambique, Zimbabwe, or any of a dozen other countries. During the period of the anti-apartheid struggle, Tanzania's first president, Julius Nyerere, played a key role in organizing the Frontline States alliance, a group of newly independent African countries located literally and figuratively at the forefront of the struggle to bring liberation to the southern African region. Following their president's lead, Tanzanians shouldered the burden of harboring political exiles and humanitarian refugees, providing military training and logistical support to guerrilla armies, and engaging in extensive diplomatic efforts to bring an end to colonial and white settler rule in South Africa, Mozambique, Angola, Rhodesia (Zimbabwe), and Southwest Africa (Namibia) (see chapter 1).

It thus came as a particularly ironic twist when Tanzania emerged as a preferred destination for South African capital seeking outlets in the region after 1994. By then, the Tanzanian government had abandoned the *"ujamaa"* socialist principles espoused by Nyerere in favor of a wide-ranging program of neoliberal economic reforms. Among other policy adjustments, the post-socialist government opened Tanzanian markets, privatized state-run firms, and removed regulatory barriers blocking direct foreign investment in the country. South Africans led the group of outside investors who took advantage of these favorable conditions by acquiring controlling interests in a number of Tanzania's most high profile parastatal corporations (see chapter 2).

This was a stunning change of circumstances as far as many Tanzanians were concerned. Not only was their economy suddenly saturated with South African capital and imported goods, but Tanzanian citizens who had long been active in the anti-apartheid struggle were now forced to engage their long-time enemies, the "Boers" (in Kiswahili, *makaburu*), face to face on Tanzanian soil. This new presence sparked controversy in nearly every major sector of the economy and ultimately surfaced as a wedge issue in a protracted national debate, pitting successive regimes of neoliberal economic reformers against die-hard Nyerere loyalists for whom the South African "invasion" was a bitterly painful affront to national dignity and sovereignty (see chapter 3).

The mining sector vividly illustrates the political fault lines that opened up in the debate surrounding South Africa's growing presence in Tanzania. Corporate involvement in gold, mineral, and gemstone mining has seen dramatic expansion over the past two decades, in part because of heavy South African investment in these industries. At the same time, the sale of rich assets to foreign firms has meant negating the preexisting claims of artisanal and small-scale miners who employ tens of thousands of Tanzanian workers. Moreover, most Tanzanians have seen little change in their relative standard of living, despite massive extraction of minerals from their national territory. To the great consternation of locals, Tanzanian nationals have also been repeatedly subjected to violence at the hands of corporate security guards in and around South African-controlled mining compounds (see chapter 4).

Objectionable actions by foreign investors such as these produced a spike in race consciousness in Tanzania. The white South Africans who chose to move there in the 1990s and 2000s represent a broad spectrum of social and political attitudes and practices. Many socially progressive South African whites living in Tanzania have, for example, spoken out to strongly condemn the racist actions of their peers. Whether they were once supporters or opponents of apartheid, however, their life experiences as South Africans were unavoidably shaped by their country's system of racial segregation and its systematic protection of white privilege. The post-apartheid transition was accordingly painful for apartheid apologists and critics alike (see chapter 5). Most saw the move to Tanzania as an opportunity for a fresh start, a chance to reengage "Africa" and Africans on new terms. This hopeful outlook notwithstanding, the encounters that ensued between South Africans and their Tanzanian hosts were often fraught with tension, inflamed by racial, class, and nationalistic animosities dating back to the years of the liberation struggle. The emergence of de facto all-white bars, clubs, and restaurants, which catered in part to a South African clientele, did nothing to dispel local fears. These and other troubling developments have led many Tanzanians to voice concerns about the future of race relations in their country (see chapter 6).

Memory and Forgetting

Tanzania's involvement in the anti-apartheid movement was once the source of tremendous national pride. Indeed, I argue below that widespread involvement in the liberation struggle was an integral component in the formation of Tanzanian national identity. By the early 1990s, however, neoliberal economic reforms had been in force for nearly a decade. The generational cohort that lived the history of the liberation struggles was aging, and the extent to which its influence would continue to be felt in Tanzania was unclear.

Two developments coincided to revive nationalistic fervor in Tanzania. The first event, ironically, was the death of Nyerere in 1999. The passing of the man known affectionately as *Mwalimu*, or "teacher," brought with it an outpouring of reminiscences selectively extolling the virtues of his government.[1] These reminders allowed civil society activists and other government critics to use his memory as a moral cudgel. The question, "What would Mwalimu think, say, or do in these circumstances?" was a common refrain.[2] Nyerere's memory was thus often invoked in attempts to instill discipline in the country's political leaders and curb the worst excesses of the neoliberal reform program. Coincidentally, the anniversary of Nyerere's death is recognized in the month of October, which is when national elections are held in Tanzania. This means that candidates for national office have been forced each year to campaign in the face of an outpouring of affectionate testimonials extolling the virtues of Nyerere's policies. Mwalimu's legacy still casts a long shadow (Chachage 2004; cf. Ulimwengu 2010).

The second development prompting a reawakening of old memories was the arrival of the South Africans, who served as a convenient foil for government opponents. According to these critics, foreign acquisition of national assets that might otherwise have been used to serve the general good in Tanzania represented a clear violation of the principles of economic independence that Nyerere espoused. The presumption that white South African investors were fleeing the consequences of their apartheid crimes and reproducing abhorrent social relations in Tanzania simply fanned the flames of xenophobia directed against the Boers.

Scholars have argued that social or collective memories are always partial and selective, as much constructed *representations* of the past as they are any sort of faithful rendering of fact or truth.[3] In this sense, memories of national triumphs and traumas are often deployed to serve specific political purposes and are for that reason hotly contested. As I explain in subsequent chapters, the process of neoliberal reform in Tanzania has entailed what Pitcher (2006), drawing on Cohen (1999), has called "organized forgetting" or "forgetting from above."[4] Pitcher, whose work features post-socialist Mozambique, defines "organized forgetting" as "a conscious process of dissociation from the past, engaged in for the purpose of constructing a new ideology, creating new institutions and organizing new networks to confront the present."[5] She argues that such erasures and distortions are commonly undertaken by neoliberalizing regimes in the interest of suppressing populist sentiments and communitarian values associated with earlier socialist nation-building projects (Pitcher and Askew 2006, 5–6). In the Tanzanian context, the invocation of Nyerere's memory and the rehearsal of the liberation struggle narrative in the press and popular discourse can be seen as a kind of "counter-memory" deployed to prevent the country's neoliberal government from draining the past of its contemporary political significance.[6] The countering of "forgetting from above" with "memory from below" thus represents an important objective for Tanzanian civil society activists who seek to hold on to the political values of the past.[7]

South Africa's Region

The significance of post-apartheid South Africa's economic presence "in Africa" is the subject of heated debate within South Africa and in the field of African studies more generally.[8] Nelson Mandela's successor, South African president Thabo Mbeki, sought to frame the relationship between the "new" South Africa and the rest of the region as part of a latter-day "African renaissance."[9] The form this initiative eventually took was a loose alliance known as the New Economic Partnership for African Development, or NEPAD. Ostensibly designed to spur the flourishing of regional development, NEPAD promised much needed investment to a capital-starved region. These investments would theoretically generate jobs, expertise, and local multiplier effects that would be felt from Cape to Cairo. The representation of NEPAD and the African renaissance as serving purely altruistic, or mutually beneficial, purposes has been challenged by critics, however. Among other arguments, they note that the ANC government has derived considerable political benefit from promoting these "partnerships" and that private South African firms and individuals have often profited handsomely in the process.[10]

For those who reject the official rationale for South Africa's expanded presence in Africa, like Issa Shivji, an internationally prominent Tanzanian scholar, legal expert, human rights activist, and social critic, the sweeping nature of South African investments constitutes nothing less than a "second wave of primitive accumulation," an attempt to extract the region's natural wealth on concessionary terms and redraw the boundary of the capitalist frontier.[11] Critics are divided on the question of whether the new wave of investments means that Pretoria is playing a proxy role, opening doors for international capital to enter spaces it has yet to fully exploit,[12] or is narrowly centered on achieving a dominant political position within the region.[13] In my view, these two positions are not as incompatible as partisans on either side of the debate suggest. Either way, in terms of the issues I address in this book, NEPAD provided "an ideological excuse for white business's return to its former colonial-era stomping grounds" (Miller, Oloyede, and Saunders 2008, 5).

The notion of South Africa as a hegemonic force in the region does, however, suggest the need to acknowledge the significance of South Africa's presence as a *national capital*. There are a number of ways to theorize this key concept. The term refers to a set of economic actors—investors, traders, industrialists—whose actions

serve both individual and national intentions, whose national origins are clearly
marked, and whose goods and services carry related associations and meanings
abroad. Shivji and others have argued that the actions of South African firms are not
parochial in this sense but are instead part of a larger pattern of imperialist expansion in Africa. While I do not dispute such claims, my interest in applying the idea
of a national capital in this instance derives from the fact that South Africa's recent
forays into the region have set in motion cultural and social dynamics that are not
reducible to economic explanation. The attitudes and actions, beliefs and behaviors,
cultural traits and social practices of South African investors have, in and of themselves, generated meanings and influenced material outcomes across the region (see
Miller, Oloyede, and Saunders 2008). Thus, even when a particular intervention is
consistent with broader structural economic logic, capital often shows up, as it were,
with a particular face (Mitchell 2004). Over the past two decades in Africa, that face
has, as often as not, been that of a white South African.[14]

The empirical case of Tanzania vividly demonstrates this point. Situated on the
northern edge of southern Africa, Tanzania has historically escaped the full brunt of
South Africa's political and economic influence. Since 1994, however, the continent
has taken a dramatic tilt to the south. Tanzania has accordingly experienced a surge
in foreign direct investment, a rapid influx of retail and commercial imports, and a
flood of mostly white neo-settlers from South Africa. In addition, South Africa has
emerged as an all-purpose model of a developed society that the Tanzanian government has repeatedly invoked. South Africa has been held up as an example of how
to run national elections, expand agricultural productivity, promote entrepreneur-
ialism, and manage valuable mineral resources. Its expertise has been solicited in
the fields of wildlife management, medicine, and crime prevention, and its cultural
influence is increasingly felt through television programming, magazines, movies,
music, and sports. Tanzanians have been sent to South Africa in increasing numbers
for educational purposes or to upgrade skills in areas as diverse as trade unionism,
tourism marketing, and athletics. Thus, the very *idea* of South Africa has come to influence the way Tanzanians lead their lives in ways that would have been unthinkable
a scant two decades ago at the height of the anti-apartheid struggle.[15]

African Whiteness

The inescapable fact that nearly all of the South African investors in Tanzania
are white connects this case study to a broader theoretical discussion taking place
within the field of "whiteness" studies. Several million people claim white African
identities. By far the largest group is found in South Africa, where many whites can
point to hundreds of years of personal family history on the continent.[16] In this sense,

South African whites' "African-ness" is hard to dispute. At the same time, under apartheid, whites did not live their lives as "Africans"; they lived them as whites or Europeans, and they enjoyed a host of related perquisites and privileges. "Africans," by contrast, were natives, Bantus, "kaffirs," people without rights or privileges who belonged elsewhere, people who were hardly people at all. While whites shared none of these aspects of the "African" experience, they nonetheless selectively assert a distinctive sense of belonging to, and in, Africa.[17] Indeed, this sense of being African is what led many of the new South African residents in Tanzania to move there in the first place rather than relocate to Europe, North America, or Australia/New Zealand.

The "whiteness" of white South Africans is seemingly more straightforward than their "African-ness" per se, but here, too, there are important nuances that need to be recognized. The field of whiteness studies emphasizes the fact that whiteness is frequently unmarked among those who self-identify as white. For whites, "race" is typically understood to apply only to peoples of color, the racialized "others," and not to themselves. Thus, one of the field's central projects has been to enhance the "visibility" of "racial privilege, the assumptions, the taken-for-grantedness, the identities and 'raced' subjectivities" of whites (Steyn and Conway 2010, 285). In apartheid South Africa, however, the problem of "invisible" whiteness was arguably not as pronounced as elsewhere (Steyn 2007, 421–22). Indeed, it might be argued that white South Africans under apartheid were *hyper*-visible, the *whitest* of whites. This has nothing to do with skin color, obviously; nor am I referring to blood purity—these biophysical attributes do not equate to racial identity in any useful sense. Instead, the idea that South African whites were the "whitest of whites" derives from the fact that South African whiteness was so clearly marked *as such*. This was true in a legal sense, in terms of the privileges enshrined in apartheid laws; in a social sense, in terms of the stark spatial divides that shaped interactions between whites and South Africa's other racialized groups (blacks, coloureds, Asians); and in a moral sense in terms of the stigma and shame that were eventually attached to white South African identity due to the presumption of guilt by association with apartheid.[18] Notably, the spread of *these* whites with their problematic historical baggage has given pause to Africans and white expatriate groups elsewhere in the region, and race consciousness has been heightened as a result.

In this regard, contemporary African contexts represent important sites for the study of whiteness, and there is a growing body of scholarship devoted to this topic.[19] The field has emphasized a series of recent crises that have occurred within white communities and their significance in causing a re-racialization of whiteness in different contexts (Steyn 2004, 150). The end of apartheid in 1994 was one such moment; the Mugabe government's violent eviction of hundreds of white farm families from land they had occupied for generations in Zimbabwe in the early 2000s was another; a third was the public trial of a white settler twice accused and finally convicted of shooting unarmed black trespassers on his family's Kenyan estate. Not since the end of the colonial period have white groups experienced such dramatic upheavals or been forced to confront such painful questions about their own unstable position within Africa's rapidly changing social landscapes.[20]

In Tanzania, the arrival of white South Africans (and to a lesser extent Zimbabweans, Namibians, and other white "southerners") has constituted a whiteness crisis in its own right. Unlike many other parts of the region, Tanzania (known as Tanganyika at the time) was never host to a full-fledged settler society populated by large numbers of whites from a single European nation.[21] The displacement of the German colonial regime (1884–1918) and the establishment of British rule (1922–1961) under a League of Nations mandate following World War I effectively ensured that a white settler colony would not take shape in Tanganyika. The British were preoccupied with their much more important Kenyan colony to the north and the Europeans who eventually filled the partial void left by the departure of Germans were a multinational lot with disparate political and economic interests. This set of historical precedents partly accounts for the fact that the transition to independence was relatively smooth in Tanzania, inasmuch as the level of black-white animosity that characterized the liberation struggles in Zimbabwe, South Africa, and the Portuguese colonies failed to materialize there.[22]

The absence of a dominant white settler class did not mean that colonial rule had no impact on race relations in Tanganyika, however. To the contrary, four distinct racialized groups were routinely identified in colonial Tanganyikan "race thinking": Africans occupied the lowest rung on the social ladder, Asians (i.e., Indians and Pakistanis) and Arabs were in the middle, and Europeans held the top position. None of these categories had any clear-cut basis in biology or genetics, nor were they coherent as historical-geographical or cultural units. The fact that they were treated as distinct "races" by colonial rulers had weighty material implications nonetheless.[23] As imperial British subjects, Asians in particular enjoyed certain economic and social privileges under British rule in Tanganyika that were otherwise denied to Africans. When Tanganyika finally achieved independence in 1961, a backlash against Asians immediately took shape.[24] Until recently, scapegoating of a relatively large and wealthy class of Asian entrepreneurs diverted attention from the exploits of white investors from Europe, North America, and Australia who operated with relative impunity in the country for decades (Aminzade 2003).

It is worth noting in this context that many of the European whites who came to assist Tanzania in its nation-building efforts in the early decades of independence were themselves ideologically committed to the socialist and liberation causes. Indeed, a great deal of early development assistance came from the social democratic countries of northern Europe, including Sweden, Denmark, Norway, and Finland. As a rule, these whites were not bent on extracting Tanzania's wealth for private gain.

Their relatively benign presence undoubtedly contributed to better social relationships between whites and blacks in Tanzanian society.

In sum, there are a number of reasons why black-white race relations in postcolonial Tanzania were relatively unproblematic on the domestic front until recently. Internationally, the picture was much different, however. Indeed, prior to 1994, Tanzania was actively, virulently opposed to the "white, racist, imperialist" regimes to the south, where the worst forms of racially motivated human rights violations were perpetrated. The history of this deep-seated animosity and its implications for contemporary social relations in Tanzania form the focus of the next chapter.

1
Frontline Memories

One of the more perverse features of apartheid was the creation of black "homelands" or "bantustans." These nominally autonomous territories were run by puppet governments and were expected to pursue independent development paths without assistance from Pretoria. Located on some of South Africa's most desolate wastelands, they were dumping grounds for displaced blacks who were forcibly evicted from areas that were coveted by whites elsewhere in the country (Butler et al. 1977).

The territory known as Bophuthatswana was perhaps the most infamous of the fictive homelands, in part because it contained the Sun City resort complex.[1] Sun City, or "Sin City," as the resort was known colloquially, traded on Bophuthatswana's quasi-independent status to offer forms of entertainment, such as gambling and topless female dancing, that were illegal in South Africa proper. It also afforded opportunities for South African audiences to witness performances by international musicians and other artists who were discouraged from performing in South Africa under the terms of the cultural boycott adopted by anti-apartheid campaigners in 1966.[2] From the perspective of anti-apartheid activists, a performer's decision to "play Sun City" was tantamount to providing support for the apartheid system.[3]

The pretense of independent Bophuthatswana, and its use by performers to skirt the constraints of the cultural boycott, rankled many anti-apartheid campaigners. Performers affiliated with a group known as Artists United against Apartheid took it upon themselves to challenge the status quo. Led by Steven Van Zandt[4] and including such notable musicians as Miles Davis, Bob Dylan, Herbie Hancock, Bruce Springsteen, Pat Benatar, Ringo Starr, Ruben Blades, Run DMC, Lou Reed, Bonnie Raitt, Jimmy Cliff, Gil-Scott Heron, Joey Ramone, U2, and Keith Richards, this group produced a key anti-apartheid album entitled *Sun City* in 1985 (Marsh 1985). The title track contained a refrain voiced by each of the musicians: "I-I-I . . . ain't gonna play Sun City." The song became the unofficial anthem of the international anti-apartheid solidarity movement in the United States and Europe (Thörn 2009, 434).

The *Sun City* project generated renewed interest in the cultural boycott and brought additional pressure to bear on those who sought to break it (Reed 2005, 165–72). It also yielded roughly a million dollars in profits, which organizers donated to the anti-apartheid cause. The primary recipients of *Sun City* largesse included the South African Council of Churches, which was led for many years by Nobel laureate Archbishop Desmond Tutu; two of the leading U.S.-based anti-apartheid organizations, Transafrica and the American Committee on Africa (ACOA); and a seemingly obscure educational facility in rural Tanzania known as the Solomon Mahlangu Freedom College (SOMAFCO).[5] That an organization in Tanzania was singled out for such significant support at the height of the anti-apartheid struggle may seem surprising in retrospect. However, for the better part of three decades, Tanzania formed a crucial hub of political activity focused on the southern African liberation struggles. SOMAFCO itself hosted thousands of exiled South Africans under the auspices of the African National Congress from 1978 to 1992. Dozens of foreign delegations visited this "showpiece of the liberation struggle" in the 1970s and 1980s and subsequently contributed substantial sums to it (Morrow et al. 2004, 3; cf. Shubin and Traikova 2008, 1022; SADET 2008, vol. 3).

The prominence of SOMAFCO in the eyes of international anti-apartheid activists highlights the distinctive geography of the anti-apartheid struggle. A great deal of attention in the scholarly literature has been paid to the relative importance of "external" contributions by the international solidarity movement in comparison to the "internal" struggle being waged by combatants in South Africa itself.[6] In this regard, Tanzania constituted neither an "external" nor an "internal" force, but instead occupied a third, interstitial space that remains relatively underexplored in histories of the period.[7] Like Zambia, Botswana, and, later, Mozambique, Zimbabwe, and Angola, Tanzania was located on the "front line" of the region-wide struggles for southern African liberation. Its government provided refuge and respite to thousands of foreign nationals in exile even as it sought to secure its *own* borders and meet its obligations to fulfill the nation-building aspirations of its people.

SOMAFCO was in fact one of over a dozen Tanzanian sites that provided shelter for war refugees, served as military training bases, or hosted diplomatic conferences devoted to the liberation struggles. These installations provided Tanzanians in all corners of the country with opportunities to meet their "brothers and sisters" from the south and absorb the ethos of the liberation struggle through firsthand social contact. Tanzanians who came of age during this period recall with pride the central role their country played in the liberation struggle. As I show below, the political consciousness that emerged in Tanzania during this period has been long-lived. Indeed, it continues to shape Tanzanians' attitudes toward South Africans well after the formal end of apartheid in the early 1990s.

Regional Solidarity in "The Struggle"

For Tanzania, efforts to end white domination in southern Africa actually began in the late 1950s, and President Nyerere quickly became a leader of the international solidarity movement (Houser 1989; Minter 1994; SADET 2004, 2007, 2008; Khadiagala 2007). "The struggle," as it was known in the political parlance of the time, moved forward on several fronts simultaneously. These included the anticolonial wars leading to independence in the former Portuguese colonies of Mozambique (1975) and Angola (1975); the ensuing civil wars in each of those countries against counterrevolutionary forces backed in part by South Africa (mid 1970s through 1990s); the overthrow of the white settler regime in Rhodesia/Zimbabwe (1980); the fight for independence in South Africa–occupied Namibia (1990); and the anti-apartheid campaign in South Africa itself culminating in the election of the ANC government in 1994. Though each of these national liberation movements had its own political character, as far as Nyerere was concerned, they were all ideologically linked. His position, which he shared with Nkrumah and other prominent African leaders and helped establish as a guiding principle of the Organization of African Unity (OAU), was quite clear: "We shall never be really free and secure while some parts of our continent are still enslaved."[8]

Safe Haven

Tanzania's support for the liberation struggle ultimately took several forms. One of its earliest objectives was to provide humanitarian relief services to civilian groups fleeing war and political repression. When the army of the Mozambican liberation front (Frelimo) began attacking Portuguese colonial forces in northern Mozambique in 1964–65, and the Portuguese retaliated by burning dozens of Mozambican villages along the border, many of the displaced Mozambicans fled into Tanzania.[9] By 1965, some 7,000 Mozambican nationals had taken refuge in Tanzania, and that number grew to an estimated 50,000 by the early 1970s as the war against the Portuguese colonial regime intensified (Chaulia 2003, 156). In order to meet the needs of this large refugee community, Nyerere's government allowed Frelimo to set up facilities offering a range of social services to Mozambican nationals, including a secondary school in Bagamoyo, a center for women and children in Tunduru, and a hospital serving war wounded in Mtwara (see map 1).[10]

The story was much the same with respect to South African refugees. When thousands of young South Africans fled their country in the wake of the apartheid regime's crackdown following the Soweto uprising of 1976, many found their way to Tanzania.[11] The ANC's Solomon Mahlangu Freedom College (SOMAFCO)—the recipient of funds from the *Sun City* project—was subsequently opened on a sisal plantation provided by the Tanzanian government in the community of Mazimbu in Tanzania's Morogoro district in 1978.[12] A second facility was later opened by the ANC in the nearby town of Dakawa. The two ANC camps eventually housed some 5,000 South African exiles and provided services to them via a secondary school, a primary school, a nursery, a farm, and a development skills training center. Their goal was to ensure that the exiles would be "practically and intellectually equipped to make their contribution [to] the struggle . . . and to take their rightful place as citizens in a free and democratic South Africa of the future" (Morrow et al. 2004, 15). They pursued this mission until 1992 when Nelson Mandela, newly freed from prison, paid a historic visit and called his countrymen and women back home again.[13]

The residents of these camps had extensive economic ties with surrounding communities: SOMAFCO hired a significant number of Tanzanians as farm laborers, its farm surpluses were sold in local markets, and traders from nearby communities bartered cigarettes with SOMAFCO students in exchange for clothing and other items sent through foreign aid channels (Morrow et al. 2004, 113–31). To facilitate communication, ANC members learned to speak Kiswahili, and Tanzanians in the area picked up South African dialects. South Africans also played in local sports leagues. Binational marriages were not uncommon. In these respects, the refugee and military encampments that dotted the Tanzanian landscape left a lasting impression on neighboring Tanzanian communities.

In addition to land for the camps themselves, the Tanzanian government and its citizens made a number of other contributions to the needs of the refugee groups. Early on, the government committed one percent of its national income to the Liberation Fund of the Organization of African Unity (Chaulia 2003, 155), and for a brief period, it paid some refugees a daily living allowance.[14] The Tanzanian government helped stock Frelimo shops by exchanging everyday necessities for goods that were produced in the liberated zones of northern Mozambique.[15] Ordinary Tanzanian citizens routinely donated clothing, blood, and money to support the exiled groups.[16] Thus, for example, when Tanzania's ruling party, the Tanzania African National Union (TANU), declared 1974 the "year of liberation," Tanzanians contributed a total of four million Tanzanian shillings (approx. $286,000) to assist Frelimo in its final push to free Mozambique from Portuguese rule (Kisanga 1981, 113).[17]

Military Involvement

Tanzania's proximity to the Mozambican battle lines made its direct military involvement in the struggle virtually inevitable. At the same time, its relative *distance* from the core of South African influence meant that its national territory was strategically significant as a training and staging area for nearly every set of freedom fighters active in the region:

> It is a well-known fact that guerrilla fighting for the liberation of Rhodesia, Angola, Mozambique, and South West Africa has been able to occur largely because of the fact that there are bases for training of troops and launching of attacks in the neighboring Zambia, Tanzania and Congo. Were those three countries to discontinue their policy of harboring liberation movements, the struggle for freedom would virtually be rendered impossible.[18]

During the early years of the liberation struggle, Dar es Salaam was the terminus of an extensive underground railway that funneled exiled military personnel from all over the region into and through Tanzania for training (Ndlovu 2004, 454–60). Indeed, the Tanzanian countryside was dotted with military installations hosting foreign guerrilla armies. Frelimo established as many as ten different military bases and supply camps on Tanzanian soil, including its headquarters in Nachingwea. The battle for Namibian independence was launched directly from a military training camp in Kongwa in Tanzania's Dodoma district in 1966. South Africa's ANC had four different military camps in Tanzania (Kongwa, Mbeya, Bagamoyo, and Morogoro), and its rival, the Pan-Africanist Congress (PAC), had camps in Mbeya and Ruvu. Zimbabwean guerrilla forces were trained and staged at bases in Mgagao, Morogoro, and Itumbi (see map 1).[19]

These various groups of "freedom fighters" received instruction from Cuban, Russian, Algerian, and Chinese military trainers, among others, both on Tanzanian soil and abroad. They availed themselves of military supply chains that ran through Tanzanian ports—Chinese military funding and weapons supplies delivered via Tanzania, for example, had reached a level of over $40 million by 1972. And they took advantage of countless donations ostensibly contributed for "humanitarian" purposes to help support military personnel exiled within the country. Much of this funding was funneled through the OAU's Liberation Committee, but direct bilateral donations to the Tanzanian government were also often destined for redistribution in the liberation camps.[20]

Tanzanian civilians and military personnel were killed in Tanzania in repeated cross-border incursions by Portuguese colonial forces in the early 1970s. Thousands of Tanzanian troops also became directly involved in military action outside its borders, most notably to help defeat counterrevolutionary forces in Mozambique. Operation Safisha ("Cleanup") launched in Mozambique in 1976 resulted in over a hundred Tanzanian casualties. Tanzanian soldiers also participated in military actions in Rhodesia.[21] Additionally, Tanzania's police and army were deployed internally to help defend the liberation camps. The Tanzanian military helped protect the ANC, for example, which was in a state of perpetual alert against the prospect of an attack on SOMAFCO by South African security forces:

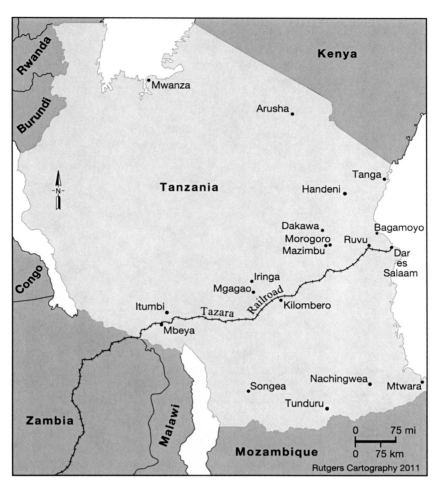

Map 1. Sites of solidarity in Tanzania. Over a dozen different Tanzanian communities supported the southern African liberation struggles by sheltering war refugees or hosting military training bases and diplomatic conferences.

MICHAEL SIEGEL, RUTGERS CARTOGRAPHY.

The sense of threat from the South African regime was also noticeable . . . [SOMAFCO] authorities continually emphasized that being outside South Africa did not mean that they were safe, and that vigilance was essential. In the early 1980s there were rumours that the regime was going to attack SOMAFCO, and that South African forces would use Malawi as a staging post to fly to Mazimbu. It was said that the official opening of the school in 1985 was to be targeted . . . As a result of such fears, trenches were dug all over the Mazimbu campus . . . In one incident, the water supply from the nearby

Map 2. Key frontline states. The four presidents of Tanzania, Zambia, Mozambique, and Botswana led the Frontline States alliance in opposition to the "white, racist, imperialist regimes" to the south.

MICHAEL SIEGEL, RUTGERS CARTOGRAPHY.

Ngerengere River was poisoned. Luckily, local people noticed that fish were dying in the river, and they notified the SOMAFCO authorities.[22]

Similar threats were directed at the Zimbabwean camps in Tanzania.[23]

On two separate occasions, prominent members of the liberation movements living in exile in Dar es Salaam were assassinated. The most sensational of these events was the killing in 1969 of Eduardo Mondlane, the president in exile of Frelimo, who died instantly when a parcel bomb sent by the Portuguese political police exploded as he opened it (Brittain 2006). The second incident involved PAC leader David Sibeko, who was killed by PAC comrades in 1979 (Kondlo 2008, 177–78). Tensions within the liberation movements also erupted when Zimbabwe African National Liberation Army (ZANLA) forces attacked and killed "a considerable number" of Zimbabwe People's Revolutionary Army (ZIPRA) guerrillas at their joint military bases in Mgagao and Morogoro in 1976 (Martin and Johnson 1981, 243; Chung 2006, 315).

Strategic Infrastructure

Tanzania also provided strategic logistical support to its neighbors. Tanzania's most important ally in the region, Zambia, shared borders with Rhodesia, Mozambique, Angola, and Southwest Africa (Namibia), and was thus much more directly exposed to attack by anti-liberation forces than Tanzania. Zambia was also economically vulnerable because it was landlocked; its primary routes to port accounting for nearly all its imports and exports in the early 1960s ran through white-held Rhodesia, Angola, Mozambique, and South Africa (see analysis in Mwase 1987, 191–98; Griffiths 1969, 214; see also map 2). In 1965, this situation reached crisis proportions when Ian Smith's government in Rhodesia issued its "Universal Declaration of Independence" (UDI) from Britain and placed an embargo on oil deliveries to Zambia in retaliation for Zambia's support for Zimbabwean guerrilla groups.

To break the stranglehold on the Zambian economy and promote development within both Zambia and Tanzania, three parallel infrastructure projects were undertaken. Presidents Kaunda and Nyerere coordinated plans for the construction of an oil pipeline (TAZAMA) and a new rail line (TAZARA) (see map 1). Simultaneously, a highway connecting the two countries was built by an American construction firm.[24] Of the three projects, the Italian-funded pipeline provided the first relief from the Rhodesian oil blockade (Griffiths 1969, 216), but it was TAZARA that arguably carried the greatest symbolic significance.[25]

Initially, Nyerere and Kaunda sought funding for TAZARA from western governments and multilateral donors.[26] When these actors denied support to the project, the two presidents were forced to seek help from the Chinese government, which seized the opportunity to align itself with the liberation struggle and gain political capital at the western governments' expense:

> The Chinese-sponsored TAZARA was known as the "Freedom Railway," the critical link to the sea that landlocked Zambia desperately needed in order to break free from her dependency on Rhodesian, Angolan, and South African rails and ports. TAZARA was therefore also an anti-apartheid railway, a symbol of revolutionary solidarity and resistance to the forces of colonialism, neo-colonialism, and imperialism . . . By breaking free from the southern African mining interests, Zambia could provide inspiration for those fighting against white settler and Portuguese colonial rule in Rhodesia, Mozambique, Angola and South Africa. The railway would also assist Zambia and Tanzania in their support for these liberation struggles: with an independent outlet to the sea, Zambia would no longer be as vulnerable to trade sanctions or border closings

in retaliation for supporting the anti-colonial forces. Meanwhile, the railway could provide the means for shipping supplies, including military supplies, to the liberation forces in exile through a friendly neighboring country. (Monson 2009, 2, 22; cf. Monson 2006, 118–20)

Construction of the gargantuan project, which eventually involved some 15,000 Chinese and 45,000 Tanzanian laborers and engineers, began in 1970, and the line opened to commerce in 1976.[27] In developmental terms, the economies of both Tanzania and Zambia were enhanced outright as the new rail line helped integrate rural areas and markets. The use of the slightly larger rail gauge also linked Tanzania for the first time into the southern African rail network, which extended all the way to Cape Town.[28] Thus, the idea that TAZARA was the "Uhuru," or "Freedom," railway had a double meaning: the project fostered liberation but also helped promote economic self-reliance (Bailey 1975, 47; see Monson 2009, ch. 5).

The strategic significance of these infrastructural developments was multifold. First, they cut off an important source of Rhodesian revenue in the form of freight charges attached to Zambian use of Rhodesian rail lines (Bailey 1975, 47–48). The opening of alternative routes to market for Zambian goods also made the Beira-Umtali railway line in Mozambique a legitimate military target for Frelimo, which had avoided attacking the line previously because of its significance to Zambian trade (Bailey 1975, 48). Finally, and perhaps most significantly from Tanzania's perspective, these developments meant that the threat of sabotage on Tanzanian territory increased, as a series of coordinated attacks carried out in Tanzania in 1969 attest:

Tanzania and Zambia moved jointly to tighten their security measures as a result of the sabotage of the oil and road links between the two countries which took place at the end of December. Both countries believe this sabotage marks the beginning of a tougher policy against them by Portugal, Rhodesia and South Africa. Although Portugal and Rhodesia have been suspected of undertaking sabotage operations against Zambia and Tanzania, there has been nothing as ambitious, or as carefully planned, as the blowing up of the pumping station on the 1,058-mile long oil pipeline, severing Zambia's crucial fuel supplies. Damage is estimated at $240,000. It is thought that the damage cannot be repaired in less than a month. Zambia's oil reserves can last at most for six weeks. The attack on the station, near Iringa, the main town in Tanzania's Southern Highlands, was carried out with considerable skill. It came simultaneously with a less successful attempt to destroy a vital bridge near Mikumi on the [American-built] highway linking the two countries. The attack was seen as clear evidence of a carefully thought out plan to halt the growing cooperation between Zambia and Tanzania. The pipeline, built by Italians for $38.4 million, was opened only last September. There is not much doubt in either Dar es Salaam or Lusaka that the saboteurs, probably Africans, were agents working for the Portuguese and their allies in Southern Africa.[29]

Similar attacks on road and railway bridges were launched by Rhodesian forces on the Zambian side of the border in 1979 (Fleshmen 1980, 4).

Diplomatic Support

Because Tanzania played host to so many of the liberation groups in exile, it served as a central location for diplomatic efforts centered on the different national struggles. Dar es Salaam in particular "drew political refugees like a magnet" (Houser 1989, 247), hosting offices of the major political factions active in Mozambique (Frelimo), Zimbabwe (ZANU, ZAPU), Angola (MPLA), Namibia (SWAPO) and South Africa (ANC, PAC).[30] This concentration of regional politicians in Dar es Salaam grew so great that it posed a security problem for the host government, which feared attack on its largest city. In 1969, Nyerere's government insisted that the liberation groups restrict the size of their offices in Dar es Salaam to just four representatives; all other personnel were relocated to regional camps scattered throughout the country (Ndlovu 2004, 445–46).

Several of the exiled political groups held meetings in Tanzania that represented pivotal points in their respective liberation struggles. The founding congress of Frelimo, the Mozambican liberation movement, was held in Dar es Salaam in 1962 (Minter 1994). The ANC's Morogoro Conference in 1969 represented a "watershed" moment in the group's history, which led to the establishment of the group's "Revolutionary Council," the opening of ANC membership to people of all races, and the formal election of Oliver Tambo as ANC president (Ndebele and Nieftagodien 2004, 573–74; cf. Lissoni 2009). SWAPO made the fateful decision to take up the armed struggle at a clandestine meeting in Mbeya in 1962 and developed a full-blown strategic plan for achieving Namibian independence at a major party congress in Tanga in 1970.[31] Competing factions in the Zimbabwean liberation struggle, ZAPU and ZANU, met in Mbeya circa 1972 to negotiate the merger of their respective armies, and the so-called Mgagao Declaration issued at the ZANU military camp near Pomerini in 1975 helped pave the way for Robert Mugabe's ascendancy to ZANU party leadership (Sibanda 2005, 162; Chung 2006, 148; Martin and Johnson 1981, 200–202). Finally, a series of meetings in 1973 in Dar es Salaam and Mwanza helped lay important groundwork for the transition to Angolan independence (Ishemo 2000, 88–89) (see map 1).

In addition to the dozens, if not hundreds, of meetings launched by and for the liberation movements per se, Tanzania hosted other important events involving international actors in the solidarity movement. For example, in 1971, representatives of the West German International Cooperation Committee, Dutch Angola Comité, British Anti-Apartheid Movement, and French National Committee of Support for the Liberation Struggle in the Portuguese Colonies met together with Organization of African Unity officials in Dar es Salaam to coordinate efforts on behalf of the liberation movements. In 1972, the United Nations Committee on Human Rights met in Dar es Salaam to hear testimony from Frelimo members on alleged atrocities committed by the Portuguese. In 1973, the International Labor Organization invited liberation movement leaders to address their delegates at a meeting in Dar es Salaam. In 1985, the United Nations held an International Conference on Women and Children under Apartheid in Arusha. And in 1987, a meeting of 500 delegates representing anti-apartheid organizations from around the world met once again in Arusha under the banner, "Peoples of the World against Apartheid for a Democratic South Africa."[32]

Much of the diplomacy surrounding these events was conducted personally by Julius Nyerere. Even before Tanganyika obtained its own independence, Nyerere asserted his leadership in the struggle to unseat the apartheid regime. Joining British anti-apartheid campaigner Trevor Huddleston, Nyerere made an early call for a boycott of South African goods that helped launch Britain's anti-apartheid campaign. He summarized his position shortly after this meeting took place in an open letter to the editor of *Africa South* in 1959:

> We in Africa hate the policies of the South African Government. We abhor the semi-slave conditions under which our brothers and sisters in South Africa live, work and produce the goods we buy. We pass resolutions against the hideous system and keep hoping that the United Nations and the governments of the whole world will one day put pressure on the South African Government to treat its non-European peoples as human beings.
>
> But these resolutions and prayers to the United Nations are not enough in themselves. Governments and democratic organisations grind very slowly. Individuals do not have to. The question then is what an individual can do to influence the South African Government towards a human treatment of its non-white citizens.
>
> Can we honestly condemn a system and at the same time employ it to produce goods which we buy, and then enjoy with a clear conscience? Surely the customers of a business do more to keep it going than its shareholders. We who buy South African goods do more to support the system than the Nationalist Government or Nationalist industrialists.
>
> Each one of us can remove his individual prop to the South African system by refusing to buy South African goods. There are millions of people in the world who support the South African Government in this way, and who can remove their support by the boycott. I feel it is only in this way that we can give meaning to our abhorrence of the system, and give encouragement to sympathetic governments of the world to act . . .
>
> I must emphasise that the boycott is really a *withdrawing of support* which each one of us gives to the racialists in South Africa by buying their goods.

There is a very real sense in which we are part of the system we despise, because we patronise it, pay its running expenses.[33]

By September 1963, a total boycott of South African goods had been declared in Tanganyika, and restrictions had been imposed that prevented travel between the two countries (Niblock 1981, 25).

Nyerere was also active on behalf of the liberation movements within the context of the British Commonwealth. Three key moments illustrate the force of his considerable diplomatic skills. In early 1961, South Africa petitioned the Commonwealth to retain its membership following its status change from dominion to republic. As a prospective commonwealth member—Tanganyika's independence was scheduled for December of that year and its entry into the Commonwealth was pending—Nyerere responded to the South African overture in an open letter to the Commonwealth prime ministers, which Cassam paraphrases:

> How could Africa join an organization which had as its member a state which applied apartheid and white supremacy as its official policy[?] . . . [Nyerere] explained that his country would decline to seek membership in such a situation, for "to vote South Africa in is to vote us out." Furthermore, [Nyerere argued] Tanganyika's example could well be followed by other African, Asian and Caribbean countries soon to gain independence from the UK. (Cassam 2010, 66–67)

The threat of a multi-party boycott of the Commonwealth carried the day, and South Africa was forced to "withdraw . . . rather than face being expelled" (Cassam 2010, 67).

In 1965, Nyerere again challenged the status quo within the Commonwealth by protesting Britain's ongoing support of the Rhodesian government. When Ian Smith's white minority government issued its "unilateral declaration of independence" (UDI) from Britain, and Britain's prime minister, Harold Wilson, failed to intervene to thwart Smith's efforts, Nyerere broke off diplomatic relations with Britain, a step that led to the cancellation of a £7.5 million loan, which had been earmarked as a source of funding for a range of development projects in Tanzania (Pallotti 2009, 71–76).[34] Nyerere then orchestrated a vote by the African members of the Commonwealth to override British objections and adopt a principle of "no independence before majority African rule," which effectively delegitimized the UDI government in Rhodesia. Finally, in 1971, Nyerere led a group that challenged and forced British prime minister Edward Heath to back down over proposed arms sales to South Africa (Cassam 2010, 68).

Under Nyerere's leadership, Tanganyika became a founding member of the OAU, and he, along with Zambian president Kenneth Kaunda, "dominated" the

OAU meetings for the better part of two decades (Sahnoun 2010, 63).[35] Nyerere was the principal force behind the creation of that body's Liberation Committee at its first meeting in Addis Ababa in 1963. This body "provided funding, logistical support, training and publicity to all liberation movements officially recognized by the OAU. The committee also organized their presence and campaigns on the diplomatic front through conferences, visits, press campaigns and radio broadcasts" (Sahnoun 2010, 62). At Nyerere's invitation, the committee's secretariat was located in Dar es Salaam, which meant that Nyerere was privy to the latest political developments and was in a position to establish strong relationships with the generation of nationalist leaders who would go on to run their independent governments (Khadiagala 2007, 25).

Tanzania lobbied hard on behalf of the liberation movements within the OAU and the UN, helping to win them official observer status in the latter prior to their achieving independence.[36] It also became a leading force within the so-called Front-line States (FLS). This crucial political alliance began as a series of meetings between Nyerere and his closest ally, Kenneth Kaunda.[37] Botswanan president Seretse Khama later joined the group along with Samora Machel, the president of newly independent Mozambique.[38] At this point, according to one Zambian official, "the term 'Frontline' became more than a fact of geography" (quoted in Khadiagala 2007, 25). Instead "active commitment against minority rule in southern Africa" served as the litmus test in determining whether a given country was actually a "frontline" state (Khadiagala 2007, 25). The FLS were formally recognized by the OAU in 1975, and "the four presidents"—Nyerere, Kaunda, Khama, and Machel—went on to play a major role in shaping the politics of the struggle (see map 2).

The key tasks facing the FLS allies were to reconcile tensions between competing liberation movements (for example, between South Africa's PAC and ANC, and between Rhodesia's ZAPU and ZANU) and counter the initiatives undertaken by South Africa to undermine political solidarity among the newly independent African national governments (Khadiagala 2007; Ishemo 2000). The diplomatic chess match between the Frontline States, on the one hand, and South Africa and its allies, on the other, continued for the better part of three decades. A detailed examination of this history is well beyond the scope of this book. The point here is that, for Nyerere (and Tanzanians more generally), the individual liberation struggles throughout the region were directly linked to the anti-apartheid effort in South Africa. The ideological basis for this claim has already been stated: no part of Africa could be free until all of Africa was free. As for the strategic linkages, Nyerere himself stated, "I used to tell [the freedom fighters living in Tanzania] that after their independence, we needed a liberated zone of independent states in southern Africa . . . Once we had these independent countries stretching from the Indian Ocean to the Atlantic, that would be a really powerful challenge and deterrent to South Africa. We all agreed on this" (Julius Nyerere, quoted in Khadiagala 2007, 25). The idea that conflicts elsewhere in southern Africa were strategically linked to the anti-apartheid struggle was shared by South Africa's leaders as well. Pretoria's defense minister, Piet Botha, was quoted in 1970 as saying, "South Africa has an interest in what happens in Angola and Mozambique. The onslaughts there are aimed at the [South African] Republic in the final instance. About that we can have no illusions" (quoted in Khadiagala 2007, 19).[39]

South Africa accordingly worked hard to exploit weaknesses in the FLS alliance, and within the OAU more generally, offering to sign a "nonaggression treaty" or open up a "dialogue" with any willing African country (see discussion in Ndlovu 2007a, 616–31; Khadiagala 2007, 19–36; Kisanga 1981, 105). These efforts eventually led to the defection of Malawi and Zaire, and the co-optation of a number of other moderate governments elsewhere, all of which destabilized the regional military situation. Even Zambian president Kaunda was tempted by the offer of a peaceful settlement with Pretoria.[40]

Tanzania's position within these debates evolved in response to changing circumstances in Angola, Mozambique, and Zimbabwe. Nyerere and his government were nonetheless resolute as they sought to articulate key principles to guide the response to South Africa's regional diplomacy. Thus, for example, in 1970, Nyerere argued forcefully against the signing of "nonaggression" pacts with Pretoria in a speech at the United Nations:

> For Africa there is no choice. We have to support the Freedom Fighters. Theirs
> is merely a continuation of the freedom struggle which has already resulted
> in 41 African nations being represented in this General Assembly. For the na-
> tional freedom and human equality for which these people are fighting are not
> only the same rights which the rest of Africa claimed—and won. They are also
> the only basis on which the free states of Africa exist. . . . This is why talk of a
> Non-Aggression Treaty between South Africa and Tanzania is such nonsense.
> Our conflict is not that of two states quarrelling about a border or something
> of that nature. The conflict is about apartheid versus humanity, and about our
> right to freedom. For racialism is itself an aggression against the human spirit,
> and colonialism is the result of past aggression against a people and a territory.
> We in Tanzania, and the other peoples of Africa, have been—and still are—the
> victims of those aggressions. It is impossible for us to sign a Non-Aggression
> Treaty with aggression itself. (Nyerere 1970)

Nyerere's government was similarly unequivocal on the possibility of engaging in a direct "dialogue" with South Africa:

> There is no doubt, however, that a diplomatic dialogue between the states of
> free Africa and racialist regimes of Southern Africa would, in fact undermine
> the cause of liberation—as the South Africans intend that it should. It certainly
> cannot serve the cause of freedom . . . The leaders of African peoples of South

Africa are in South African gaols, the South African government could free those leaders and then talk to *them*.[41]

In sum, Nyerere's willingness to stake out and defend his strong pro-liberation positions carried a great deal of weight in international diplomatic circles, and firmly established his reputation as "the conscience of Africa on decolonization issues" (Khadiagala 2007, 43).

Nationalist Mobilization

The citizens of Arusha, Bagamoyo, Dakawa, Dar es Salaam, Itumbi, Kongwa, Mazimbu, Mbeya, Morogoro, Moshi, Mtwara, Mwanza, Nachingwea, Pomerini (Mgagao), Ruvu, Tanga, Tunduru, and other unspecified locations throughout Tanzania played host to the liberation struggle for the better part of thirty years, often at considerable risk to their own livelihoods and safety. As the Portuguese attacks on southern Tanzania, the bombing of Tanzania's transportation infrastructure, and the occasional violent clashes within the liberation movement groups residing in Tanzania demonstrate, Tanzanians had good cause for concern that the liberation wars might spill over into Tanzanian territory. Tanzanian citizens were accordingly exhorted by their government to remain vigilant and be on the alert to the possibility of foreign military incursions. The mobilization of nationalist sentiments against a potential attack was carried out in a number of different venues, among which was an institution known as "National Service" (Kiswahili: "Jeshi la Kujenga Taifa" or JKT).

National Service

National Service initially consisted of "a voluntary corps of young men and women who would undergo political, military and agricultural or vocational training as a prelude to nearly two years spent working on 'nation building' projects" (Ivaska 2005, 90). In effect, JKT formed a military reserve army. In 1966, the government took the controversial step of making National Service mandatory for all high school and college graduates whose school expenses were covered by the national government. This arrangement, which entailed six months of training and eighteen months of on-the-job service (for example, building roads or teaching), was conceived as a way for students to repay society for the costs of their education. University of Dar es Salaam students initially protested the compulsory nature of this new plan, revealing cracks in the veneer of national unity. To Nyerere, their actions suggested that the university was generating a political elite that might one day undermine his vision for a socially egalitarian society. To prevent this from happening, Nyerere had the university shut down and vowed to root out elitist tendencies both at the university and within his own government. With respect to the latter objective, he docked his own salary by 20 percent, and lowered the salaries of his cabinet members shortly thereafter. Later that year, he issued his famous "Arusha Declaration" of socialist principles and published a seminal tract, "Education for Self Reliance."[42]

The early tensions surrounding JKT notwithstanding, it ultimately played an influential role in indoctrinating the Tanzanian public. Former journalist Godfrey Mwakikagile described how important a 1971–73 stint in National Service was in forming his own political consciousness and sensibilities:

> It was a two-year programme, from the time we first went in, and it taught us discipline and helped instill in us not only egalitarian values but a strong sense of patriotism. We already loved our country. But we were at the same time constantly reminded that there were enemies within, working with enemies outside, to try to destroy our country, sabotage our economy and independence . . . "Be vigilant,'" we were always reminded in speeches and patriotic songs. Some of the patriotic songs we sang in National Service training camps concerned apartheid South Africa and other white minority regimes in southern Africa. . . . They were pretty violent songs, ready to irrigate our land with the blood of the enemy, reminding ourselves that we were on the frontline of the African liberation struggle and should be ready to defend our country, anytime, and at any cost, and be prepared to fight alongside our brothers and sisters still suffering under colonialism and racial oppression anywhere on the continent. . . . Apartheid South Africa was the primary target as the most powerful white minority regime on the continent and as the most stubborn. And it evoked some of the strongest feelings among us because of the diabolical nature of the regime and its abominable institution of apartheid. (Mwakikagile 2006, 33–34)

In this context, the term *kaburu* (pl. *makaburu*), which is the Kiswahili word for Boer, took on strong pejorative connotations. The term's origins trace back to a contingent of Afrikaners, or Boers, who fled to East Africa between 1904 and 1907 in the aftermath of the (Second) South African War (1899–1902).[43] The group that settled north of Arusha along the Kenyan border consisted mostly of relatively poor livestock keepers who were offered substantial plots of land by the German colonial government—up to 1000 ha per family—in the hopes that they would spur agricultural development in the area.[44] When the British assumed control of Tanganyika in the 1920s following World War I, Boer land rights were reaffirmed, and they were renewed once again in the late 1940s.[45]

It is not certain in retrospect which aspect of the Afrikaner presence was most objectionable to Tanganyikans, their usurping of locals' land rights or the fact that they "had a reputation for exploiting their squatters."[46] What is clear from numerous conversations with my research informants is that, by the time Nyerere had launched independent Tanganyika on its anticolonial and anti-apartheid mission, the term *kaburu* had become synonymous with "white South African racist imperialist," and was in wide use as a politically charged epithet. Several Tanzanians I interviewed vividly recalled the days when they were secondary school students, cadets in the National Service camps, members of the ruling party's youth league or soldiers in the military, how they marched to the cadence of chants and songs that called for the violent death of any white South African found within Tanzanian borders. The chant most frequently mentioned was delivered in call and response fashion: [call] *"Kaburu akije . . ."* ("If a *Boer* comes . . . ") [response] *". . . chinja!"* (". . . slaughter him!").[47]

The memories of marching around school yards and JKT training camps, chanting in unison against white-dominated regimes, could not help but leave a powerful impression on young minds, and my informants often linked their own enduring antipathy towards white South Africans directly to that experience. For example, an NGO representative working in Arusha in 2005 described how several of her acquaintances were still carrying on the old economic boycott of South African goods and services. There was the elderly gentleman who refused cell phone service from Vodacom, the largest supplier of such services in Tanzania, because it was owned by a South African firm; and the middle-aged community activist who categorically refused to dine at Steers, a South African-owned fast food chain. These decisions were a product of the indoctrination her friends had received during the liberation struggles of the previous decades. As she explained, "To read and to see are two different things [she takes her head between her hands]. For those who were there, you can't rub it from your memory."[48] At the same time, there was at least some recognition among my informants that the chest thumping and blood lust expressed in chants against the *makaburu* represented a hollow threat. As one informant drily put it, "What we tend to forget is that, if the South Africans had, in fact, invaded, chances are *we* would have been the ones getting '*chinja*-ed' [that is, "slaughtered"], not them" (author field notes, 2005).

Popular Media

A second mechanism used by the state to shape popular opinion was the mass media. Government pronouncements and official reports on the battles being waged in the region-wide liberation struggle appeared regularly in the state-run press, always characterizing the white governments in the south as "racist" and "imperialist." News briefings and press releases offered by the liberation movements themselves often first saw light of day in the Tanzanian press. For example, the newsletter *Southern Africa,* which was published between 1967 and 1983 by the New York–based Southern Africa Committee, routinely drew on the *Tanzanian Standard* and other national newspapers as primary sources for information on events taking place elsewhere in the region.[49]

Even more significant was Radio Tanzania Dar es Salaam (RTD), which played a "pivotal role" in the propaganda wars launched over radio airwaves (Mosia et al. 1994, 6). Mytton estimates that some 500,000 radio sets were in use in Tanzania in 1967, and that that number had increased to 1,787,000 by 1973, so the "reach" of the political broadcasts was substantial (1983, 109; cited in Patterson 2004, 12). Even these numbers likely underestimate the full extent of listenership, however, given the fact that multiple users often shared transmitters: one survey in the largely rural Lushoto district in northeastern Tanzania in 1969–70, for example, indicated that roughly 80 percent of men and 60 percent of women listened to the radio on a regular basis (Molloy 1971, 148; reported in Feierman 1990, 252). The fact that Kiswahili was so quickly established as a national language greatly facilitated the use of mass media for political purposes.

RTD regularly broadcast President Nyerere's speeches and reported on diplomatic efforts relating to the various liberation movements. As early as 1956, Radio Tanzania's "External Service" operated a shortwave service with a broadcasting range extending as far afield as Johannesburg; in 1970, this service was enhanced to extend coverage over the entire continent (Patterson 2004, 10; Konde 1984, 223, 230). By 1968, RTD hosted the radio programs of eight different liberation groups, including the ANC's "Radio Freedom" (Davis 2009, 360–67).[50] At its peak, it devoted roughly 17 percent of its programming, or over ten hours a week, to broadcasts prepared by the liberation movements in exile (Mosia et al. 1994, 7).

On the occasion of Nyerere's death in 1999, a Tanzanian journalist working for the BBC's Swahili Service, Vicki Ntetema, recalled how important RTD radio broadcasts were in shaping her political consciousness growing up in the southern highlands in Tanzania. She noted that these broadcasts portrayed Nyerere's efforts in glowing terms and religiously followed his efforts to work with other African leaders to promote liberation on the continent. In this sense, the broadcasts were a source of great inspiration:

> There was no single day which passed without hearing songs praising Mwalimu or Baba (Father) Nyerere. Tanzania Bands sang of how he fought for the country's independence "without spilling blood" and how he was still fighting for the liberation of those nations under colonial and apartheid regimes . . . Listening to Radio Tanzania we followed the struggle of Mwalimu and other African leaders for the liberation of the whole of the continent. Twice a year we donated blood and clothing to our brothers and sisters in the struggle in Mozambique, Zimbabwe and Namibia. We had to welcome and accommodate exiles from South Africa. They became our half-relatives and were given the best of everything, from education to health.[51]

A Revolutionary Education

Even as the masses were bombarded with pro-liberation messages via RTD broadcasts, a different set of social dynamics was taking shape in Dar es Salaam. For in the period in question, Dar became a revolutionary "Mecca" for members of the various liberation movements and their supporters in the international solidarity movement.[52] Prominent African leaders who spent extensive time in Tanzania in exile included Eduardo Mondlane, Samora Machel, and Joachim Chissano from Mozambique; Sam Nujoma from Namibia; and Oliver Tambo and Thabo Mbeki from South Africa. Augustinho Neto from Angola was also a frequent visitor. International personages who either lived in Tanzania or traveled through to lend their support for the liberation struggles included Malcolm X, Angela Davis, Che Guevara, Stokely Carmichael, and Fidel Castro (see Campbell 2010, 49, 51; Mwakikagile 2006, 106–15; Tasseni 2006a).

Many of these international politicians as well as a star-studded roster of leftist academics spoke to student audiences at the University of Dar es Salaam (UDES) where the campus community was deeply immersed in an extended debate regarding the ideology and tactics of the liberation struggle:

> In the ten-year period between 1967 to 1977, the university was a major cooking pot of ideas, and provided a splendid platform for debate and discussion. No African scholar, leader or freedom fighter could ignore its environs. While the government brought its official guests to see its picturesque Mount Olympius-like [sic] exterior, others came to seek knowledge or refine their ideological positions. Here, the East and West Germans, who officially were not talking to each other; the Chinese and the Americans who officially could not stand each other; and the white and black South Africans, who at home could not even sit together in the same church, met in the seminar rooms built by Swedes and the British to debate not only on Tanzania's development path but also the Vietnam war, the Palestinian Question, apartheid, the Chinese Cultural Revolution and countless other subjects. Very intense were these debates, and a huge number of discourses and manuscripts were churned out.[53]

The university was, thus, a critical site for nationalist indoctrination and the development of pan-Africanist sensibilities, which informed Tanzania's relationship with South Africa for decades.

Frontline Memories

Memories of Tanzania's involvement in the liberation struggle give rise to mixed feelings on the part of Tanzanians who are old enough to recall both the sense of pride they felt as Tanzanian citizens and the costs their country endured to support their African comrades. Three sets of extended comments by contemporary observers of the period help flesh out the competing feelings of nostalgia, regret, and confusion that Tanzanians feel as they survey both their country's past and the contemporary circumstances it faces with the recent influx of South African investors.

JK, a retired civil servant, explained the unwavering commitment Tanzanians once felt toward the liberation cause and how that sense of solidarity has continued to shape their view of South Africans in the post-apartheid period:

> When it comes to South Africans, Tanzanians will always react with emotions ranging from the violent to the ambivalent. For us, South Africans are always Afrikaners. When we think of South Africans, we do so inevitably against the apartheid backdrop. We always think of this period and the impact this had on our way of thinking. This was not just a relationship where we gave refuge to a few chaps in the ANC training camp. We sent our own boys to teach the Mugabe fighters down in Rhodesia that if you shoot a white man, he will bleed and he will die. If a liberation person met a white person, he would be afraid because of the mystique surrounding white settlers during the colonial period in Zimbabwe. So we had to go and teach them how to kill. It sounds brutal and callous, and we lost some of our own boys in the process, but it was a form of contribution we made to the liberation struggle.[54]

He invoked pan-African solidarity as the key motivating factor behind Tanzania's staunch defense of anticolonial political movements:

> To be serious, at least initially, the liberation struggle was a Tanzanian show. Even if we didn't want it, Nyerere would have done it. And we paid dearly, in terms of both support from abroad and in terms of the drain on the few resources we had, to go out and bankroll the liberation struggle. But we never asked ourselves the question: okay, we brought independence to Rhodesia, South Africa—what did we get from it? We had a one-track mind. We didn't think about how we might recoup our losses. Back in those days there was the PAC, the ANC, Frelimo; and Mandela, Sobukwe, Mondlane . . . It was us against them, and the "them" was Pretoria, Lorenzo Marquez, and Salisbury. Those were the "them," and they had to be pushed off the seat of economic power. There was no possibility whatsoever for "dialogue." The ethos was clear.

Another informant, MM, a journalist with close ties to Nyerere's inner circle, expressed similar views regarding his country's support for the liberation movements and the material and psychic costs of undertaking this mission:

> From the very word "go," we were in a confrontation. Like, you had Nyerere saying to the Commonwealth that if South Africa is a member of the Commonwealth then we won't join. And that was very hard, and very controversial,

and was again very concrete, a real challenge to the Commonwealth and to imperialism, as we called it then. And doing that was important in my opinion, not necessarily because South Africa lost anything in the trade, but because it was the first attempt to *isolate* South Africa. It was the first *effective* attempt to isolate South Africa. It formed the platform upon which all other policies for the isolation of South Africa were built . . . it was the *pillar* of our foreign policy.

Well, the Tanzanian granting, of course, of facilities to the liberation movement and so on created a very serious issue [because] South Africa infiltrated the liberation movements. Some were killed. And we thought that South Africa, Portugal were all working together with imperialist countries: the U.S., France, U.K. and so on, Belgium. And so there developed here, whether perhaps we liked it or not, a kind of also, a siege mentality. We thought, "This is *serious*. It's real. And we are the targets." And there were attempts, there was an attempt to blow up this bridge here [beckons at the bridge across the street from the restaurant where we are meeting], Salander Bridge, you must remember. And that's why this police station is here. It wasn't a police station; that used to be a hotel, the building there. They tried to blow it up. . . . And then, the whole propaganda, the information for people about the influence of apartheid, the dangers of apartheid and so on. And then, of course, the boycott of anything South African built up a feeling here that really, this was evil. It was *real evil*. It went simply beyond politics.

MM explained how bilateral tensions between Tanzania and South Africa played into the formation of Tanzanian national identity:

It is true, that our identity was Mwalimu Nyerere, Mwalimu Nyerere's voice in the world, that we were actors in the world. And we were *important* actors—people looked up to us. The United Nations, in the OAU, people said to their government, "Just look at what Tanzania is going to do, and vote the way Tanzania votes. You don't have to think: the Tanzanians have got it all wrapped up, so just do what they do." We played a very, a much bigger role in African affairs and world affairs than we really had a material base for. But we were very strong and obviously people felt very proud. *Very* proud . . . But it did take a lot of time . . . I think probably that more than 30 percent of Nyerere's time was on these questions. Possibly a little bit more . . . and that's a lot of time to take out of national issues and put it into that. And even when he was doing national issues they were also always related somehow to some aspect of liberation and the prices we had to pay and so on, to be prepared. . . . Now if we . . . talk in terms of figures now, and I don't have figures, and nobody had those figures. But if you spent five, ten million dollars maybe per year on national liberation, that was a lot of money. I think we may have spent in that neighborhood, of that kind of . . . money. I think we had. And not only that, the fashioning of the military, fashioning of the intelligence, the community. All those were big sums directly related to the threat.[55]

The gist of these comments is that Tanzanians were keenly aware of the costs Nyerere undertook on their behalf. There is also an unmistakable sense of pride in the level of influence such a small country was able to exert on regional geopolitical events. Whether that meant bolstering the courage of guerrilla fighters and convincing them that "if you shoot a white man he will bleed and die," or shaping high-level diplomatic discussions concerning the future of the continent, Tanzanians possessed a "one-track mind" in service to the cause.

What no one at the time could have guessed is how radically the relationship between Tanzanians and South Africans would change after the end of apartheid. A faculty member at the University of Dar es Salaam, whom I will call N., characterized the dramatic shift that unfolded from the 1990s onward. Leaning back in his chair in an office decorated top to bottom with posters of Lumumba, Cabral, Machel, and other African revolutionary heroes, he began by recalling his own student days at UDES in the 1970s, when "there was a lot of radicalism . . . a lot of purpose." He noted that there was a contingent of South African students who attended the university at the time and that the campus as a whole was much more "ideological" than it is today: "Even the student government: you wouldn't be elected if you were not politically active." When I asked N. how things had changed between Tanzania and South Africa after 1994, he responded bitterly:

> So basically this is what I can say: we see a total, 180 degrees change from the '80s—from the '60s, '70s, and '80s—to the '90s where you lose patriotism completely. There's no patriotism now. Now when you see the same government which we were fighting, which is more or less in power economically—the South African whites *still* control the [South African] economy; not the politics, maybe, but the economy, they still control it—so when you see the South Africans coming [to Tanzania], taking over the economy, it pains you, because you saw the liberation struggle . . . When you look at what is happening today with people [Tanzanians] who used to pay what I can call lip service to liberation now really coming out in their true colors, almost *selling the country,* one gets a little bit—not a little bit—one gets disturbed. And the South Africans are doing what they want. . . . You really visibly *see* the South African presence here. Highly pronounced. . . . So you get a lot of xenophobic, almost, attitudes from Tanzanians against South Africa. Just the opposite of what we used to do in the '80s when we were discussing liberation of Mozambique, liberation of Namibia and South Africa, and the liberation of Zimbabwe. It's just the opposite. People are calling the South Africans Boers [that is, *makaburu*] . . . These are the people we [fought]; these were the backbone of apartheid . . . Actually they are laughing at us: "You fought us, huh? We are here now. You fought us

in South Africa, now we are here!" . . . they're very callous. We're dealing with the crudest of all South African, if I may use the word, whites, who actually were being *fought* by the ANC and the PAC. . . . They're not coming to invest; they're coming to *rip* [off] the country. And they have no bones about it.[56]

MM, the journalist quoted above, echoes N.'s sense of disbelief at how suddenly fortunes have changed in Tanzania:

When in a very short time you have to change and get over [the old animosities from the liberation struggle], it's not easy. You know, I think Tanzania was the last country to actually recognize the South African government. We had others as early as 1990, Kenyans were already doing business with South Africa and had already gone there. We were not; we were the last. We said no, we will not believe this until we're really quite sure. We were the last country to recognize South Africa's government. . . . And then all of a sudden the South Africans were saying, "Let us come and do business here. We want to invest [because] times have changed." So solidarity is not the same thing now as it used to be. Strategic relationships are shifting from only politics to economics and business. So only the *businessmen* are in solidarity much more than the general population. That is something that maybe we should all be aware of.

The impression these speakers leave is that there is a line of continuity between the past and the present: the white South Africans who have shown up in Tanzania in the post-apartheid period are understood to be the same whites who controlled the South African economic system under apartheid. At the same time, there is a break in that historic relationship on the Tanzanian side: one now finds Tanzanian business people, who may have once paid "lip service" to the struggle but are now willing to meet the new investors more than halfway.

Solidarity No More?

Somewhat surprisingly, the negative attitudes Tanzanians express toward South Africa are not confined to white investors but also embrace the ANC government and the country's black majority population. The roots of these problems can be traced back in part to Nyerere's involvement in the OAU's Liberation Committee and the Frontline States alliance, in which capacities he was forced to juggle sometimes competing allegiances to several national liberation movements at once.[57] Some Tanzanians speculate that festering resentments pertaining to these issues lay behind the unfriendly treatment they have experienced at the hands of their black South African comrades in the post-apartheid period. Tanzanians have been particularly incensed by the lack of recognition Tanzania has received for its contributions to the anti-apartheid struggle, visa restrictions Tanzanians face in traveling to South Africa, and the general pattern of xenophobia expressed by South African citizens against African foreigners.

The Nyerere Snub

In 2002, as part of its efforts to jettison the baggage of apartheid, the ANC government created a new list of national honors. Among them was an award known as the "Order of the Companions of O. R. Tambo," which was created in honor of Oliver Tambo, the leader of the ANC during its many years in exile. The prize is the "highest civilian award for foreign nationals . . . who, through their roles in the struggle against colonialism worldwide, served as inspiration for the fight against apartheid."[58] Its first recipients were Mahatma Gandhi, Olaf Palme (the prime minister of Sweden), and Nyerere's long-time ally in the Frontline States alliance, Kenneth Kaunda of Zambia—but not, for some reason, Nyerere himself. It was not until 2004 (no awards were issued in 2003), that Nyerere, along with a number of other contemporaries (Amilcar Cabral, Patrice Lumumba, Eduardo Mondlane, Agostinho Neto, and Kwame Nkrumah), received the honor.[59] When these results were published in Tanzania, they caused a tremendous uproar, as the journalist MM explains:

> Tanzanians were really shocked when in the first list of people who, important people who were supporting the liberation in South Africa, Nyerere's name was not listed. . . . It was official, official government-awarded prizes. Nyerere's name was not on that list. I think it came [that is, Nyerere was later recognized] in the second or third year. But people here were really, really, really, *really* upset. I was [he pauses as he struggles to find the right words to express himself], I thought it was completely, I don't know, *unacceptable,* that his contribution had not been recognized *immediately* with others, after all. And not just simply in terms of South Africa alone, because [Nyerere's interest] was not just South Africa; it was Angola, Mozambique, Burundi, Rwanda, Congo, Vietnam, everywhere . . . So, I tell you, you know, it was in the papers, in the headlines and so on. We were *really, really* upset.

An Asian Tanzanian shopkeeper recalled the same incident:

> I personally feel that Tanzania was left in limbo after the apartheid was dissolved. Because I think Tanzanians, Tanzania as a nation and its people, both went through a great deal of sacrifice, both financially, materially, and physically, in the struggle against the apartheid. The founding fathers, especially Mwalimu Nyerere, to a great extent occupied his nation's wealth towards [ending] the apartheid regime, you see. And after the whole apartheid system was dissolved, I think Tanzania was not acknowledged as much as it should have been . . . A particular incident, which I very vividly remember, is the

award that was given by the South Africans to the very "founding fathers" who
fought for the [anti-] apartheid [cause]. Like, it was presented to, I think . . . I
do not very well remember, but one of the African leaders. Whereby Nyerere
particularly should have been given that award *first*. Okay, he was given it only
in the second year, which leaves me as a Tanzanian very bitter about it. I'm
sure you're aware . . . we had the camps here in Morogoro, whereby they were
being trained, they were being educated. Like, you can see so many South
African leaders, southern African leaders, have come from Tanzania . . . that
have been educated in Tanzania and gone back to their countries and they're
rulers right now. So in that particular sense, I feel Tanzania was left in limbo
basically. It has *never* been acknowledged.[60]

The omission of Nyerere's name from the initial list of Tambo's "companions" after
everything he had done to support the anti-apartheid cause was scandalous.

The Visa Debacle

Beyond the lack of formal recognition, Tanzanians have also felt slighted because they have been made to feel unwelcome in South Africa. They find it especially
galling that they are required to obtain a visa to visit South Africa. Witness the following op-ed piece in a Tanzanian newspaper, which emphasizes how difficult this is
for Tanzanians to understand given the sacrifices they once made on behalf of South
Africa's black majority:

> Why does a *Bongoman* [local slang for Tanzanian] need a visa to visit Azania
> [South Africa]? We gave them freedom-fighting Azanians our blood, food,
> money, clothing, land and all manner of hospitality from our ever-smiling
> people. We even gave them Tanzanian passports when they had no documents
> so they can travel abroad. We believed we were not free until they were free.
> Didn't we use to sing, dance and chant from primary school to University,
> and from Bagamoyo to the top of the Kilimanjaro, that our comrades and
> brothers[,] Nelson and his fellow inmates[,] should be set free? For decades we
> did this and now they subject us to the third degree (it feels that way) when we
> want [a visa] to do a short visit. If it was a remnant of the *ubaguzi* [Kiswahili:
> apartheid; literally, segregation or discrimination] days, why is the practice
> still there a decade after the end of racial segregation? (Zacharia, 2005, 5)

Professor N. finds an explanation for the visa debacle in the distortions of South
Africa's political economy, which he traces back to apartheid:

> You know it is the old arguments of the strong hitting the weaker, the weaker
> hitting the weaker down, and so on. Like now, you go to South Africa today as
> a black. If we go together, even among the black [people], you [he refers to me]
> will be acceptable [as a white person]. I won't be acceptable in South Africa
> right now, because . . . the economy has remained intact in the hands of the

white South Africans. So the blacks think that the problem is the other blacks from elsewhere in Africa who are the problem. . . . We are no longer accepted. The people who *assisted* liberation are not acceptable in South Africa. I can enter Zimbabwe, I can go to Swaziland, Botswana; I can go to Namibia, to Malawi without a visa [but] I need a visa to enter South Africa.

The absurdity of this situation was made painfully clear when N. was told that he needed a visa to attend the World Conference against Racism, Racial Discrimination, Xenophobia, and Related Intolerance, which was held in Durban, South Africa, in April 2001. He explained how conference organizers were worried about demonstrations in and around the conference venue, and how they had actively tried to discourage the residents of other African countries from attending. Would-be participants were told that they would need a letter demonstrating that they had prepaid airline tickets and hotel accommodations. So he and others in his group acquired the necessary paperwork and submitted it to the South African High Commission in Dar es Salaam, only to be told that each member of the party would need a *personal* letter of invitation from the UN Commission for Human Rights, which was sponsoring the event.

By then there was a lady, the high commissioner. . . so we went there. Now they were just pushing us from the desk. We said, "No, we're not going to leave this place. We want to speak to the high commissioner." Now, they said, "She has traveled," which was not true. So there was a white guy who was the deputy. So he called us inside: "We have heard there is a lot of noise. What is happening?" My colleague . . . said, "You're the wrong person to talk to. We wanted to speak to the high commissioner, because she's black. Not you." He said, "Oh, I represent South Africans." We said, "No, you cannot understand our problem. You see, we want to go to South Africa. We want to attend, have all the letters allowing us to go to Durban for the racism conference. Then we're being denied visas. The first day they give this reason, the next day there's this, and so on. We wanted to inform the high commissioner that when they came here for liberation, not only did they come without visa, they came without *passports.* And we as Tanzania accommodated them without passports and visa. Now we want to go [to South Africa]; we have passports, they say we need a visa. You cannot understand us." So the gentleman stood up. He asked us, "Where are your passports?" We gave him our passports. He told us, "Come tomorrow." We didn't even fill the forms. That [next] day we got the visa.

Xenophobic Violence in South Africa

As Professor N. suggests, the issue of discriminatory visa policies against Tanzanians is seen in Tanzania as part of a broader pattern of xenophobia in South Africa. The strong negative reaction to black African in-migrants intensified in South

Africa for over a decade and finally came to a head in 2008, when several black townships erupted in full-scale anti-immigrant riots that left sixty-two dead, about a third of them South African citizens. Tanzanians living in South Africa at the time were forced to flee, and false rumors circulated that Tanzanian nationals were among those killed by the mobs. As a measure of the sensitivity of these attacks, the South African High Commission in Tanzania quickly issued a press statement clarifying that none of those who lost their lives were Tanzanian.[61]

This disclaimer notwithstanding, the issue of xenophobia captured a great deal of attention in the Tanzanian press, and it was almost always set against the backdrop of the liberation struggle. Thus, for example, the following column appeared in 2008 under the heading, "I Sadly Sing the *Nkosi Sikelel*" (the South African national anthem),[62] which the author used to invoke the bonds of solidarity that once joined the peoples of Tanzania and South Africa:

> I learnt to sing *"Nkosi sikelel"* some 30 or so years ago. Then, every Sunday morning, at around 10 a.m. we would assemble inside a small National Housing Corporation house at Kinondoni, in Dar es Salaam, with some African National Congress of South Africa "comrades" and get the latest appraisal of the situation in the then land of apartheid. At this session, which lasted for about four hours, we would always commence and conclude it with an emotional rendition of the "Nkosi sikelel i Afrika" heart-rending song [sic].
>
> We were a group of young, energetic and idealist Tanzanian men and women, mostly journalists, lawyers and employees of various public and Government institutions who strongly believed in Nyerere's philosophy on liberation. Mwalimu Nyerere had drummed into our young minds that Tanzania would never consider itself free until every part of the African continent was liberated and gained its independence.
>
> This was a very powerful message which rallied almost every able bodied Tanzanian to contribute morally and materially to the liberation of Africa, mostly South Africa. No wonder Dar es Salaam, in no time, assumed the mantle of being the cradle of the African liberation and rightly housed the head office of the Liberation Committee of the then Organisation of African Union [sic].
>
> It was therefore no big surprise then to bump into the likes of Oliver Tambo, Thabo Mbeki, Sam Nujoma, Samora Machel, Robert Mugabe and Augustihno Neto in the dusty streets of Kinondoni, Temeke and Ilala in Dar es Salaam.
>
> Most Tanzanians who were in their teens and above in the 60s, 70s and even in the early 80s must have at one time or another contributed some cash, clothes, food and the like, including donating blood to the liberation forces of the African peoples in Mozambique, Zimbabwe, Namibia, Angola and South Africa. It was, simply put, a national duty.

In the Kinondoni house, we joined the hundreds of ANC comrades residing in Dar es Salaam in the important solidarity sessions. No wonder we learnt to sing that signature song. To this date I sing with my heart, and with a haunting and nostalgic emotion, the "Nkosi sikelel" song.

This week, I again sang the song. However this time I sang the song with a sad heavy heart. I sang it wondering as to where would have all those South Africa comrades gone? Where would all those whom we used to share with [sic] a bottle of beer and "konyagi" in the "Bonga Nikubonge," "Villa de Tanzania" or "Matumbi" bars in Kinondoni and Mwananyamala areas in Dar es Salaam gone to? Where are those comrades, the Ndlelas, Mfekanes, Zumas, Dlaminis . . . . ?

I sang wondered in sadness [sic] because reports coming from South Africa this week say at least 23 people have been killed there by local mobs roaming townships looking for foreigners in that land of Mandela.

As of this week the wave of attacks on foreigners in only four areas in Johannesburg had forced 13,000 others to flee their homes. They have sought refuge in police stations, churches and community halls.

The situation has become so grave that the army has been called to compliment [sic] police efforts to arrest the situation. Reason behind the killings: the local mobs believe foreigners who have fled their lands in oppressive places like Zimbabwe are stealing their jobs. Simply put: this is xenophobia at its best.

But do these mobs remember how they were welcome in places like Mazimbu in Morogoro, Pomerini, in Iringa, in Handeni, in Songea and many other places in Tanzania when they sought refuge when fleeing the racist and apartheid South Africa? Do they really remember what it means to be a refugee? Do they?[63]

In sum, the relationship between Tanzania and democratic South Africa has proven difficult at times. The depth of feeling with which Tanzanians responded to perceived slights by the post-apartheid regime in South Africa is eloquent testimony that memories of Tanzania's years on the front line of the liberation struggle continue to serve as a source of deep national pride in Tanzania long after the end of apartheid.

Conclusion

Tanzania's involvement in the anti-apartheid movement, and the southern African liberation struggles more generally, began even before the country achieved its own independence. With Mwalimu Nyerere providing a moral compass, the early years of nationhood in Tanganyika were profoundly shaped by the anticolonial battles being waged elsewhere in the region. Positioned on the front line, Tanzanians provided safe haven to politicians, guerrilla armies, and thousands of civilians displaced by fighting and political repression elsewhere. They subsequently endured a state of perpetual anxiety and fear of attack as the liberation wars sporadically spilled over into Tanzanian territory. They debated theory and tactics and were themselves indoctrinated through contact with liberation movement leaders at the university. They chanted, sang, and marched in the army and National Service camps as they were mobilized to thwart the country's enemies. They closely followed news of the struggle on daily radio broadcasts, and when called upon to perform what was presented to them as a patriotic duty, they donated blood, clothing, money, and time to the cause. Thus, the decision by Artists United against Apartheid to send *Sun City* profits to Tanzania in recognition of its role as a critical site in the anti-apartheid struggle was clearly well founded.

Given the obvious importance of the liberation struggle to Tanzania's national history and identity, Tanzanians have had difficulty making sense of the contradictory encounters they have had with the "new" South Africa in the post-apartheid era. The South Africa they recall from the years of the liberation struggle, the ANC and PAC comrades with whom they shared food and drink, sang hopeful freedom songs, and hammered out a sense of mutual political purpose—that South Africa seems to have vanished. In its place, Tanzanians find a regime that they consider cold and unwelcoming, even hostile, and a citizenry that has seemingly forgotten the sacrifices others made to help secure their freedom. At the same time, they contend, the South Africa that created the hated system of apartheid, the *makaburu* who ran the "white racist regime" and profited from the exploitation of their black brothers and sisters—*that* South Africa has suddenly shown up on Tanzania's doorstep seeking to do business.

In many respects, the changed social and political-economic dynamics underway in Tanzania mirror the painful transition South Africa itself has undergone in the post-apartheid era. This should, perhaps, come as no surprise. Whether one considers the apartheid regime's direct involvement in attempts to undermine the southern African liberation struggles in Mozambique, Angola, Rhodesia, and Namibia, the nature of the apartheid economic system, which was premised on access to surplus labor from throughout the region, or the frontline alliance itself, which made common cause around the goal of ending apartheid, the influence of South Africa's iconic system of racial segregation was widely felt. The *undoing* of apartheid, then, the dismantling of its structures and the launching of efforts to reconcile historical animosities, is likewise playing out in more remote contexts elsewhere in the region.

Tanzania and the other Frontline States have been confounded by South Africa's new presence on the continent. Whereas white-held South African firms and white South African citizens were once denied entry to most other African nations on political grounds, they have taken up residence on the continent with a vengeance in the aftermath of 1994. In this context, the memories of the liberation struggle, and its meanings, are being relived and reconfigured to serve specific purposes (cf. Confino 1997, 1388; Olick and Robbins 1998, 110). Through the telling and retelling of the liberation story, and claiming it as a vital part of their national legacy, Tanzanians have constructed a platform from which they can critique their own government's neoliberal economic policies. This critique emanates partly from a generational cohort that finds its influence on the wane in Tanzania and partly from civil society organizations whose mandate is to promote more equitable distribution of the nation's wealth. Mobilization of their frontline memories has proven to be a symbolically potent political tool in an ongoing debate over national economic policies, which is the subject of the next two chapters.

2
Invasion

The billboard greeting arriving passengers outside the Dar es Salaam airport in 2005 seemed to say it all. Erected on behalf of the South African cellular telephone giant, Vodacom, the sign depicted tourists craning their necks through the overhead hatch of a Land Rover as they snapped pictures of a giraffe in the background. The caption read, "Feel free to roam." While the ad agency's allusion to the firm's newest service option and the image's visual pun of an off-road safari vehicle "roaming" across the Tanzanian countryside offered a clever double entendre, it also effectively, if unintentionally, captured the attitude of Tanzania's economic policy makers toward foreign investors.[1] Beginning with the election of the country's second president, Ali Hassan Mwinyi (1985–1995), and extending through the political regimes of Benjamin Mkapa (1995–2005) and Jakaya Kikwete (2005–2015), the country's open-door policies were responsible for a dramatic economic transformation. The image of foreigners roaming across the Tanzanian landscape looking for investment opportunities is one that grew commonplace throughout the 1990s and into the new century.

While it is fair to say that Tanzanians were not wholly prepared for the policy changes undertaken by their government under its neoliberal economic reforms, the pivotal role of South African capital in that process came as an even greater shock. In the decade and a half following the dismantling of apartheid in the early 1990s, the economic geography of sub-Saharan Africa was radically reconfigured, with South Africa assuming the role of the continent's leading economic power. More than 150 South African firms entered Tanzania during this period, for example.[2] Once obsessed with the prospect of the South African Defence Force invading their national territory to pursue exiled ANC activists, Tanzanians were forced to come to terms with a bitter irony: the long-awaited South African invasion had come in economic rather than military form (Rwambali et al. 2000).

They also had to adjust to the fact that their own government's policies helped make this happen. To encourage further investment and expand trade relations, Tanzanian officials implemented a sweeping set of economic reforms designed to dismantle the socialist state. By eliminating protectionist barriers and relinquishing control of state-owned enterprises, government planners sought to promote greater innovation and efficiency. The adoption of these reforms also played a major role in Tanzania's successful renegotiation of its national debt. Indeed, in the eyes of the World Bank and the IMF, Tanzania firmly established itself as a star economic performer. Keeping an open door to South Africa was thus part of a broader strategy to restructure the national economy and reposition Tanzania in the world economic system.

The influx of South African capital was accordingly hailed by the Tanzanian government as a boon to national economic growth. Instead of honing the knife's edge of Tanzanian national identity on the rough politics of the southern African liberation struggle, the Tanzanian government actively sought to rehabilitate South Africa's image domestically and curry favor with the post-apartheid regime. Government officials repeatedly exhorted the Tanzanian body politic to set aside their historical animosities, stop calling the South Africans "Boers," and welcome South Africa's ANC regime as a vital economic ally (Mhawi 2004, 1). Answering critics who claimed South African companies were "colonizing" Tanzania, President Mkapa stated bluntly, "I wish we could have more South African investment in this country. The old apartheid South Africa was our enemy . . . The new independent South Africa is a friend and partner in development."[3]

The close association of South African capital with the economic reform process, however, created a series of unforeseen problems. The highly visible presence of South Africans in the Tanzanian economy was a thorny public relations problem for officials from both South Africa and Tanzania given the history of acrimonious relations between the two countries during the apartheid years (Bandawe 2006). When South African firms took the lead in acquiring parastatal companies auctioned off by the Tanzanian state under the privatization program mandated by the IMF and the World Bank, they were forced to shoulder much of the social burden of implementing unpopular reforms such as the retrenchment of civil servants. The result was a moral economic landscape full of political pitfalls, which the proponents of the new economic "partnership" between South Africa and Tanzania had great difficulty navigating.

South Africa in Africa

In the first decade and a half after 1994, South Africans made tremendous inroads into the rest of the continent, both as a source of investment capital and as a leading exporter of goods and services to the region. Freed from the constraints of the anti-apartheid economic boycott, South Africans' "pent-up entrepreneurial energy . . . explod[ed] all over Africa" (French 1995). The percentage of South Africa's overall exports sent to other African countries tripled between 1991 and 2001, producing substantial trade surpluses with several neighboring countries and an overall balance of trade with the region that was tilted 5 to 1 in South Africa's favor.[4] Its dominance as a source of foreign direct investment (FDI) was even more dramatic. Investments by South African companies in the thirteen countries that share membership in the Southern African Development Community (SADC) averaged over $800 million per year between 1994 and 2004, accounting for roughly a quarter of all FDI into the sub-region over this period (UNCTAD 2005, 7; cf. Rumney and Pingo 2004). South Africa ranked among the top three sources of inward FDI in ten of the thirteen SADC countries (Rumney and Pingo 2004, 18). Ninety-two of the largest 100 companies in South Africa contributed to this effort, and their activities embraced every economic sector.[5] Continent-wide, South African firms averaged well over $1 billion in outward-bound FDI annually between 1994 and 2003 (Itano 2003), effectively challenging, if not replacing altogether, both subregional economic powers such as Nigeria and Kenya and the continent's neocolonial trading partners in Europe, North America, and Asia as the dominant economic force in many areas.

As dramatic as these statistics are, they only begin to capture the extent of South Africa's economic presence. Most of the sources cited above define "South African capital" conventionally with exclusive reference to firms that are legally registered and/or maintain their corporate headquarters in South Africa, including government parastatals. This definition, however, omits a number of prominent firms that were once based in South Africa but have since relocated elsewhere, such as the industrial giants Anglo-American and South African Breweries, both now based in London and merged with international partners.[6] The narrower definition also neglects firms incorporated by South African nationals in offshore tax havens, such as Mauritius or any of several Caribbean countries.[7] Finally, the more exclusive definition of South African capital leaves out multinationals such as Coca-Cola and Barclay's Bank, which frequently staff their national offices throughout the region with South Africans who report to superiors based in regional hubs in Pretoria or Johannesburg (Sanchez 2008). In short, there are a number of routes by which South Africans and their economic interests have found their way onto the continent, not all of which would fall under a conventional understanding of the term "South African capital."

For the purposes of the discussion that follows, then, I use the terms "South African capital" and "South African presence" expansively to embrace firms with diverse national origins and decidedly different legal and structural profiles. For most Tanzanians, the salient social fact connecting these different firms is that the managerial and technical personnel who are actually posted to Tanzania are almost always white South Africans. The fact that black South Africans hold substantial *financial* stakes in many of the firms investing in Tanzania under South Africa's Black Economic Empowerment (BEE) program is of seemingly little consequence.[8] These firms are still firmly associated with the old *kaburu* regime.

South African State Policy vis-à-vis Foreign Direct Investment "in Africa"

The official South African government position on investment in Africa was outlined for me in an interview with a representative of the South African High Commission (SAHC) in Dar es Salaam in 2006. He began by explaining that part of the impetus for the expansion of South African capital onto the African continent was strategic. South Africa's isolation during the apartheid era had produced circumstances under which it had aggressively pursued national development objectives and ultimately succeeded in achieving "First World" socioeconomic standards, at least for ruling whites. This accomplishment stood in sharp contrast with the rest of the region, however, which remained deeply impoverished. Political analysts within the ANC argued that the dramatically different development standards experienced by South Africa and its regional neighbors threatened South Africa's political-economic stability.

It was in this context that South African president Thabo Mbeki adopted the concept of the African renaissance, originally developed by Kwame Nkrumah, and deployed it via the New Economic Partnership for African Development, or NEPAD.[9] As Mbeki put it, "It's very directly in the interest of South Africa that there should be development in the rest of the continent . . . I don't think you can have sustainable, successful development in this country if the rest of the continent is in flames" (quoted in Swarns 2002).

Mbeki's argument was echoed by an official at the South African High Commission in Dar es Salaam:

> When we attained freedom [in 1994] . . . we said the battle of reconstruction
> and development is our war. In South Africa, in the region of southern Africa,
> in the continent of Africa, the battle of reconstruction is our war. And how are
> we going to do that reconstruction, if [we] want to survive surrounded by a
> sea of poverty? . . . there is no way that we have a policy of reconstruction and
> development in South Africa and that policy does not benefit the surroundings
> that are of course severe in terms of the poverty [sic]. So the policy of recon-
> struction and development . . . had to now be taken. . . . Kwame Nkrumah['s]
> "African Renaissance" . . . the rebirth of Africa . . . that is what drives the
> foreign policy of South Africa.[10]

The idea here was that South Africa could put its economic muscle to work on behalf of the rest of the continent in ways that would be reminiscent of the role the United States played when it implemented the Marshall Plan in post–World War II Europe:

> "Every continent needs an America . . ." This is how one South African inves-
> tor responded when questioned about the importance of South African invest-

ment in a country like Mozambique. This comment immediately conjures up the image of the bully on the block, but the intention is subtler. It is widely accepted that the economic growth of Western Europe after World War II and the Asian economic miracle are a direct result of American investment and aid in those regions, and the opening of its market to their exports. (Grobbelaar 2004, 5)

While the lofty rhetoric of an African renaissance seemed to embrace the noble cause of creating a robust, interdependent Africa, Mbeki's own objectives in pushing the NEPAD agenda forward were considerably more pragmatic. As he revealed in an op-ed piece in the *New York Times,* Africa's relative poverty represented an opportunity for advanced capitalist countries to extract super profits from the region:

On offer to the investors from the highly developed economies are sound prospects in countries whose infrastructures—limited telecommunications systems, poor roads, rail and port facilities, sometimes dilapidated cities—hold the promise of *exponential improvement.* Where [other markets] are approaching saturation, Africa offers rapid growth. (Mbeki 2002, emphasis added; cf. Hudson 2007)

This proposition was especially attractive to South Africa's own corporate community, which had effectively exhausted the potential of the home market during the years of isolation under apartheid.

Pretoria offered South African firms substantial incentives for investing in the region. Between 1997 and 2004, for example, Pretoria increased the amount of capital South African investors could commit to new projects in the region forty-fold. Rules on repatriation of profits, exchange rates, and taxation were all similarly relaxed during this period (see Miller, Oloyede, and Saunders 2008 for a full discussion of these reforms). The combined effect of these state incentives, the availability of lower labor costs beyond national borders, and the efforts by host governments within the region to attract foreign investment was that continental Africa offered significantly higher rates of return on investment than either the South African home market or other parts of the world. Select industries were said to offer returns as high as 30 to 50 percent.[11] On average, analysts estimated that profits were four times higher than investors realized in advanced capitalist countries and twice as high as in Asia (Grobbelaar 2004). Given these favorable conditions, South African firms moved onto the continent in droves. Indeed, by the early 2000s, some earned more from their offshore activities than they did from their home markets (Miller, Oloyede, and Saunders 2008).

All of this begs an obvious question: if profits in Africa were so high, why were capitalists from other countries not more heavily involved in tapping into these opportunities? Or to put it differently, how did South Africans achieve so much success investing in a region that was generally avoided by investors from other parts of the world?

Tight Briefs: Masculinist Hype for South African Business

Throughout the period of South African expansion onto the continent, the African business press built up an elaborate mythology that essentially located the explanation for South African business success in the cultural realm. The basic argument began with the premise that the prevailing political economic and social conditions in much of the African continent in the decade following the end of apartheid made any investment by outsiders extremely risky. The risks to investors included "externalities" such as natural disasters (drought, floods), unstable governance and corruption, disruptions wrought by civil conflict, and the ravages of HIV/AIDS on workplace productivity, as well as a number of factors with a more direct bearing on the business climate, including "nationalisation, expropriation, confiscation . . . restrictions on the repatriation of dividends . . . [and] nonpayment for goods or services" (Duncan 2005). Viewed from this perspective, the prospect of successfully extracting profits from African business ventures was presented as daunting in the extreme.

According to risk assessors such as U.S.-based Aon Insurance, no African country qualified to be listed in either the "low-risk" or "medium-to-low risk" categories (these designations were reserved for the advanced capitalist countries of North America, Western Europe, Australia, and Japan). Only five African countries—South Africa, Namibia, Botswana, Morocco, and Tunisia—were included in the "medium-risk" category, which also included the "emerging" economies of Brazil, India, China, and Russia. Sixteen African nations, including Tanzania, were included in the "medium-high risk" group, and the remaining countries on the continent—the majority—were grouped together in the "high risk" category (Rose 2005b).

This pernicious geography of "risk" was reinforced by tropes of African primitivism and backwardness. Thus, one observer felt compelled to stress, "The terms of a written agreement can change *if you happen to offend the tribal headman*" (Green 2005, emphasis added). Another invoked the "black hole of reliable information about the continent," reproducing the image of Africa as terra incognita (Rose 2005b). A third quoted an Afrikaner who ran a hotel in Tanzania as saying, "Before we came, they were eating grass" (Martin 2001).

The implication of all of this riskiness and backwardness was that Africa required a special breed of investor, one who embodied corporate machismo. "Africa is not for sissies" or for "the faint of heart," so went the refrain; it offered "rich pickings" but only "for the brave."[12] In this context, a decidedly masculine hype surrounding South African investors materialized. An advertisement for Roshcon, a subsidiary of

South Africa's giant energy parastatal Eskom, that appeared in the trade magazine *African Business* in 1997 provides an especially evocative case in point.

> The brief: Installation of an emergency power plant. The reason: A chronic shortage of electricity. The client: The Tanzanian Electricity Supply Company Limited [TANESCO]. The place: Tanzania. The logistics: A nightmare. The deadline: 160 days. No margin for error. No time to talk.
>
> Together with joint venture partners from the USA and Canada, Roshcon International took up the challenge. A challenge which drew on every project management skill. Every shred of experience. Innovation. Teamwork. And luck.
>
> In this case, bad luck. The breakdown of the carrier vessel transporting the huge GTG units from Houston.
>
> Despite this setback, and the sheer magnitude of the project, Roshcon International accomplished a truly remarkable achievement in power generation. Within 134 days.
>
> 134 days that not only brought power to the Tanzanian people. But built the nation through the empowerment of its people.
>
> 134 days. Now let's talk tight briefs.[13]

This ad copy adopts the voice and tone of a tough male South African working in the rough-and-tumble energy supply industry. It was a "nightmare" of a project, intones the imaginary speaker. The odds against success were huge to begin with and grew steeper with a near catastrophe at sea. Despite all that, the firm brought the project in *ahead of schedule!* The disembodied speaker pauses to rhetorically hitch up his pants, his macho swagger and pugnacious attitude almost palpable: "Now let's talk tight briefs."

The recurrent motif of masculine bravado among South Africans was matched by a sense of nostalgia for colonial adventure and the romantic allure of life on the "virtually virgin terrain" (SARPN 2004) of the underdeveloped African frontier. This neocolonial derring-do is very much on display in a tongue-in-cheek advertisement for Sea Cliff Hotel in Dar es Salaam. One of Dar's premier luxury hotels, the Sea Cliff and an adjoining deluxe shopping center are both South African-designed and -managed. Situated on the Msasani peninsula, arguably the most elite section of Dar es Salaam, the shopping center contains a high-end grocery store featuring South African products, a popular South African steakhouse franchise (Spurs), an office for South African Airways, and the offices of the South African–run risk insurer Alexander Forbes, among other boutique shops and restaurants. The familiar luxury surroundings and attendant shopping amenities make the Sea Cliff a prime social venue for the female spouses of South African businessmen, in particular, who frequently use the hotel's bars and restaurants for birthday parties and other gatherings.

The Sea Cliff's status as a leading destination for South African business travelers was featured in a humorous advertising campaign the hotel launched in the early 2000s. A mock-up of a movie poster depicted the hotel manager as a kind of latter-day Indiana Jones, dressed in old aviator glasses and headgear (see figure 1). The poster was emblazoned with the heading: "Jo'burg Jones is back in 'The Treasure of Dar es Salaam.'" The "plight" of the South African investor seeking suitable business accommodations was captured in deliberately florid prose:

> Soaring high above mere mortals, famed adventurer and business tycoon, Jo'burg Jones, is back to face the challenge of a lifetime. For discovering the truth behind that remarkable East African legend of "THE PERFECT BUSI-NESS HOTEL" is only a prelude in this epic adventure, as breathtaking panoramas and elegant surroundings provide the backdrop for what quickly becomes a seductive lifestyle. One where prompt attentive service and minute attention to detail are only the more visible enticements. Constantly assailed by a cornucopia of culinary delights and thoroughly enjoyable activities, only skill, daring and a will of iron can prevail against the tendrils of luxury.[14]

Tongue in cheek notwithstanding, this ad worked on a number of levels to reinforce the neocolonial chic of South Africans working abroad. Tanzania was represented as a space where "mere mortals" feared to tread. Only "tycoons" from Johannesburg possessing "skill, daring and a will of iron" managed to prevail in "the challenge of a lifetime." It also reinforced the image of Tanzania as a developmental backwater, a place where finding a "perfect" business hotel is the stuff of legend.

South African *Savoir Faire*

More generally, South Africans were represented in the African business press as possessing an intimate familiarity with all things African, a kind of *savoir faire en Afrique*. In this discourse, investors from America and Europe were disparaged as being "hugely ignorant about African affairs and open only to hearing bad news from the continent." They were accordingly much more likely to invest in Asia "where it is safer" (Graham 2003). By contrast, it was presumed that South Africans understood Africa better than anyone else:

> [South Africa] has executives who feel little of the trepidation that deters many Western investors. They know that the number of stable democracies in Africa has grown over the past decade and that the phenomenon has created new business opportunities. Many are familiar with poor communities where crime rates are high and recognize that few people have credit histories since most of South Africa's population still lives in poverty. (Swarns 2002)

They knew from personal experience in South Africa that these constraints did not necessarily preclude the development of new markets for goods and services. This knowledge was said to give them a more realistic set of expectations:

> The standard response from South African business people, asked about why [sic] they do so well in Africa, is often "because we know Africa so well." Although there is some truth in this assessment, the key feature distinguishing South Africa from other foreign investors in their assessment of risk relates to the issue of *expectation*. South African investors *expect* to be faced with logistical and bureaucratic hurdles when contemplating investment on the continent, even though most agree that they evaluate risk in exactly the same way as their foreign competitors do. There is no magic bullet to overcome the many barriers and pitfalls that accompany investment in Africa. However, South African investors who are often relative newcomers to other countries on the continent have shown remarkable skill at developing coping strategies. (Grobbelaar 2004, emphasis added).

And with such low expectations, South Africans were wont to travel prepared for anything, "even if this means bringing your own water, generators and waste disposal equipment" (Green 2005).

South Africans also supposedly succeeded in business ventures on the continent because of their "African-ness," and the key insights they possessed into how to "do business" in an African cultural milieu (Miller 2005). Shared cultural knowledge was said to give them a "competitive edge" over investors from the rest of the world (Grobbelaar, cited in Itano 2003). Exactly what this meant in practice was often left unstated, however, as the following comment by a conservative middle-aged Afrikaner living and working in Tanzania illustrates:

> You don't actually think about South Africans being "in Africa," but it's a very important factor in our being able to succeed here where others have failed. You understand the local person better because it's a part of your own history. At [our firm], we've hired South Africans, Brits, Americans, Europeans, and Australians to come out for two-year contracts . . . For most of the others, it takes a good year to get used to it, but the best workers we've had by far are those from South Africa because they know what to expect.[15]

This characterization begs several questions. The speaker asserts that "you understand the local person because it's a part of your own history." One wonders just what part of this man's personal history gave him an "understanding" of "the local person" in Tanzania, and to what ends the insights derived from this "understanding" were applied. He describes South Africans as the best workers "because they know what to expect." What exactly *did* they expect, and how did this shape their interactions with Tanzanians so decisively as to ensure success where others had failed?

Clearly they expected privation. Whereas others had to "get used to it," South Africans were portrayed as already tough enough to withstand "Third World" living conditions, circumstances where, according to one South African worker newly arrived to take up a job in the safari industry in 2004, there was "not even a proper cinema." Among other bits of business savvy, South Africans depicted themselves as knowing how to effectively deal with, and within, systems of corruption:

> When I first arrived here, the police used to pull me over for not wearing a seatbelt. And I'd say to them, you mean just like those taxi drivers over there and there? And they'd have to agree. Then they'd say that they were going to charge me a 10,000 shilling [US $10] fine. So I'd say, fine, I needed a receipt. And they'd say the receipt could only be had at the police station. So I'd say, fine get in the car, and let's go to the police station. And eventually, they'd just wave me on. See, for people who haven't lived here, or who don't have experience in Africa, they wouldn't know what might happen. But now, the police all know me, and they know they can't get anything from me, so they let me go.[16]

They also aggressively defended their homes and investments abroad with elaborate security measures. Many South Africans living in Tanzania took up residence in gated communities or walled compounds and carried out their business in workplaces protected by electric fences, armed security personnel, and/or guard dogs. Indeed, one of the special niches occupied by South African capital on the continent was in the area of paramilitary security forces (Reno 1997; Howe 1998).

In sum, an elaborate mythology has been constructed around South African business culture. Whether South African investors have succeeded in their African ventures because, or in spite, of their cultural values is highly debatable, however, as the Tanzanian case demonstrates.

South Africa in Tanzania

Near the end of Benjamin Mkapa's second term in the Tanzanian president's office, he clearly and unambiguously articulated an official line that was strongly in favor of expanded South African investment in Tanzania: while the old South Africa was surely among Tanzania's worst enemies, he argued, the new South Africa should be embraced as a "partner" in development (Moses 2002). Given prevailing trends in bilateral trade relations and investment patterns, however, this was a tough case to sell to the Tanzanian public. Indeed, to the extent that relations between Tanzania and South Africa could be considered a partnership at all, it was one that was notably lopsided.

While Tanzania was not the largest recipient of South African capital on the continent, it nonetheless ranked as a *preferred* investment target in a number of surveys of South African corporate heads, including the Johannesburg Metropolitan Chamber of Commerce and Industry and various mining investors.[17] Indeed, virtually every major South African firm actively pursuing investment targets in the region included Tanzanian assets in its portfolio (Southern African Regional Poverty Network 2004; cf. Gibbon 1999). In little more than a decade, South Africans acquired controlling interests in Tanzania's largest banking chain, the national airline, and the national brewery. They purchased or built hotels, gold and gemstone mines, and hunting and photographic safari companies. They were awarded a contract to run the national electric utility, and they set up the country's largest cellular telephone and satellite television networks. They bought factories producing plastics, cement, sugar, and fertilizer. And they quintupled their exports to Tanzania by marketing a wide variety of middle-class consumer items ranging from furniture and ceramic tiles to clothing and fine wines.[18] The influx was relentless. South African presence grew so pronounced that Kenyan observers began disparaging Tanzania as "little Jo'burg" (Hudson 2007, 130).

One of the most important reasons South African investors moved so aggressively into Tanzania was because of its comparative advantages in specific economic sectors. Representatives of the South African mining and tourism industries in particular sought to tap into Tanzania's rich endowment of natural resources. Thanks in part to substantial inflows of South African capital, Tanzania is now the third largest producer of gold on the African continent after South Africa itself and Ghana. And the South African safari industry now routinely books tours for international clients that include stops in both South Africa and Tanzania.

Others saw Tanzania as a stepping stone en route to the realization of more systematic corporate expansion strategies. Explicit references to Cecil Rhodes's dream of establishing a continental railroad linking "Cape to Cairo" are recurrent in this connection.[19] The CEO for Miller SAB, for example, which in 2005 operated forty-four breweries and ten bottling plants in sixteen different African countries, including Tanzania, said, "If there were more of Africa, we would invest in it."[20]

Tanzania also presented opportunities for gleaning windfall profits from initiatives aimed at promoting regional integration (cf. Roodt 2008). One vivid example was the role South African firms played in building an "inland port facility" in Tanzania to link the otherwise incompatible southern and East African rail networks. Southern African railroads were constructed with narrower gauge tracks than those maintained by the Tanzanian Railway Corporation (TRC) and the rest of the East African railroad industry, and for decades this represented a serious impediment to free-flowing regional trade. In the Tanzanian town of Kidatu, where the two rail networks pass within meters of each other, South African investors erected a set of cranes to lift cargo containers directly from one track to the other using specially modified train cars. This facility cut weeks off the time required to ship South African goods by ocean freighter through Tanzanian ports, a critical factor for firms working in the mining industry in northeastern Tanzania in particular (Robertson 1999; see further discussion of the regional rail system in chapter 1).

Finally, many of the firms that moved to Tanzania were simply reproducing vertically integrated business relationships that were already in place in South Africa. Thus, for example, the heavy investment by a number of South African firms in the gold and gemstone mining industry in Tanzania dramatically reshaped the economic geography of the region from the perspective of firms that serviced the mining industry in South Africa. Among the corporations that subsequently established branches in Tanzania were African Explosives, which supplied blasting materials to engineers at mine sites; construction firms such as Murray and Roberts, Group Five, and MDS Architects, which helped construct mining compounds; and specialists in medical insurance such as Medex, which promised timely evacuation direct to South Africa's "First World" medical centers in the case of mine-related injuries. These firms were joined by banking, accounting, and other legal service providers.

The close business ties between South African firms was a source of tremendous frustration on the part of Tanzanians who might otherwise have been engaged to provide these services. A woman from a relatively wealthy Asian Tanzanian family with multiple business interests, for example, claimed that South Africans closed ranks when it came to sourcing materials for any kind of investment project:

> If you are bidding for a tender for some job with a South African firm, it's like there's a secret handshake that they do—some sort of oath that they take that: "I will only do business with South Africans." Because it is impossible to win those bids. Your bid could be thousands of dollars less than the South African bidder, but he's still going to get the contract. It's only when there is absolutely no alternative that they will offer bids to other bidders . . . This is true of even the international firms—as long as there is a single South African working there, they will always look for another South African when it comes time to award contracts.[21]

When I repeated this assertion to a South African businessman in Dar es Salaam, he scoffed at the notion that national identity would skew his business decisions in this way. "I mean it adds value, or it doesn't add value. It can't just be pre-sourced directly because of South Africa. I honestly can't think of anybody that would do that. Certainly not in my experience. It's just silly." At the same time, when choosing a firm to erect a new building to house his business in 2002, he selected a South African general contractor for the job. When challenged to explain this apparent contradiction, he scrambled to explain:

But you know *there* was a partnership, and . . . you go into partnership with
someone that you *trust* because we were going to invest $15 million . . . You
want to make sure you know who your partner is and they're going to deliver
on time . . . We were putting our bucks down. This thing better open on time
because otherwise we're going to be in trouble. So yeah, we worked very, very
closely. And maybe nationalities are the same—we know each other—but
that's just sound business. If you look at . . . where we were *procuring* from, the
staff we were using, the *expertise* we were using, [it was] Tanzanian, Tanzanian, all first choice . . . And we're delighted with the standard of work we got.
It far exceeded what we could get in South Africa in terms of finish and things
like that. Tanzanians. You can't say it was some Afrikaans guy skimming the
walls [laughter].[22]

In sum, South Africans pursued a number of different business strategies in
moving to Tanzania. The overwhelming impression left in the wake of these efforts
was that they had taken over nearly everything of value in the Tanzanian economy.
One expatriate businessman traveling in Tanzania in 2003 commented,

Tanzania is experiencing a new kind of colonialism it seems. South Africans
are managing the hotel where I am staying. They are managing the beer that
I am drinking. They are managing the aircraft that I will fly to Mwanza.
And, there, they are managing the gold mines. . . . With the new commercial
invasions from the South and the nostalgic reminders of the colonizing west,
Mwalimu Julius Nyerere must be turning in his grave. (Fox 2003)

Nyerere's memory was similarly invoked by a research contact in 2004 who vented
his frustration: "Some people are saying that if our first president could come back
to life today, he would die again to see what has happened. You can't just keep selling everything!" A local community activist alluding to South African capital's new
transcontinental footprint concluded simply, "We now live in the United States of
South Africa."[23]

Managing Public Relations

The political sensitivity of South Africa's presence was not lost on the Tanzanian
government, which was at pains to downplay its significance. Ever the apologist for
foreign investors, President Mkapa called attention to Tanzanian Investment Center
(TIC) data showing that, of the roughly 2,500 projects approved by the TIC between
1995 and 2004, only 24 percent were *wholly* owned by foreigners; 44 percent were
owned by Tanzanians, and 32 percent were joint ventures (Luhwago 2005).[24] In 2001
and again in 2006, the TIC released additional data showing that the country's leading foreign investor was not South Africa, as was widely assumed, but rather the
United Kingdom.[25] Despite receiving prominent mention in the Tanzanian press,

however, these data were misleading. In presenting *cumulative* totals dating back to 1990, they failed to capture historical trends, notably obscuring the peak of South African investments in the early 2000s. South Africa emerged as the *leading* source of FDI in the 2001 fiscal year, for example, when its largest inputs in the mining sector were recorded.[26] It was also the leading source of imports into the country for the period 2000–2005, accounting for 20 percent of the total during those years.[27]

South African officials were similarly attuned to public relations problems associated with their country's large and growing presence in Tanzania. The South African High Commissioner's office sought to blunt criticism of South African investors by stressing not only that South Africans were *invited* to come to Tanzania, but that South Africans were morally obligated to invest. As the high commissioner himself put it at an event sponsored by the South Africa Business Forum in Dar es Salaam:

> Tanzanians are saying: "Why are they coming here? Why aren't they happy in South Africa?" And I keep telling them that we came here by invitation from [former president] Mwinyi. That we have invested here in recognition and gratitude for what Tanzania did for us during the liberation struggle . . . We have an economy with a certain level of development, and Tanzania deserves to have the same development standards. So that is what we are doing: helping Tanzanians to reach those standards for themselves.[28]

Who could be against Tanzania finally receiving just compensation for its contribution to the cause of liberation? A second SAHC official echoed the point:

> [South Africans were in Tanzania] not necessarily to come and make profit but to come and assist Tanzania, because what Tanzania needs is a sizeable financial injection, a capital investment, foreign direct investment in the country . . . It was because of the [unintelligible] that was made by President Mwinyi of Tanzania and President Mandela. And President Mandela went back to South Africa and requested South Africans to come and assist Tanzania, to come and invest in Tanzania. So that is the reason.[29]

This SAHC representative, himself a black South African, went on, struggling to articulate the relevance of the ANC government's "color-blind" race policies to Tanzania:

> And of course then you'll find that a majority of the people that come here, who are in business here, of course, are of a particular color . . . which becomes a question to certain sections within Tanzania. But as South Africans we carry one flag, whether we're black or white. And we are past the stage of racialism in South Africa. We're talking about *South Africa*. So those South Africans are here representing the interests of South Africa . . . not . . . as individuals, people differentiated in terms of the colors and so on. So that is one thing that should

be understood. And when President Mkapa took over from President Mwinyi, he also reemphasized the criticality of the consolidation of the economic relations with South Africa, because South Africa is very important, because of its size of economy, because of its level of technologies . . . And therefore that even encouraged more South Africans to come.

He recognized, however, that the benefits of such investments were not distributed equally throughout the Tanzanian economy. In his view, the concentration of economic control in the hands of a few elite Tanzanians carried with it the sizable political risk of exacerbating class tensions within Tanzanian society. In South Africa, he argued, representatives of the majority had seized upon the end of apartheid to renegotiate the social contract between poor and wealthy citizens in that country. But that discussion had not yet started in Tanzania: "You can't talk about black economic empowerment in Tanzania, as is the case in South Africa. But you need something more that's not here . . . Because if the population of this country is not taken care of, especially the disadvantaged communities, then it's a recipe for disaster in the long run."

"Investor Friendly" Tanzania

While officials in the South African and Tanzanian governments sought to highlight the fact that "South Africa" was acting on its moral obligation to invest in Tanzania, individual investors took a much more pragmatic view. A leading member of the South African Business Forum in Dar es Salaam agreed that he and his colleagues in the business fraternity were "generally . . . supportive of NEPAD. . . . We're very patriotic, so whatever South Africa is doing to fly the flag, we'll very proudly go along with." When pressed, however, on whether he felt there was a particular moral obligation for South Africans to invest in former frontline states given the legacy of apartheid, he replied, "I don't think we're picking and choosing anymore. I think they were the first part of the outreach, if you like . . . But now it's going beyond that."[30] A director of ABSA bank, which held a controlling interest in Tanzania's National Bank of Commerce, put the case succinctly: "We believe we understand African risk and can mitigate the risk . . . But we're not investing in Africa for altruism. We're investing in Africa to make some money."[31]

In this regard, South African firms found a willing partner in the Tanzanian government. Indeed, Tanzania's attractiveness as a destination for foreign corporate capital stemmed from the country's deliberate policies to make itself "investor friendly." This process dates to the regime of President Ali Hassan Mwinyi, whose laissez-faire attitude towards foreign investors led to his being dubbed "Mzee Rukhsa."[32] Loosely translated as "Mr. Anything Goes," Mwinyi's nickname marked the sharp break he made from the austere and tightly controlled socialist policies of his predecessor, Julius Nyerere. It also signified his greatly relaxed attitude toward the business activities of civil servants and foreign investors, a posture that was reflected in the rampant corruption of his regime. The process of deregulation that he set in motion was extended and intensified under each of his successors, Benjamin Mkapa and Jakaya Kikwete.

While there were many critics of the social disparities produced under the neoliberal policies of successive Tanzanian regimes, the government's efforts resulted in Tanzania achieving relatively high economic growth rates and a dramatic increase in foreign direct investment.[33] Net foreign direct investments in Tanzania were negligible between 1970 and 1993, averaging only slightly more than US$5 million per year. Beginning in 1994 and extending through 2006, however, investments soared to an annual average of roughly US$280 million, with the peak year of 1999 totaling nearly half a billion dollars (UNCTAD 2009).

The cornerstone of the country's neoliberal economic policies that paved the way for this surge in foreign investment was the privatization of nearly 400 state owned enterprises. The privatization exercise centered on many of the country's most prized economic assets as well as dozens of run-down and bankrupt manufacturing concerns and derelict properties. By the time the Parastatal Sector Reform Commission, the government body created in 1992 to oversee divestiture of national assets, was disbanded in 2007, it had successfully disposed of over 350 parastatal enterprises. South Africa was a key player in this process (Waigama 2008).

The availability of valuable assets alone may not have been sufficient grounds for investors to undertake new business ventures in Tanzania, however. The Tanzanian Investment Center highlights fifteen major legal reforms that were enacted in the late 1990s and early 2000s, all with the purpose of streamlining the investment process.[34] The goal of these regulatory reforms was threefold: to increase foreign investment, to secure continuing donor aid, and to qualify for debt forgiveness. In order to achieve each of these targets, Tanzanian economic policy makers became obsessed with the question of how they measured up against regional competitors in providing a business-friendly investment climate.[35]

Throughout the early 2000s, state policy makers were routinely quoted in the regional business press, where they drew elaborate comparisons between Tanzania, its East African neighbors, Kenya and Uganda, and their peers elsewhere on the continent. Miniscule ratings shifts from one study period to the next were cause for celebration, and gains in one arena were selectively reported even when performance in others was poor. Thus, for example, the press highlighted key findings contained in the "Africa Competitiveness Report 2000–2001," which listed Tanzania as tops in the "improvement index" and second in the "optimism index," both indicating changes that had occurred since the previous report in 1997. The article went on to say, however, that Tanzania ranked only fourteenth overall out of twenty-nine countries surveyed due to relatively low scores on such measures as tax evasion, irregular payments, paved roads, electric power supply, infant mortality, import tariffs, openness to trade, certainty of rules and laws, HIV screening and education, primary school enrollment, and gross domestic savings. It also duly noted that Uganda ranked seventeenth in the survey while Kenya occupied the twenty-second position.[36]

The dubious methodologies and interpretive techniques employed by the authors of such studies notwithstanding, this is one arena where perception was at least somewhat connected to reality. Due to its stellar performance in meeting a broad and disparate range of economic reform objectives, Tanzania was rewarded by being named one of the first five countries in the world to qualify for debt forgiveness under the World Bank's Heavily Indebted Poor Countries (HIPC) initiative (Kelley 2000; Mariwa 2006). It was also one of only twenty-three countries worldwide to qualify for initial donor grants under the U.S. government's Millennium Development Challenge program (Edwin 2005). These reforms significantly buoyed the confidence of foreign investors.

South Africans and Economic Reforms

Through a number of high-profile acquisitions of state-run firms, South African capital gradually assumed a more central role in Tanzania's transition from state socialism to private-sector management. South African managers were accordingly thrust into the role of instilling new forms of fiscal discipline on Tanzanian workers. Thousands of former public servants lost their jobs and the government sinecure they once enjoyed in a wave of retrenchments launched by private South African employers.[37] Bitter battles resulted as workers displaced by the privatization exercise staged strikes and work stoppages, engaged in arson, and launched other forms of protest against their new employers. Workers at the National Bank of Commerce, which transferred 70 percent ownership rights to ABSA banks of South Africa in 2000, took NBC to court within months of the privatization agreement to force recognition of job security guarantees previously negotiated by the government (Rwambali 2000e, 4). They then staged a series of strikes over the next several years demanding better pay and working conditions (2002, 2006), improved job security (2003), and payment of terminal benefits for 600 workers who were eventually retrenched (2005).[38]

A similar pattern was observed when the South African utility management firm NetGroup Solutions was awarded a contract to run the Tanzania Electric Supply Company (TANESCO) in 2002 (see chapter 3). Fearing the loss of jobs and benefits, TANESCO workers barricaded the entrances to TANESCO company headquarters and prevented NetGroup executives from entering management offices for five months. It was only when the government guaranteed that it would provide a severance package for workers that the standoff was ended. According to the negotiated settlement, 1,200 workers agreed to be "voluntarily" retrenched (Ghanadan 2009, 412–13).

Finally, the Kilombero Sugar Company, which has been controlled by the Natal-based Illovo Sugar Company since 1998, was hit by a four-week general strike in 2000, with workers demanding greater job security in the face of corporate restructuring. A site of labor unrest even before the arrival of South Africans (Tripp 1997), the factory at Kilombero was occupied by government riot police to quell the labor action. In an effort to keep Illovo from leaving the country, the state eventually terminated all 3,000 of the company's workers and agreed to pay their terminal benefits and pension costs itself. This left Illovo in the position of being able to rehire less militant workers from among those who were retrenched (Rwambali 2000c, 1; July 3, 2000, 1.) A second sugar company operated by South Africans in the Moshi area in northern Tanzania, the Tanganyika Plantation Company, was hit by arsonists twice in 2007 after several workers were sacked and forcibly evicted following a succession of "illegal" strikes.[39]

A Tanzanian executive working for one of the largest South African firms operating in Tanzania tried to rationalize this trend towards downsizing within the parastatal sector: "One of the biggest negatives through time was painful job shedding. That was one of the things which caused some sort of a stigma that, okay, if South Africa comes in, you lose jobs. But it's not South Africa [per se], it's an economic reality."[40] A representative of the Parastatal Sector Reform Commission (PSRC) put the case more bluntly:

> You need someone [in a managerial position] who won't sleep night and day to see that the company fares better. A private business, private ownership, is ruthless. The only thing they understand is profit. If they can walk across your head to get a benefit, they will. This is the bad side of privatization. The good side is efficiency. If you can get a job done with 100 workers, why have 200? People complain about the retrenchment that accompanies privatization, but these efficiencies are necessary to ensure that the firms remain viable. (Kavishe 2005)

The basic idea was that efficiencies could only be achieved through layoffs and that it was only through efficiencies that moribund firms could be made profitable once again. In the eyes of reformers, this could only happen if a wholesale reworking of the culture of work was undertaken in Tanzania, complete with the implementation of a meritocracy:

> [Regarding job] pruning . . . of course you have to prune. How did people come by these jobs in the first place? It used to be you'd get a phone call from this or that government minister or high-ranking official, and he would say, "I have this nephew or relative, can you find a place for him?" That's how people were

employed. By that time, there was no SMS [that is, there were no cellphones], but if they had it, you would probably have gotten a job by text messaging or email! [laughter] If you have 200 people doing jobs that 100 people could normally do, the surplus 100 are not doing productive work, and thus are not really employed. In fact, they suck up resources. An idle mind is a dangerous thing. It is better you pay them to stay at home as a woman industrialist in Zanzibar has done than have them come to work with nothing to do where their creative talents can be put to destructive use. Rather than have a lot of workers and pay them poorly, it's better that you have only a few and pay them well. Because if you have 200 workers instead of the 100 you actually need, what happens is you pretend to pay them, and they pretend to work, and nothing ever gets done. (Kavishe 2005)

The struggle to negotiate better severance packages and secure pension payments often took years to resolve and was a recurrent source of bitter resentment for Tanzanian workers.[41] Under the terms of privatization, there was legitimate ambiguity over who bore responsibility for the pension payments of parastatal retirees, the government or the new owners of privatized firms. Indeed, as the case of TANESCO detailed above illustrates, this was often a key bargaining point when it came to negotiating the sale of an ailing government asset (Kavishe 2005). But structural problems with the pension funds ran deep. Large numbers of workers reaching retirement age discovered that their pension programs had been dramatically underfunded through the years:

Most of the pensions started around 1967, when most of our firms were nationalized by our former president. If you begin counting from that time, what you see is a very large cohort of workers. . . . But [due to] the social transformation from the socialist system to the arrival of market forces . . . they are going out at retirement age with a salary that is ten times more. And when you calculate your pension on the basis of the salary that you *retired* with, you discover the system cannot support the number of claims . . . Therefore there has been a lot of friction. I don't think the pension fund had enough funds because of that aging population.[42]

This executive explained further that the government's raiding of pension funds to pay salaries did not make it any easier for subsequent regimes to deliver on the moral obligation to supply full retirement benefits:

Past pilferage from pension funds has left current retirement packages un- or underfunded. . . . The government portion of the pension has been paid, but most often the firms' portion has not been paid. The automatic response is that "they should be hung from the next tree!" But the situation is often more complicated. The perpetrators reply, "We had to rob the pensions to keep the firm afloat because of poor productivity of labor. The option was to either pay salaries from the pension, or not pay salaries at all." (Kavishe 2005)

Finally, technical problems with outmoded record keeping presented the Parastatal Sector Reform Commission with a procedural nightmare:

> Now the PSRC and other government agencies are left with the huge task of tracking claims, because all records were kept manually. It requires a massive effort to check all firms, private and government, over a thirty year period, with thousands of employees, and with payments coming from both government and the firms themselves. It's a big, big problem when companies have not been remitting funds into the pensions, or have only been remitting piecemeal whenever they choose. (Kavishe 2005)

Clearly the structural and technical problems with the pension program and the legacy of socialist-era patronage systems made the transition to neoliberal economic governance especially complicated. This fact notwithstanding, South Africans' central involvement as investors and managers charged with implementing reforms and imposing new forms of discipline in so many companies left them open to scrutiny. Persistent press reports of layoffs, pension disputes, and related strike actions and work stoppages had a strong impact on public opinion. The impression that South African managers were especially ruthless in their dealings with workers was widespread among Tanzanian trade unions, whose members were quick to link this perceived callousness to apartheid. The white South African managing director of an insurance firm in Tanzania alluded to the rising tensions that emerged in this context: "I do not know what has gone wrong because Tanzanians' attitude towards South African investors has changed . . . This *mzungu* (white) notion [the singling out of whites for vilification] should come to an end, to create a conducive working environment" (quoted in Rwambali et al. 2000, 2). The director of the Tanzanian Investment Center, whose job it is to promote foreign investment, weighed in with a cautionary message for all of the parties concerned:

> Both Tanzanians and South African investors should be careful because we are in a situation where working styles in South Africa could be translated as harassment in Tanzania. . . . Most South African investors are white. When anything happens at a working place, Tanzanian workers are reminded of (apartheid) South Africa. I think we need to educate our people and investors should spare a little time to study Tanzanian culture. (Quoted in Rwambali et al. 2000, 2)

The shop floor struggles surrounding the generation of new workplace efficiencies and the fallout from layoffs and pension payment problems served to reinforce preexisting negative attitudes toward South Africa originating in the anti-apartheid movement of previous decades. The government's aggressive attempts to court South African investors were at least partly counterproductive. Instead of ushering in a new social contract premised on greater fiscal discipline and workplace efficiency, the efforts of the government and its new South African partners polarized the Tanzanian body politic even further.

Conclusion

Tanzanians could not have anticipated in 1994 that the trickle of investments and imported South African goods would become a torrent by the end of the century. Nor did they expect that South African presence would be led almost exclusively by whites rather than ANC comrades like those who had lived in exile in Tanzania for decades prior to the end of apartheid. Finally, no one would have predicted that their own government would have welcomed these white foreigners with such open arms, effectively handing them control over so much of the national economy.

In retrospect, the investment climate of the 1990s created the perfect conditions for the expansion of South African economic interests in Tanzania. In South Africa, the end of the economic boycott, the enactment of policies facilitating capital expenditure on the continent, and the need to expand beyond saturated national markets all favored a move onto the continent. Meanwhile, in Tanzania, the presence of a wealth of exploitable natural resources, the dismantling of protectionist trade barriers, the streamlining of investment procedures, and the auctioning off of dozens of viable parastatal enterprises dramatically opened up the national economy to outsiders. These and other unprecedented changes resulted in hundreds of South African firms, large and small, trekking to Tanzania in search of profits.

The upshot was that South African investors and the Tanzanian state under the Mwinyi and Mkapa regimes found themselves entangled in an awkward and occasionally embarrassing embrace. For South Africans, the new partnerships meant that they were often left to do the dirty work of neoliberalism for the Tanzanian regime. They handled the layoffs, the messy renegotiation of pension payments, and decisions on whom to hire and train and where to obtain supplies. It was they who were left to impose quality control standards, instill workplace discipline, modernize production systems, and promote new forms of consumption in the interests of expanding markets. As a result, South Africans often took the brunt of the resistance generated by neoliberal reforms, absorbing criticism that might have been directed at the state itself, at Tanzanian entrepreneurs, or at other international firms, all of whom were engaged in much the same endeavor of restructuring the Tanzanian economy to their own advantage.

Similarly for Tanzanian politicians, what was already a highly painful transition out of the doldrums of socialist privation and into the glories of unfettered global capitalism was made more complicated by the fact that their partners in crime, so to speak, were white South Africans. South African involvement meant that state functionaries were saddled with not just the task of living up to the larger-than-life moral legacy of saintly Julius Nyerere but also the challenge of overcoming the apartheid-era stigma and moral opprobrium that were attached to their white South African business partners. The state's efforts to rebuild the Tanzanian economy were already the object of intense scrutiny by critics who lamented the social and economic disparities accompanying neoliberal reforms. South African involvement added racial injustice and the erosion of national sovereignty to the list of issues the state had to finesse as it worked to implement its post-socialist transition.

The ongoing tussle between Tanzanian workers and the neoliberal alliance of South African and Tanzanian national capitals and their state governments was similarly inflected. As far as neoliberal apologists were concerned, arguments about race and national culture and the anachronistic invocation of decades-old sociopolitical battles waged under the anti-apartheid banner were simply out of place in a modern economy. The fiscal discipline leading to job losses and more "efficient" managerial styles ushered in by expatriate investors were a matter of "economic necessity," an inescapable aspect of doing business in a globalized world. Critics of South African investment often resorted to a similarly reductionist logic, albeit by erring in the opposite extreme. For them, South African management practices could only be interpreted as the benighted reenactment of apartheid race relations. The tension surrounding the fact that their new managers were white and South African was inevitable: these were *makaburu,* holdovers of the old South African regime who were expected to, and sometimes did, treat Tanzanians with unbridled contempt.

Neither of these groups was particularly well served by their partial and skewed representations of Tanzania's contemporary political economy. The actions of South African managers, the resistance they engendered among Tanzanian workers, and the policies that shaped the contradictory milieu in which the two groups interacted were simultaneously economic *and* social, a fact that emerges all the more clearly in the broad national debate that accompanied both Tanzania's neoliberal reforms and South Africa's key role in their implementation.

3
Fault Lines

"People are complaining . . ."—so goes the beginning of a joke that circulated in northern Tanzania in 2005. "People," not "*the* people": a subtle but telling linguistic marker of the populist character of public opposition to the country's "post-socialist" economic policies. "People are complaining about the beer." *The* beer. There was only one possible referent: beer brewed by Tanzania Breweries, Ltd., or TBL, the formerly state-owned monopoly, controlling shares of which were sold to South African Breweries under the parastatal privatization program in 1993. The joke continues with a false lament, typically delivered in deadpan fashion: "It used to be that if you bought a crate of beer, you'd get twenty-four different flavors. Now it all just tastes the same!"

Contrasting the way "it used to be" with the way things are "now" is a code of sorts in Tanzania, calling to mind the way things were during the country's socialist period under Julius Nyerere and juxtaposing that image with the dramatic changes that accompanied the economic reforms enacted in subsequent decades. Recalling the twenty-four different "flavors" that one used to find in a crate of beer provides a pointed reminder of the sometimes dubious quality of the commodities produced under the state-run system. Any beer drinker who came of age during the socialist period could not help but remember what a dicey proposition it once was to buy a case of beer. They would recall not just the variable flavor, which ranged at times from the unrecognizable to the unpalatable, but also the inclusion of foreign matter *in* the beer, corroded bottle caps, and loss of carbonation due to improper sealing of containers. Buyer remorse was commonplace, matched only perhaps by frustration at not being able to find beer at all given its chronic short supply. The idea that one would long for *those* days gone by is laughable on the face of it.

While there could hardly be a more tangible illustration of the improvements that accompanied economic reforms than the quality of the local beer, the joke suggests that all is still not well, because now "the beer all just tastes the same." Here the joke reverses expectations and attaches regret to the new, clearly improved quality control standards that have been introduced by South Africans in the brewing industry. The reminder "it used to be" invokes the nostalgia that many Tanzanians feel for the socialist period. The subtext seems to indicate that something important, something ineffable, the flavor of life itself perhaps, has been lost in the rush toward economic liberalization. It conveys the sense that a steep price has been paid for the impressive economic gains of recent years. The beer produced by the old TBL may have been bad beer, but it was *Tanzanian* beer, and that fact still matters at a basic level. The joke then, from this perspective, is on anyone who would uncritically accept the compromise of gaining better living standards at the expense of national sovereignty and identity.

The Drumbeat of Controversy

The double-edged, poignant, and wry social commentary embedded in this joke reflects the painful ambivalence that accompanied Tanzania's neoliberal reforms. In some ways, South African presence was incidental to this emotionally charged domestic policy dispute; in others it was a central concern that drove partisans on all sides further apart. Conservative Tanzanian commentators praised South Africans for their work ethic and their forward-looking business culture, both of which, they argued, stood in sharp contrast to the moribund thinking that characterized their own national entrepreneurial class. Progressive Tanzanian commentators, on the other hand, argued that the Tanzanian economy had been overrun by South African capital. They viewed their government's complicity in this process as a total abandonment of Tanzania's founding values and principles. And they found vindication of their position in the long string of controversies spawned in the wake of South African investments in the country.

In some cases, the impact of South African investment was immediate and concrete: it meant the loss of jobs, the denial of access to resources, and the alienation of profits. In others, the effects were more intangible: loss of national heritage, erosion of national sovereignty, and damage to national pride. This mix of material and symbolic effects was felt in nearly every branch of the Tanzanian economy, as the following discussion of specific economic sectors demonstrates.

Brewing/Beverage

South African Breweries (SAB) was one of the earliest investors in Tanzania, acquiring a 46 percent controlling stake in Tanzania Breweries Limited (TBL) in 1993. It quickly established itself in the Tanzanian market and confronted a challenge from East African Breweries (EAB) based in Kenya to the north. As was the case with a broad range of consumer goods, the beer market in East Africa was substantially controlled by Kenyans during the socialist period. In the Tanzanian market, this was partly by default, given the inconsistent production by TBL. All of this changed with the arrival of SAB, however, and the two brewing giants became enmeshed in a full-scale cross-border "beer war." Both EAB and SAB launched brands that were deliberately intended to undercut their competitors in their respective "home" markets.[1] And both built branch facilities on the other's turf: EAB undertook a $30 million refurbishment of a small family brewing company in the northern Tanzanian city of Moshi and renamed it Kibo Brewery; SAB built its own state-of-the-art $45 million Castle Brewery in Thika, Kenya. A price war ensued and partisan attempts to sabotage opposing advertising efforts were widespread (Otieno and Tagama 1999).

The two firms eventually ended up in court, where, somewhat incredibly, they sought to block one another's use of images of Tanzania's Mount Kilimanjaro in advertising campaigns. EAB uses the name of the mountain's highest peak, "Kibo," as one of its leading brands, whereas SAB's premier Tanzanian-brewed beer is called "Kilimanjaro." In an interview with the BBC, the CEO of SAB/TBL sought to parse the distinction between the rival branding exercises. He explained that SAB felt compelled "to stop [EAB] from using the peaks of Kilimanjaro because we felt it is a national icon, it cannot be a registered trademark." When pressed to explain SAB's own use of the iconic mountain's image on its Kilimanjaro beer labels, he offered a rationale that underscored the absurdity of the dispute: "Yes, well we have registered the *name* and we have got the *name* Kilimanjaro premium lager and that was used long before Kibo came onto the market. We have never registered the *peak* or the mountain as a trademark, we have just registered the brand, as in the name, as a trademark" (Ashurst 2000; emphasis added).

Eventually the two brewers declared a truce of sorts, culminating in the closure of both the Thika and Moshi facilities and an agreement allowing each brewer to distribute its competitor's brands in its home market.[2] The general issue of foreign firms trading on Tanzanian landmarks resurfaced again, however, when Associated Breweries, a Tanzanian firm with ties to Belgian and Danish brewers, began marketing a series of beer brands under the "Serengeti" label.[3] This led to the suggestion that all private firms seeking to make commercial use of park place names should be required to pay a premium to the Tanzanian National Parks Authority. This was the only way, critics argued, to protect against the usurpation of Tanzania's national heritage.[4]

In 2000, TBL's Arusha branch caused an outcry on a more local scale when it erected a public fountain in the shape of a giant beer bottle in the center of a well-traveled roundabout where a memorial statue to former president Nyerere had been proposed (wa Lutenango 2000; cf. Bwire 2005). During a visit to Arusha in the midst of his presidency, it came to Nyerere's attention that a local businessman was planning to construct a petrol station at the roundabout in question. Upon hearing of these plans, Nyerere intervened to block commercial development of the site, arguing that the roundabout should remain a green space for the enjoyment of future generations. Thus, when TBL installed its beer bottle fountain on the site, it was roundly disparaged as a "sacrilege" that defiled Nyerere's original vision.[5] The fountain further outraged local residents because it spewed water at the height of a severe drought (Nkwame 2000, 1).

The response in the press was scathing. One writer sarcastically suggested that the fountain should be viewed as Tanzania's answer to the British national monument dedicated to Lord Nelson at Trafalgar Square (wa Lutengano 2000, 3). Another voiced outrage at the dual slight to civic and national pride:

And situated directly in the center of this roundabout, tipped at a cocky angle and shining offensively in the sun, is an imposing replica of a beer bottle. I bristle with indignation that such a tasteless display be allowed to represent our town, and that an oversized beer bottle now sits where a statue honoring the founder of our nation was expected to be. Is the spirit of Arusha really better represented now by a beer bottle, than by a statue of our founding father? (Simonson 2000, 7)

Other commentators argued that national heritage was a "priceless" commodity that should not be commercialized in this way (Nkwame 2000, 2). A letter to the editor of the *Arusha Times* addressed the brewers directly:

People of Arusha have pride in their town. As a large investor in Arusha you need to be more sensitive to this pride. Your crass attempt to take advantage of some prime advertising space has given people a beer that they now associate with tawdry commercialism . . . Try thinking a bit broader than mere bang for your buck and realize the impact you could have on the dignity of this town if you invested in a civic project that invoked local pride. Why not consider investing in the donation of a statue in honour of the late Mwalimu Julius Kamberage Nyerere? On that site . . . he could welcome one and all to Arusha reminding visitors that he was a peoples [sic] person treating dignitaries and farmers as one. Mwalimu was a highly respected statesman of international status. He made mistakes, but he had the humility to face up to them. Perhaps it is time for you to show a little humility and reconsider the mistake you have made in alienating the people of Arusha. (Saunders 2000, 6)

Bowing to public pressure, TBL moved quickly to dismantle the fountain. The public relations damage had clearly already been done, however, as observers seized on the opportunity to ridicule TBL itself. One letter to the editor summed up the correspondent's feelings by saying, "The project is completely bad taste and hopefully not reflecting to the taste of the beer [*sic*]" (Masoy 2000, 6). Another Arusha resident wryly noted, "Well, this has confirmed my earliest fears that the beer brand is simply water!" (quoted in Nkwame 2000, 1).

An interview with the managing director of the TBL plant in Arusha, who is himself a Tanzanian, shed additional light on the situation. Abashed, he explained how the idea of erecting a fountain on the site originated:

> For fifteen years, the Mwalimu Nyerere Park and that roundabout has been maintained by TBL. I don't know when we started that one. I think in the mid-90s. We plant the trees, we keep the grass. I've been paying someone full time to manage the park. But maintenance does not mean ownership. Unfortunately that's the mistake we made . . . Because we are managing this one on behalf of the Arusha people . . . So the idea of putting a beer bottle came out of that mistaken thinking that because we maintained it, we owned it. We know that we manage it on behalf of the Arusha people, and if we want to do such a thing, we have to have a medium of communication between ourselves and the Arusha people.[6]

While acknowledging his firm's missteps regarding the fountain project, he nonetheless maintained that the acquisition of TBL by SAB had played an important role in boosting Tanzanian national pride in other respects. An extended excerpt from our conversation illustrates the complexity of national branding exercises. I asked him to explain how beer brands had come to carry such heavy symbolic weight in the relationship between Tanzanians, Kenyans, and South Africans:

> Tanzanians and Kenyans have been strange bedfellows since the years of our former President Nyerere and Kenyatta in Kenya. It actually came from the social policies which we had. The Kenyans were accusing Tanzania of being the source of people who produced nothing. And the Tanzanians were accusing Kenya of being the source of bloodsuckers . . . [Then] when Kenyans were using the Tanzanian national identity to promote their tourism—the Kilimanjaro mountain, the Serengeti, and other things—those are the things that infuriated the Tanzanians for a long time. Therefore, it didn't start with beer. It started a long time back with other things . . . The beer [eventually] became a part of it. Basically, that's why Tanzania Breweries became one of the more successful companies. Because it actually rode on that wave of Tanzanians mistrusting Kenya. Then came the time when Tanzanians started to drinking their own beer, which had the best quality, and in the right quantities. And new [TBL] brands came in, local brands came in, which could compete anywhere else in the world. They just perceived this as something that was taken out from Kenyan domination . . .

I asked him whether SAB had consciously sought to build national pride in Tanzanian beers and he replied that this goal had played a "huge" role in the company's marketing efforts:

For example, we had Safari [the oldest TBL brand]. Safari, basically if you look at the message through the years . . . its sale line was national identity, "authentic Tanzanian." We actually rode on that wave for a long time . . . The perception by Tanzanians is that Kenyans don't want South Africans because Kenyans [themselves] want to bleed us to death . . . But if you reflect among Tanzanians [sic], one of the things which actually they are proud [of], that helped them get out of Kenyan domination, it's Tanzania Breweries.

Whether Tanzanian beer drinkers see SAB's claims of success in wresting control of the Tanzanian beer market from EAB in the same light as this TBL executive does is debatable. The situation was complicated further in 2010 when EAB bought Serengeti (Associated) Breweries, granting it control of roughly 29 percent of the Tanzanian beer market (Turana 2009). TBL has yet to respond to this challenge to its dominant position within the industry, but it is clear from this salvo that the beer wars being fought by international brewers over the Tanzanian national market are far from over.

Tourism

The safari tourism industry is second only to agriculture in its contributions to GDP in Tanzania and was a natural target for South African investors. In 1997, ConsCorps Africa (CCA), one of the continent's largest tourism companies with forty properties in six different countries, made a splashy debut in Tanzania by purchasing several sites on the northern safari circuit.[7] It promptly razed the well-known Ngorongoro Crater Lodge and replaced it with the first of several ultra-luxury tourist facilities established by South African investors in the past decade. Rates for the lodge, which was marketed to the world under the dubious rubric of "Maasai meets Versailles" due to its eclectic mixture of design elements, were listed at $1,500 per person per night for high season in 2011. Its appeal to neocolonial sensibilities is unmistakable in the breathless ad copy that appears on the firm's website:

> Guests can be forgiven for losing track of which era, or even continent, they
> are experiencing at Ngorongoro Crater Lodge. Nowhere else on earth can
> you wake up among all the trappings of an elegant baroque chateau—brocade
> sofas, gilt mirrors, beaded chandeliers and panelled walls—and be instantly
> transported into one of the most famous African landscapes with just one
> glance out the window of the lodge. In this place of dramatic contrasts, where
> Versailles meets Maasai, anything is possible.[8]

The construction of these luxury accommodations on the northern safari tourism circuit led South African safari industry observers to claim that they had introduced new "standards" to Tanzania. As a South African active in the industry in the Arusha area put it, "Tanzania is 'wild Africa' compared to the South African hospitality industry. South Africa is *light years* ahead of Tanzania. When they say five stars in South Africa, you know it is really five stars."[9] Commenting on the new Ngorongoro Crater Lodge, another said,

> [When] CCA demolished the old Ngorongoro Crater Lodge, [it] was falling apart. You can say what you want about the new lodge, but that lodge is responsible for Tanzania being featured in more issues of tourist magazines all over the world than any other site in the country! [South Africans] were breaking the mold and a lot of people resented it. We are brash and a little proud about the way we do things, but there's definitely more good than bad that has come from it.[10]

Some of this South African "brashness" carried over into the branch of Tanzania's tourism industry devoted to trophy hunting where "southerners" were accused of engaging in unsustainable hunting practices. Both more reputable hunters and proprietors of traditional photographic safaris lamented the presence of South African hunters who "had no great love for Tanzania," and who, it was alleged, would "shoot the hell out of the local wildlife" and move on to the next hunting ground without a second thought.[11] A South African hunter based in Arusha concurred with this representation. Alluding to the caricature of southern African whites wearing khaki shorts, he quipped: "The shorter the pants get, the lower the morals go." Regarding the allegations of unsustainable hunting, he acknowledged that the perception was widespread even if he could not conclusively verify the behavior:

> That's certainly the message that goes around and it's what I feel, although I couldn't tell you a single name of a single South African that's hunting illegally. I just don't know them, but they are. I mean the Selous is just filled with South Africans. . . . And if you look in the hunting magazines, you'll see there: "Come hunt Tanzania!" Yeah, there are tons of them. And what about the Zimbabweans that are now pouring in? I guess it's a similar set of circumstances that led them all here . . . Come up, do their safaris and go back again. What is that doing for the country? But yeah, I've got that impression really strongly that there's a lot of trash out there. . . . But you know if someone actually said to me, "Oh, you're accusing South Africans here. Give me one name!" I don't think I'd be able to. Because I just don't know them.[12]

Finally, a South African hotel chain was implicated in a controversy surrounding the corporate tax breaks enjoyed by foreign investors. In 1995, the Sheraton company opened a luxury tourist hotel in the heart of Dar es Salaam to great fanfare. Six years later, in 2001, this hotel changed hands and was renamed the Royal Palm Hotel by its new South African owners, Legacy Hotels and Resorts. In 2005, the property was sold again to the Swiss hotel chain, Mövenpick. This rapid turnover of one of the most visible hotel assets in the country was viewed skeptically by Tanzanians. In the popular imagination, the reason the hotel had been sold and resold so often over such a short time period was because the firms in question had exhausted the benefit of a tax holiday exempting new foreign investors from paying corporate taxes for five years. These "obscene discretionary exemptions," as one columnist called them, were widely cited as evidence of the preferential treatment foreigners received at the expense of local investors who were forced to compete with them while shouldering a full tax burden.[13] Even the IMF saw fit to warn Tanzania that it had created too many tax havens for foreign investors, and was thus in danger of "adversely affect[ing] the tax base" and undermining its economic solvency.[14]

Telecommunications

In 1999, South African cellular telephone operator Vodacom was granted a license to operate in Tanzania and quickly became the country's leading network. The rapid growth and intense competition within the cellular telephone market prompted the company to undertake an aggressive publicity campaign. Billboards and pre-paid phone voucher advertisements for Vodacom and its chief rivals were ubiquitous. Vodacom outmaneuvered its rivals when it acquired the rights to re-paint a number of prominent buildings in large urban centers. In Dar es Salaam, giant multistory renditions of the bright blue-and-white Vodacom logo (see figure 2) became a fixture of the urban landscape, creating jarring sight lines along main thoroughfares. At least one major government building, the Tanzanian Commission on Science and Technology, or COSTECH, was initially included in this effort, much to the chagrin of locals: "I could understand it if it were a private building," said one, "but a *national* institution like COSTECH? It's an insult!"[15]

Vodacom's promotional activities were singled out for criticism in a focus group session organized in 2005. Participants drawn from a number of development NGOs in the Arusha area explained that when the number of Vodacom subscribers grew so quickly, consumers expected that costs to subscribers would go down.[16] Instead, they continued to rise. The group was especially upset about a sweepstakes promotion Vodacom had organized in which the prospect of winning a new house was used to entice consumers to purchase more prepaid phone vouchers. The focus group participants argued that the cost of the house being raffled off came from *their* money. Rather than waste that money on a promotion, they felt Vodacom should return those revenues to subscribers in the form of cheaper rates. This is what they would do "*if* they were genuine, and *if* they were for the people."[17]

Retail Grocery

In 2000, the South African supermarket chain Shoprite opened several outlets in Tanzania. With over seventy stores in sixteen countries outside of South Africa, Shoprite was one of the most visible South African brands on the continent.[18] The firm quickly took on a larger-than-life aura in Tanzania. In Arusha, Shoprite became the anchor tenant in a new shopping mall on a site that had previously been occupied by the dilapidated warehouses of the Tanganyika Farmer's Association. For the city's expatriate population, Shoprite's location in a gated compound monitored by security guards represented an opportunity to engage in "one-stop shopping" in a "secure" environment with ample parking. It allowed shoppers to go about their business without having to deal with thieves and street children who might accost them in other parts of the city. They also counted on Shoprite for access to certain high-quality goods:

> I go to Shoprite for those packed green beans and peas, eh? We had a safari
> once to Kilwa [a major archeological site on an island off the Tanzanian coast].
> And we had a refrigerator with us. And we took a bunch of those beans with
> us, and we had fresh vegetables for the whole week we were there . . . The other
> thing I get sometimes is garlic. I went in there once, and they had these packs
> of peeled garlic—large cloves, man—all peeled and clean. They were selling a
> whole pack for something like Tsh 500 [roughly US$.50]. Somebody put a lot
> of sweat labor into those, eh? . . . But to have them all peeled like that? That
> saves a helluva lot of time.[19]

For petty commodity producers, Shoprite seemed to offer a way to tap into the growing middle-class market for consumer goods. Indeed, judging from the expectations expressed by the small-scale farmers and cooperative members I interviewed, all roads to lucrative markets passed through Shoprite's doors. The would-be suppliers of fresh meat and produce were thus deeply frustrated when Shoprite would not purchase their goods due to quality-control concerns:

> I represent [a farmer's cooperative], and our members, many of them are into
> horticulture. And dairy. They could supply Shoprite if they were given the
> proper training. So I've told Shoprite that they should do some training. All
> they need to do is say, "Here are our standards." And then train Tanzanian
> farmers to supply them. They should set some goals. In one year, you source
> X percentage locally. In year two, you add more goods to your list. In year
> three, you add more. And by year five, you are meeting the goal of sourcing 50
> percent of some articles locally. But they are continuing to get their supplies
> from South Africa. I mean, there is no reason in the world that they should
> be getting *eggs* from South Africa! Or getting *dairy* from South Africa. I can
> understand that maybe they need to get some of their horticulture from South
> Africa, their tangerines of a certain size, and their grapes . . . But tomatoes and
> onions? Uh uh![20]

Shoprite also received criticism for the dry goods it imports, especially from South Africans living in Tanzania who knew the chain intimately. It was South Africans in particular who argued that Shoprite was using its Tanzanian outlets to dump products nearing the end of their shelf life: "All that they sell is second- or third-rate South African stuff for more expensive than you can get good Tanzanian stuff. . . . *Shoprite* can't say we're bringing a whole new higher range of standards here!"[21] The general impression was that Shoprite's stores in Dar es Salaam were better stocked than those in Arusha, and that those in South Africa were vastly superior to those in Dar es Salaam. Arusha was the end of the line.

Shoprite countered complaints that it imported too many locally available goods by placing conspicuous placards in its shops noting its reliance on local produce suppliers. At first, in 2005, these labels simply announced that a particular section of high-quality vegetables contained exclusively "Tanzanian produce." Some months later in a subtle but telling shift, this section was relabeled, "*Proudly* Tanzanian produce" (emphasis added). While the significance of this relabeling may have been lost on other patrons, South Africans recognized the direct allusion to the "Proudly South African" branding effort that was launched by the National Economic and Labour Council (NEDLAC) in South Africa in 1998 (Wilson 2001). The "Proudly South African" campaign was devised by a consortium of labor, business, and government actors to encourage conscientious consumers in South Africa "to buy local goods and services in the knowledge that this would help build [the South African] economy" (Wilson 2001). The use of a similar rhetoric by Shoprite in Tanzania was a belated, and somewhat disingenuous, attempt to lay claim to the mantle of localism. For even as the company was extolling the virtues of its "Tanzanian" produce in one aisle, shelves throughout the rest of the store in Arusha contained dozens of products imported directly from South Africa and still bearing the "Proudly South African" campaign logo.

Banking

In 2000, Amalgamated Banks of South Africa (ABSA) tendered a bid to purchase the National Bank of Commerce (NBC), Tanzania's largest banking chain. The original NBC was established under the Nyerere government and was commonly referred to as "the people's bank" because its widely distributed branch network made banking services available to residents of smaller cities and towns throughout the country. In 1997, this entity was split into three parts—NBC, Ltd., the National Microfinance Bank (NMB), and the NBC Holding Company—to pave the way for privatizing the core assets of NBC Ltd. The national press corps assiduously followed negotiations surrounding the sale of this key national icon, eventually announcing that its sale price was $18 million. At the last minute, however, ABSA's offer was withdrawn pending receipt of debt payments from the Tanzanian government on behalf of the other two branches of the original NBC. Tanzanian observers were subsequently mystified when, instead of *receiving* $18 million, the Tanzanian government ended up effectively *paying* ABSA $18 million from the NMB, plus an additional $2 million from the NBC Holding Company, to take control of the NBC banking chain. They were equally alarmed when President Mkapa then appointed a South African manager from ABSA to manage NBC through the transition period even though formal ownership of the firm had not yet been fully transferred to ABSA. Acting in his new capacity, this official promptly transferred the first installment of the interbranch arrears payments out of the country for safekeeping, all before the sale of NBC assets had even been finalized (Rwambali 2000a, 1). Locals were incensed when NBC's new managers moved to close several of its regional branches in a cost-cutting measure. Not only did this mean a loss of jobs (see chapter 2), but it meant reduced access to vital banking services in smaller towns and cities.

Meanwhile, Tanzanian entrepreneurs complained loudly about the degree to which the country's banking industry was falling under South African control. In addition to ABSA, South Africa's Stanbic Bank was an early and active participant in Tanzania's financial services industry. One local executive lamented the fact that South African banks were "now controlling nearly half of the Tanzanian banking industry," thus locking up capital available for commercial ventures in the country. He claimed that South African bankers showed favoritism to South African investors by loaning them money without security or collateral, but required well-heeled Tanzanians like himself to meet the strictest of conditions before granting them new lines of credit.[22]

Construction

In 2000, South Africa's Group Five construction firm began work on a major contract to build a new headquarters for the Bank of Tanzania (BoT). The BoT "twin towers," as they are known locally, dominate the Dar es Salaam skyline. The original project budget was set at roughly US$80 million in 2000. By 2003, however, the building's estimated cost had risen to US$200 million; and by September of 2007, it had ballooned to $358 million (Mande and Edwin 2008; see figure 3). The building's furniture alone was said to cost the government US$3.5 million, and a "resounding" US$44.5 million was allocated for the acquisition of a state-of-the-art security system.[23]

Anonymous sources quoted in the press declared these figures to be an "absurd" amount of money to be spent on a monument to the prestige of the country's central bankers. They claimed (erroneously) that "the headquarters of the central bank is now arguably the most expensive building in the world";[24] and that "the total value of all the skyscrapers in the country put together in the past few years is much below what taxpayers will spend on the BoT project alone."[25] The growing expense of the building generated heated debate in parliament, where the twin towers' cost was decried as being "at least four times higher than similar buildings in some of the world's most expensive cities like London, New York and Tokyo."[26]

A columnist writing for *The Citizen* newspaper, which helped break this story, juxtaposed the extravagant expense of the BoT project with the country's widespread poverty. He acknowledged the prominence of the central bank and the need to provide it with accommodations befitting its role in the nation's economy, but had difficulty reconciling the building's expense with the opportunity costs incurred by the project:

> [S]uppose the [funds were] spent in construction of secondary schools, the country's education interface could have been greatly transformed and justice would have been done to the innocent poor young boys and girls who work hard in pursuing education but are denied opportunity due to what is seen to be society's lopsided priorities.

He concluded that what might have been viewed as a "symbol of benefits accruing from liberalisation policies" was now "a subject of discontent" (Msombeli 2006b, 13).

Energy

In 2002, the South African energy management corporation NetGroup Solutions assumed control of TANESCO, Tanzania's national electric utility, amid high hopes by the government that the new managers would deliver reliable electric services to a desperately needy nation. The new firm was tasked with expanding the national power grid to allow greater access by the country's citizens, especially in rural areas where only one percent of the population had access to reliable energy sources.[27] It was also given responsibility for reducing power outages and setting up a more efficient system of collecting payments for services.

Initially, the arrival of South African contractors was represented as a major breakthrough for a beleaguered nation:

> The arrival of the NetGroup Solutions was noisy and our rulers went on the rampage kicking out Tanesco['s] local senior experts for alleged incompetence. NetGroup Solutions was hailed as a panacea to the ills of Tanesco: we were bombarded with factual information on the level of competence, efficiency and experience the NetGroup were bringing to our besieged Tanesco. NetGroup boasted of its ability to rein in on non-paying clients and in the process widening the revenue base . . . [It] swore to do away [with] the power outages which were prevalent at the time of its arrival. (Nestory 2006, 6)

As the first two-year contract was concluded, however, the firm had made much greater progress in collection of fees than on the delivery of services (Ghanadan

2009). Its contract was renewed but concerns were rising over intermittent power outages and the failure to more substantively address the broader goal of rural electrification.

In 2005, the nation was plunged into a period of rolling blackouts as the region was beset by a severe drought. One by one, the country's main hydroelectric reservoirs fell below minimum levels required to run generators safely and went off line. Tanesco officials scrambled to patch together supplies from a variety of irregular and expensive sources, and placed a rush order for the delivery of new gas turbines to help offset the dire shortages facing the country. At the same time, the electric grid was hit by vandals who targeted transformers and generators in an effort to pirate engine oil or scrap metal. The net effect was that the country was left "reel[ing] in darkness." The country's industrial plant gradually ground to a halt as the steady thrum of private generators echoed throughout the night.[28]

Tanzanians were outraged, both at the shortages and at the fact that their electricity bills had risen some 20 percent under Netgroup management.[29] Editorial writers argued that the extreme drought could not be blamed for the shortages since there was ample precedent for such conditions in the historical record; they argued that NetGroup officials were "caught napping" by the drought.[30] They railed against their government's "overdependence on foreign expertise" and bemoaned the "parasitic" nature of privatization contracts, which they argued should be renegotiated.[31] They sarcastically claimed to be world record holders in running a national economy on flashlight batteries, and suggested that, under the circumstances, the nation's largest city might as well be renamed "Dark Salaam."[32]

Under mounting public pressure, the Tanzanian government and NetGroup began laying blame at one another's doorstep for the power shortages. Finally, in May 2006, the government notified NetGroup officials that their contract would be discontinued on the grounds of poor managerial performance. NetGroup's CEO vigorously denied the government's characterization of its performance and threatened legal action, but in the end opted to drop the case in the hopes that this would help it win contracts elsewhere in the region.[33]

Transportation

After failing in earlier attempts to establish partnerships with Air Tanzania (ATCL), South African Airways (SAA) paid US$20 million to acquire a 49 percent stake in the state-run airline in 2002. The plan floated by SAA in its bid to acquire a controlling stake in the Tanzanian fleet was to make Dar es Salaam into a regional hub in the expanding SAA flight network (Kizigha 2006a, 3). Shortly after establishing its partnership with ATCL in 2002, SAA raised eyebrows in Tanzania when it repainted the Air Tanzania fleet, replacing the Tanzanian national symbol of a giraffe with a stylized version of the South African Airways logo, which is based on the

South African national flag. It also stopped booking tickets using the Air Tanzania flight code, a step that rendered ATCL "technically . . . non-existent" as far as the International Air Transport Association was concerned.[34]

SAA also allegedly failed to deliver on its original strategic plan for the joint venture. According to breach of contract notices issued by the Tanzanian government, not only did the South Africans fail to make Dar a hub, but they engaged in direct competition with ATCL for lucrative routes into Zanzibar. Moreover, they allegedly "engage[ed] in acts that were meant to undermine ATCL, like not servicing its plane or train personnel [*sic*]" (Mosoba 2006, 10). At one point, the entire fleet of ATCL planes was grounded for maintenance. In lieu of paying to repair Tanzania's aging planes, however, the new managers leased several aircraft from South African suppliers. The snag in this plan was that no Tanzanian pilots were qualified to fly them. Workers for ATCL said this amounted to direct "sabotage," and relations between the two firms soured further.[35] By late 2006, amid rising losses and antagonism between ATCL and SAA officials, the "divorce" between the two firms was finalized and control of ATC reverted to Tanzanian authorities (Kizigha 2006c; see figure 4). For at least one observer, this was good riddance: "You don't want a partnership with someone who just wants to swallow you."[36]

Discussion

To say that this long string of controversies involving South African investors had a searing impact on the Tanzanian national psyche would be an understatement. The cumulative effect of these reports was to keep the South African origins of investment capital a focal point of national debate for over a decade. Competition for markets and access to resources, "loss" of tax revenues, the stripping of government assets, ineffective delivery of key services—these material consequences of the neoliberal reforms were routinely linked to South African presence. At the same time, the desecration of national symbols, the reconfiguration of public space, the assertion of foreign "standards," the denigration of Tanzanian national culture—these symbolic slights, both real and imagined, weighed heavily on Tanzanians as they watched South African presence expand. This was not some abstract capitalist force at work but a set of firms and individuals with specific national origins. Tanzanians could hardly escape the conclusion, as one woman suggested, that whenever the *makaburu* show up as investors, "disaster follows."[37]

Debating Tanzania's National Character

One of the immediate consequences of the economic exchanges with South Africans described above and the related insertion of nationality into economic discourse was that Tanzanians were forced to examine their own national character. This discussion, led by proponents of economic reforms in the private sector and government agencies alike, typically began with Tanzanians denigrating their own culture and deriding their countrymen and women for their backwardness and lack of initiative. For example, a senior economist for the Ministry of Trade and Industry speaking at a public forum in Arusha in 2005 used an anecdote about a small-scale coconut vendor plying his wares to illustrate the lack of entrepreneurial drive among Tanzanians: "You meet him first thing in the morning and offer to buy all of his wares from him. And his response is: 'If you buy all of my coconuts at 7 AM, what am I going to do with the rest of the day?'" The speaker could barely contain his scorn: "He is practicing trade like it was a hobby!" Here, he suggested, was a perfect opportunity for an enterprising entrepreneur to double his profit by restocking his stall, and yet the hapless trader seemed at a loss for what to do. This was the problem with Tanzanians, the official argued: because of their past, they lacked the experience to take full advantage of market opportunities. In his view, Tanzania's lack of business acumen was also in evidence within the government ministries, where a few old "dinosaurs" still spouted socialist rhetoric. "Some of these old guys must leave," he concluded. "We need a new brain!"[38]

Within conservative economic circles, the manifest shortcomings of Tanzanians were contrasted with what was constructed as the obvious entrepreneurial spirit of other nationalities, most especially the Chinese and the South Africans: "One of the most relevant reasons why our economy is lagging behind is simply due to the fact that a large majority of our people is lazy. If we were to leave the running of this country to say the Chinese for just two years Tanzanian's [sic] would be shocked at the level of economic and social development that the country would attain" (Kimaro 2005, 6).

The problem with Tanzanians, according to this perspective, was that they lacked the right attitude. In order to develop the proper sensibilities towards modern economic realities, the Tanzanian Investment Center launched an initiative in May 2006 known as the "Young Entrepreneurs Roundtable." This program, modeled after a similar initiative in China, was designed to "train entrepreneurs, and educate the public to change their mindset towards private sector engagement."[39] Participants wholeheartedly embraced the opportunity to network with their peers and encouraged their government to promote the new market economy "with the same spirit" that it had once devoted to the promotion of socialism.[40]

Interestingly, the guest of honor at the event was Jackie Mphafudi, a South African business executive who was director and chief operating officer at Mvelaphanda Holdings, a sprawling, black-owned conglomerate founded by Tokyo Sexwale, the former ANC stalwart who became one of South Africa's richest men in the aftermath of apartheid. The Mvelaphanda business empire reaped huge dividends from South Africa's Black Economic Empowerment (BEE) program.[41] It also, ironically, had substantial holdings in a number of prominent South African firms active in the Tanzanian economy, including ABSA Bank, Group Five Construction, and others. So while Mphafudi was represented as someone from whom Tanzanians could learn entrepreneurship skills, he was also their direct competitor, the notable difference being that, unlike the overwhelming majority of South African investors active in Tanzania, Mphafudi was black.

South Africans were held up as models by members of the Young Entrepreneurs Roundtable not just because they had economic clout and business savvy but because they supposedly possessed a superior work ethic:

> Because the thing is, they are the people who have the capital. They are the people who have the technical know-how. They are the people who came in at the time when we were saying, "We give up! We want to sell. This government is no longer a good businessman. Government will step aside . . . You do the business. Pay us our taxes. Create jobs. And that's it." And the economy is do-ing well in that policy . . . It doesn't matter *who* is doing it. [Former President] Mkapa said, "I couldn't care who skins the cat; I want a skinned cat. It doesn't matter if it is South African, or black, or white, yellow, green; I don't give a damn." And I agree with him . . . South Africa is not an issue. The issue is: there is an investor who was willing to come. South Africa will go all the way to Libya! Why? During their isolation they knew how to work and they worked very hard. So the issue is not South Africa. The issue is people and work. People who want to work, be regulated as they work, be rewarded for working hard. That is the issue.[42]

While laying stress on work habits, the speaker here seemed to contradict her-self on the question of nationality. She argued forcefully that South Africans' national identity had no bearing on their strong economic performance on the continent; na-tionality, she contended, was a non-issue. At the same time, she maintained that the particular historical experience South Africans went through under the economic boycott imposed by the global anti-apartheid movement led directly to the develop-ment of a distinctive South African national work ethic. Indeed, this was an idea with which many South Africans I interviewed strongly identified.

Critics of South African presence found it similarly difficult to form a singular line of attack on the question of South African capital in Tanzania. In October 2005, I conducted a focus group discussion with a group of representatives of nongovern-mental organizations based in Arusha. An extended segment from a debate between three participants reveals the range of perspectives observers brought to this subject.

Samwel is a middle-aged Tanzanian who currently works with a prominent NGO; Joseph and Sara are European NGO workers in their thirties who worked closely with Samwel's organization:

> **SAMWEL:** I still think that South Africans are imperialists, exploiters and oppressors who take our resources to their country without leaving anything behind. That thought hasn't left my mind, and it never will . . . There are three things I have noticed concerning investment, imports, and resident South Africans. The first one concerning investment is the question of cheating. There are more resources going out of the country than are coming in. And when you look at the national statistics, they show how much investment from the mining of precious minerals has contributed to this nation. It's very little! We all have heard the finance minister's speech about the less than three percent of national income originating from minerals. But how much money do the investors earn from minerals? It's a lot! Secondly, the issue of imported goods. I find that we've become a dump for inferior goods. I can't support this . . . How could the tomato that I harvested today [in Tanzania] be inferior and less fresh than one harvested three months ago [in South Africa]? It is not possible. Truly, Tanzania has been made a dumping ground for foreign junk. And the issue of residents, I think they have brought us new traditions and habits. It will be a challenge to live with them. They have come with their own schools, their own games, their own language—you can see some of the obstacles . . . So, I cannot support investment 100 percent . . . Really, for me, South Africans and foreign investors have serious exploitation, imperialistic, and capitalistic habits, which we must reject in the lives of Tanzanians.

> **JOSEPH:** Yeah, um, I'm uncomfortable with the focus on South African investment as opposed to any other type of investment. Firstly, any investor, whether Tanzanian or South African or Chinese, operates under a Tanzanian regulatory framework, which is determined by the Tanzanian government, voted for by Tanzanians. Ultimately, *ultimately,* countries do have choices. And the same conditions, for example, that Tanzania accepts unconditionally, so to speak, in Ethiopia are *not* accepted. The Ethiopian government makes other choices and rejects a lot of the regulations surrounding opening of markets to investment that most of our institutions ask for. The Tanzanian government doesn't. The Tanzanian government has a choice and has chosen to open its markets. *Tanzanian* investors take land from Tanzanians, sometimes illegally. They can exploit water resources at the expense of ordinary Tanzanians in the same way that South African investors can do that, in the same way that Chinese investors can do that. Some of those people are in the same government as has introduced this new regulatory framework. So I'm very uncomfortable about identifying the foreigner as the oppressor. There's a framework that allows

that to happen that was determined by Tanzanians. There are also *Tanza-nian* investors who exploit Tanzanians. There are *Tanzanian* investors that steal land; there are *Tanzanian* investors who farm land illegally. There are *Tanzanian* investors that farm land legally, but that steal water illegally from the river inflow. And I don't think that focusing on South African investors adds value to the debate. *Exploiters come in all colors. . . .*

SAMWEL: A footnote. A footnote please! *Tanzania* did not choose, did *not* . . . the framework that Tanzania is having is a *forced* one . . . It is a *conditionality,* through the World Bank, through the IMF opening our borders.

JOSEPH: Ethiopia rejected it.

SAMWEL: No . . . they are following, they have their own PRC [Parastatal Reform Commission] meeting the full conditions now, as we speak.

JOSEPH: Very different to here.

SAMWEL: I don't think so because I have read it so maybe we can debate it outside the room. What I am saying, the conditions that have been put on Tanzania . . . are really literally from *outside* our country. The invest-ment pattern, uh, the language that is being used in Uganda, in Kenya, in Tanzania, in Mozambique, is the *same!* It is global capitalism that is mov-ing Tanzania and forcing Tanzania to have the framework that we have in Tanzania at the moment. So we should not avoid the fact that we may have a framework but . . . our bargaining position is very weak. We have to acknowledge that. And our politicians are struggling to strengthen the economy, we know that. And you know there is this concept that capital-ism is the answer and some of us are saying: "No, please, wait a minute; there could be so many answers around that."

SARA: I just wanted to add to what Samwel was saying. I think, you know, you have to separate the decisions of the government from decisions of the Tanzanian people. The decision of the government is *of the government* and it doesn't necessarily represent Tanzanians . . . Because these decisions are made behind closed doors. The average Tanzanian in the village has no idea what's going on. So the government is maybe representing less than one percent of the Tanzanian population that are making these decisions. So you can't say that the Tanzanians have invited this . . . But also I think there's a reason to focus on South Africa here. *Yes,* there are Tanzanians who are oppressing their fellow Tanzanians, because there is a class system here. That's going to be there, of course. But it's the *scale* of South African investment . . . it's a *huge* scale of investment, and you can't compare it to Tanzanian investors. And South Africa has a particular historical relation-ship with other African countries that European countries don't have . . . It's different. There was a colonial relationship [with Europeans]. So that is different from the relationship that Tanzania had with South Africa, and that South Africa had with other countries in and on the continent.

JOSEPH: But I think that focusing the debates against one kind of outsider does nothing to address issues of accountability within Tanzania. I'd have rather seen [a focus] on say, government regulations for investors, on the land act, for example, and the ways it's been used and abused, rather than focusing on one outsider. I don't think that's productive.

The sharp nature of this exchange regarding the nature of South African presence in Tanzania suggests on the face of it that the idea of a national capital had a great deal of relevance for Tanzanians and expatriate residents alike. The views expressed in this focus group ranged across the ideological spectrum on the political left. Samwel initially suggested that all South Africans be branded as "imperialists, exploiters, and oppressors" in their own right, and then appeared to contradict himself by linking them to broader trends within "global capitalism." Joseph conflated race and nationality and rejected the idea that either had any place in a discussion of economic policy since "exploiters come in all colors." Instead, he asserted, Tanzanians effectively controlled their own political economic destiny through the adoption of specific national policies. These, he argued, should be the focal point of discussion. Sara acknowledged that economic oppression based on class relations existed in Tanzania, but reiterated the need to focus on South African investors as South Africans. In her view, both the overwhelmingly large scale of South African investment and South African's unique historical position vis-à-vis the rest of the continent given its apartheid past justified detailed consideration in unpacking the politics of investment in neoliberal Tanzania.

In sum, "South Africa," which is to say the national origin of South African capital, clearly *was* an issue for both conservative and progressive observers, albeit one that provoked an ambivalent response, especially when viewed against the backdrop of neoliberal reforms initiated by the Tanzanian state and the hegemonic role of the World Bank and the IMF.

Fault Lines: Debating Tanzanian Economic Reforms

In many respects, South African presence acted as a wedge issue in Tanzania, prying open cracks in the national body politic. There were many in the Tanzanian business community, for example, who avidly embraced the goals of the government's neoliberal reform policies and were accordingly very sympathetic to South African investors. They saw the arrival of South Africans as the inevitable outcome of competition fostered in the context of the country's post-socialist transition: "Privatization has been a very good process. It has meant that tenders have been granted to the most qualified firms. As far as South Africans are concerned, they grabbed the opportunities. We didn't. So more power to them."[43] The implication of this statement was that Tanzanians had had their chance to manage their own affairs but failed. State-owned enterprises foundered under the socialist system due to a mixture of incompetence and a general lack of entrepreneurial drive. "The new thinking is that Tanzanians had 40 years after independence in which they were supposed to learn to run the economy, but all they did was run it down. Another 40 years will not make matters any better" (Okema 2005a).

From this perspective, the shortcomings of Tanzania's socialist "experiment" were revealed when South African firms took over a number of formerly state-run firms. Indeed, several of the parastatals acquired by South African investors performed extremely well following privatization. Tanzania Breweries, for example, saw its market share increase from roughly 35 percent when SAB Miller first acquired controlling interests in the firm in 1993 to over 80 percent by 2009. Over the same period, Tanzania went from being a net importer of beer to a regional exporter, sending its products to Kenya, Uganda, Malawi, and the Democratic Republic of Congo.[44] In recognition of this strong performance, TBL was chosen as the "Most Respected Company in Tanzania" in an annual poll of East African business executives in 2005.[45] It was also selected as the Confederation of Tanzania Industries' "President's Manufacturer of the Year" in Tanzania in 2006 (see figure 5).[46]

Similarly strong economic performance can be cited for a number of other firms owned and/or operated by South Africans. Despite the repeated incidents of labor unrest outlined above, Kilombero Sugar increased its production tenfold over a seven-year period in the early 2000s and sugar growers at the Tanganyika Plantation Company saw equally sharp increases in productivity.[47] The cement industry was led by South African–run Tanga Cement, which doubled output following privatization.[48] And gold miners, buoyed in part by a heavy infusion of South African capital, saw a dramatic expansion of production as Tanzania became the third-largest gold producer on the continent after South Africa and Ghana.

The success of these firms stood in sharp contrast to the performance of the Tanzanian parastatal sector under socialism. An entrepreneur underscored this distinction by describing the difficulties she encountered in managing a business under the state-run economic system:

> The National Bank of Commerce was *gone*. And it was the *National* Bank of Commerce, with *full* monopoly. I've never seen in the world, read anything

about, a bank that has full monopoly, and made a loss! [The South Africans] turned it around. I never could borrow in those days . . . Loans were being given on the basis of little notes coming from politicians . . . But [today] I borrow. So if it's a South African bank that is facilitating my business, do I care? I mean, would that matter to you?[49]

South Africans' ability to turn a profit from moribund state-owned industries was not universally acclaimed, however. For some, the most relevant fault line in the debate over South African presence was the difference between privatization of bona fide national assets and the encouragement of "free market" competition between Tanzanian goods and foreign imports. They were willing to open up Tanzania's borders to increased trade but rued the loss of individual firms that were built through the sacrifice of Tanzanian blood, sweat, and tears: "If someone comes and shows you something that he wants to sell to you, you can decide if you want to buy it. That's fine. What I don't understand is when South Africans come in and buy up something that is already in place, like one of our banks or our utilities. When they take something that others made, *that's* what I don't understand."[50] The favorable terms under which these acquisitions took place were seen as giving South Africans an unfair advantage in the competition with Tanzanians:

[Government] strategy is to enlist the expertise of the international community in the hope that Tanzanians will pick up the tricks of the trade along the way. Nationalists retort that a social activity such as developing the economy is like trees growing in a forest: the fast-growing ones throw a shadow that forestalls the growth of any new ones. Tanzanians by implication are doomed to lose out in the economy forever (Okema 2005a).

Critics of the government's open-door investment policies point to the fact that prior managers were hamstrung by state policies and thus not in any position to run their operations effectively:

The government's rationale is that we have had these businesses, but we have failed to manage them ourselves, so we need to sell them to foreign investors. But these were *public* [that is, state-run] firms. And it is a public mess-up. Punishing the private sector in Tanzania doesn't make sense. They put the blame on Tanzanians *in general*. If they had first handed these firms over to the Tanzanian private sector, and then seen the Tanzanian private sector fail, *then* it would have made sense to seek out a foreign buyer. But not under these circumstances. Besides, [Tanzania] Breweries has a monopoly, so they don't even have to compete. I say, let a Tanzanian run Breweries. Then invite SAB in and let them invest on their own and build up their own plants and come and compete. Otherwise it's not fair because of the monopoly situation.[51]

The notion that South Africans had "saved" businesses run into the ground by poor local management was especially difficult for some to accept:

> They came over and grabbed up all the plums where they were available. Take Breweries. I mean you have to be a total fool if you can't make a profit with a brewery. But the Breweries were losing money before because they were being bled to death by bureaucracy. If somebody's son was being married, 100 crates of beer were hauled off, and that had to be absorbed as a cost of doing business. The government set the price of beer, so the managers' hands were tied in that regard. And any time the government couldn't pay salaries, they simply grabbed cash from Breweries (and Cigarettes). It was a cash cow for the government.

This observer went on to explain how South Africans were in a position to take advantage of strategic planning that the Tanzanian government had already done:

> There was already a feasibility study for a new brewery in Mwanza sitting on the shelf when the South Africans came. Everything was ripe for investment . . . we had already developed a plan to set up a bottle-making plant to service the new Mwanza brewery. So all of this thinking had been done already . . . And a full geological survey was already in place way back then. We knew where the gold was. We knew where the diamonds were. So if somebody comes in, it was simply, "There is gold there. Go, ye, and mine it!"

Moreover, South African investors were able to take advantage of undervalued assets they acquired when assuming control over some of the larger parastatals:

> But the government had a stranglehold on the economy. [The National Bank of Commerce] is another good example. With that broad financial network system already in place, why wouldn't you make a profit? Breweries, one of their chief assets was actually the land they sat on. And the South Africans acquired all those real estate assets along with the physical plant. So the first thing they did was liquidate all the houses and generate a bunch of working capital. So the cost of acquiring the brewery was actually minimal . . . And [the South Africans] came in and made a profit. Is that so surprising? [Scornfully] And then they go on and talk about *efficiencies* as if that were the reason for all of their success. But these are things that the government won't talk about.[52]

Imports

If the widespread perception of South Africans investing in Tanzania's productive capacity was that they were given unfair opportunities due to their acquisition of undervalued national assets and favorable tax requirements, the debate took on a different tenor when it came to trade relations, where South African dominance was everywhere apparent:

> A casual walk through the aisles of the leading supermarket chains . . . leaves one wondering what they were selling before South Africa products started entering our market. It is as though South Africa invented packed fruit juices, with the ubiquitous Ceres brand dominating shelf space in virtually all outlets. South African wines, likewise, seem to have eclipsed not only local wines, but even those from Western sources. Then there is South African confectionery, chocolates, biscuits, takeaway pizzas, chicken and hamburgers. Name it, a South African brand leads the pack. In the good old days, the Tanzania and Uganda markets were dominated by consumer products manufactured in Kenya.

After itemizing a long list of South African products being imported into the region, this writer came to the heart of the matter:

> When . . . consumers decide to pay a premium price for eggs or orange juice from South Africa, they are paying for a more efficient, cost-effective and reliable delivery system, superior packaging, better positioning, more aggressive marketing and a greater commitment to quality service delivery. They are also paying to minimise post-purchase remorse. Ultimately, they are paying a premium to get peace of mind—not just an egg. (Ohayo 1999, 27)

A commentator writing in the "letters to the editor" section of a local newspaper went even further to praise the new efficiencies being generated through competition with South African goods. He began with the standard condemnation of Tanzanians:

> Protectionism has been part of our lives for so long that we are bereft of understanding, we are dumbfounded, rendered hopelessly lost when the curtain is lifted. Whereas we should be evaluating the results of liberalization critically and starting to tend the sores exposed by the fortunate turnaround, we instead howl at the moon and cry wolf. Since independence, we have entombed ourselves in a system that secures the walls while the inside festers and crumbles. Protectionism for far too long disguised the inefficiency and backward policies that have been in place.

He then supplied a classic neoliberal economic rationale:

> Opening the doors to competition has forced many firms in Tanzania to re-think strategy and embrace hitherto novel programmes such as restructuring and retrenchment, downsizing etc. These have impacted negatively on jobs, but then they have also shorn the excessive baggage and bloatage that the companies were lugging, making them incapable of competing with more efficient competitors from outside the country. . . . South Africa has done no wrong. If anything, she is playing a commendable role of waking up other countries

in the region, and at the same time forcing them to start cutting down on the malpractices that have been bringing them down to their knees. (Bilks 2000, 5)

These paeans to the virtues of capitalist competition notwithstanding, some observers were extremely bitter that sweeping investments by South Africans had not resulted in more substantial returns to Tanzanians. They saw the effects as a dire threat to local development:

> [South African] investment . . . does not benefit Tanzanians; that everything should come from South Africa—that is not *investment* at all. In most cases, they have come to kill our businesses. Even when a businesswoman wants to sell tomatoes, she can't do so because tomatoes have already been imported from South Africa. Through such investment, they are trying to fool us. In the beginning we thought they had come to Tanzania to cooperate with us in the selling of our goods so that they would benefit us. Only to realize that they had come to establish shops and sell goods from their *own* country, not even wanting to look at domestic produce. That isn't friendship at all. It is like someone coming to practice segregation in your own country . . . it's like he's insulting you. And that's not investment. It's humiliation.[53]

Critics also challenged government policies in light of what they saw as the limited multiplier effects stemming from the actions of foreign firms. In their view, outside investments did little to produce viable socioeconomic change in Tanzania:

> I look at an investment, and I prefer to see it as something that has a meaningful residue. Whereas the South Africans, they just come and grab and run. They're likely to be here for a while, but let them tread carefully. This unconditional support for investment is not tenable. There has to be some regulation. Yes, we need expertise, exposure, experience, but what price do you pay for all of that? . . . Are they adding value? If they are seen to be making a contribution to the welfare of the country, I don't think anyone would be against their presence. But that is the question . . . They are being given credit where it is not due. And in the process, they are building up anger among some of us who are wondering how things could go so far with so little to show for it.[54]

An Asian Tanzanian commentator compared her own community's record of investing in Tanzania with the pattern she saw emerging in South African investments:

> You know, people ask me, "What about the Indian community?" And I say that at least the Indian investors are investing in building schools, health clinics, and those sorts of things. You'd never see a South African investing in those because there's no money in it . . . The South Africans could be here for a hundred years—I mean, this is an exaggeration, but still—they could be here for a hundred years and they would still not become Tanzanian. They would still be South African. They would never change.[55]

Conclusion

The national ambivalence prompted by South Africa's growing presence can be traced to the new investors' national and racial identity and how that was understood against the historical geographical background of Tanzanian's history as a frontline state (see chapter 1). As a growing body of scholarship drawn from diverse geographic settings demonstrates, capital expansion into new areas of the global periphery almost inevitably sets in motion cultural and social dynamics that are not reducible to economic logic.[56]

For several years in the late 1990s and early 2000s, South African presence dominated the national press reports on Tanzania's economic development. In sector after sector, scandals erupted as South Africans assumed an ever larger role in the economy. The summary impression gleaned from these reports is that South African investment activities in Tanzania throughout this period bore all the hallmarks of an unbridled imperialism. Anti-competitive actions designed to secure near-monopoly control over Tanzanian markets increasingly saturated with South African products; the strengthening of relations with an emergent comprador class operating under the guise of the Tanzanian state; the insistence on special corporate prerogatives regarding taxation, royalty payments, and import duties; the insensitive violation of potent national symbols—all signaled that South Africa had joined the ranks of the world's most aggressive neocolonial powers.

Given persistent press coverage, South Africa's presence in Tanzania served as a constant reminder that the country had firmly charted a new economic course "down the road to neo-liberalism" (Shivji 2006b). The expansion of that presence was politically divisive. The ensuing debate surrounding South Africa accordingly exposed deep fault lines within the Tanzanian body politic, pitting proponents of economic reforms against long-time supporters of socialist principles (cf. Goodman 1999). Among high-level government officials and the country's entrepreneurial class, South Africans were seen as potential business partners and models to be emulated. The relevant facts for these observers were that South Africans came and invested in the Tanzanian economy when few others were willing to do so, and they did so at levels that Tanzanians themselves could never match. South Africans took risks, worked hard, and ultimately achieved business success by turning around floundering state-run businesses. In the process, they introduced new quality standards and imposed a type of capitalist discipline on Tanzanian firms, forcing them to match the new standards or lose out in an increasingly competitive marketplace for goods and services. As far as neoliberal proponents within the Tanzanian elite were concerned, these were changes that were long overdue.

Critics offered grudging respect to the South African managers responsible for the dramatic turnaround of Tanzanian businesses, but they had much greater difficulty reconciling themselves to the loss of key national assets and the rise of a new moral economy premised on intense competition. They refused to accept the rough, insensitive ways of the newly dominant capitalist enterprises and felt slighted at the trampling of proud national symbols. They rejected the notion that Tanzanians could not manage their own affairs and asked pointed questions about the social consequences of a reform program that enriched a few at the expense of many. For these observers, it may have been true that South Africans made better beer, but the taste that this left in their mouths was a distinctly bitter one.

Figure 1. "Jo'burg Jones is back in 'The Treasure of Dar es Salaam.'" A humorous advertising campaign launched by the South African–run Sea Cliff Hotel in the early 2000s featured the hotel's manager cast as a latter-day Indiana Jones exploring the "legend" that a "perfect business hotel" could possibly exist in Tanzania. PHOTO BY THE AUTHOR.

Figure 2. Vodacom buildings in Dar es Salaam. Giant multistory renditions of the bright blue-and-white Vodacom logo became a fixture of the urban landscape in Dar es Salaam in the mid-2000s, creating jarring sight lines along major thoroughfares. PHOTO BY THE AUTHOR.

Figure 3. Towering cost overruns. The Bank of Tanzania's "twin towers," as they are known locally, dominate the Dar es Salaam skyline. The original budget for their construction, which was carried out by a leading South African firm, was set at roughly US$80 million in 2000. By 2007, it had ballooned to $358 million. Press accounts characterized the cost overruns as scandalous, given the poverty of the Tanzanian population. REPRINTED WITH THE PERMISSION OF THE ARTIST, KING KINYA, AND MWANANCHI COMMUNICATIONS, PUBLISHERS OF THE CITIZEN, MWANANCHI, AND MWANASPOTI NEWSPAPERS.

Figure 4. Air disaster. The acquisition of a controlling interest in Air Tanzania by South African Airways (SAA) in 2002 was originally approved with the expectation that Dar es Salaam airport would become a regional hub in SAA's growing air transportation network. By late 2006, rising financial losses led to the acrimonious dissolution of the partnership. REPRINTED WITH THE PERMISSION OF THE ARTIST, SAMUEL MWAMKINGA (SAMMI JO'UNE), AND MWANANCHI COMMUNICATIONS, PUBLISHERS OF THE CITIZEN, MWANANCHI, AND MWANASPOTI NEWSPAPERS.

Figure 5. Tanzania Breweries chosen "Most Respected Company in Tanzania." The economic performance of several formerly state-owned enterprises has dramatically improved under South African management. In an annual poll of nearly 300 East African business executives in 2005, for example, South African–run Tanzania Breweries was named the "Most Respected Company in Tanzania." It was also selected as the Confederation of Tanzania Industries' "President's Manufacturer of the Year" in Tanzania in 2006. REPRINTED WITH THE PERMISSION OF MWANANCHI COMMUNICATIONS, PUBLISHERS OF *THE CITIZEN, MWANANCHI,* AND *MWANASPOTI* NEWSPAPERS.

Figure 6. White spot. This luxurious rugby club situated at the foot of Mt. Meru is one of several bars, clubs, and restaurants that have become de facto "white spots" in the eyes of Tanzanians due to their association with South African managers and/or their primarily white expatriate clientele. PHOTO BY THE AUTHOR.

Figure 7. Trespassing allowed? In its original unadulterated form, this sign located outside a prominent "white spot" conveyed the message "No Trespassing Allowed." Locals indicated their displeasure at being excluded from the property by scratching out the first two letters of the word "Hakuna," thereby reversing the sign's meaning so it read, in effect, "Trespassing Allowed."

PHOTO BY THE AUTHOR.

Figure 8. Rugby's white history. This 1963 photo displayed on the wall of a local sports pub shows fourteen rugby players from a now defunct rugby league. The names of the players included in the accompanying newspaper clippings—Van Rooyen, Pretorius, Mallinson—provide evidence of the South African families that lived in the area in the 1960s.
PHOTO BY THE AUTHOR.

Figure 9. Rugby returns. A member of a well-established American missionary family is shown with rugby ball in hand as very young man in 1975, and again as a grizzled veteran lining up for a scrum in 2006. The gap between the photos is significant. Although rugby has been a favorite pastime of white settler and missionary families in East Africa for nearly a century, it waned in significance in Tanzania following the departure of Afrikaners not long after the 1967 Arusha Declaration. In part, this was due to the perception that rugby was a foreign game, played by whites only, and thus not worth promoting in Tanzania's public schools. Only with the influx of foreign investors from South Africa and other rugby-loving nations after the adoption of neoliberal economic reforms in Tanzania was critical mass reached once again to revive a rugby league. PHOTO BY THE AUTHOR.

Figure 10. Tanzania's "rainbow team": The Tanzania Rugby Union's rules stipulate that anyone who has spent three years in Tanzania working on a residency permit is eligible to participate in league and national team competitions. Thus, approximately two-thirds of the players on the national side in the mid-2000s were white expatriates. PHOTO BY THE AUTHOR.

4
Tanzanite for Tanzanians

God gave us the mine and gave investors the brain.
AYUB RIOBA

Our destination was a windswept hillside a few kilometers south of Tanzania's majestic Mount Kilimanjaro, the site of world's only known deposit of an obscure gemstone known as tanzanite. We entered the compound through the first of three gates, each staffed with armed guards and ringed with tall fences topped with razor wire. Two were monitored by the security personnel of a South African mining corporation known as Tanzanite One, and the third was patrolled by Tanzanian government officials. The latter marked the entrance to the Mererani Controlled Area, the core of the tanzanite deposit where access is tightly restricted to mining personnel and their official visitors.[1]

My guide, a young miner who began his career in South Africa, took me first to hear a presentation delivered by one of the firm's geologists. After learning about the unique 500-million-year-old rock formation that contains tanzanite, he gave me a tour of the mine site itself, providing a brief history of tanzanite production along the way. We drove past sorting and processing facilities, dormitories and a dining hall. At one point, we climbed down into a steeply pitched abandoned mine shaft to get a sense of the spatiality of the underground gem deposits. We then drove to the far edge of the corporate perimeter. Here, my guide stopped and explained that the fence in front of us was absolutely crucial to the mining operation because it worked, as he put it, "to keep the miners in, and the scum, if you like, out."

The "miners," in this instance, were the employees of Tanzanite One, and the "scum" were the thousands of artisanal and small-scale mining (ASM) operators and laborers who worked in rudimentary mine shafts located just beyond the fence. Many of the ASM miners operated shafts *within* what is now the corporate perimeter until they were forcibly relocated by the Tanzanian military when the mining enclave was privatized in the late 1990s. The entrances to their current mines, which were easily visible less than a kilometer from our position, ran perilously close to and occasionally intersected with corporate shafts underground. The proximity of the different mining operations made for a volatile situation: over the previous decade, dozens of ASM miners had been shot, several fatally, when they were caught "trespassing" within the corporate mining zone.

The long-running battle between corporate and ASM miners for control of the tanzanite deposits received extensive coverage in both the national press and trade publications in the mining and jewelry industries after the core of the mine was acquired by South Africans in the mid-1990s. Indeed, tanzanite mining became a national test case regarding the potential pitfalls and benefits of opening up Tanzania's economy to South African investors, throwing neocolonial economic relationships into graphic relief. In the case of gold and gemstone mining, the promise of quick riches for small-scale miners stood in sharp contrast to the generalized poverty surrounding the mining districts. The extraction of gems and precious metals was a zero-sum game, pitting technologically sophisticated, vertically integrated, multinational mining corporations against artisanal miners using flashlight headlamps and manual equipment. In the case of tanzanite mining, the situation was complicated further by the fact that the gem was strongly associated with the nation: in the view of locals, tanzanite should have been reserved for Tanzanians. Portraying Tanzanian miners as "scum" could only inflame these preexisting tensions.

Controversial South African Mining Investments

The implementation of economic reforms in Tanzania resulted in a radical restructuring of the country's mining industry. In 1994, for example, there were only 170 prospecting licenses and 22 mining licenses registered with the government; by 2005, over 2,200 prospecting licenses had been granted and 200 mining licenses were on the books, more than a tenfold increase over the course of a single decade.[2] Foreign miners, including some of the largest mining firms in South Africa, flocked to the country during this period, injecting over US$2 billion in FDI into the Tanzanian economy in little more than a decade.[3] With an initial investment of US$335 million, including US$205 million to acquire mining rights and US$130 million in project financing, AngloGold, a subsidiary of the Anglo American mining conglomerate, acquired a 50 percent stake in Geita Gold Mine from Ghana's Ashanti Goldfields in 2000 (Parry 2000). Control of the remaining 50 percent stake was acquired when the two firms merged as AngloGold Ashanti in 2004. This firm currently leads dozens of South African prospectors, miners, and service providers active in the Tanzanian gold mining industry. Similarly, South Africa's De Beers had a dominant presence in the Tanzanian diamond mining sector for decades after acquiring its initial stake in the Williamson Diamond mine at Mwadui in 1938. The mine was later nationalized under Nyerere, but a 50 percent stake was reacquired by De Beers with a fresh capital outlay of US$23 million in 1993.[4]

In order to clear the way for these foreign mining ventures, hundreds of thousands of Tanzanian gold and gemstone miners were forcibly removed from their traditional mining areas in the mid-1990s (Chachage 1995; Fisher 2007). These moves set up a confrontation between large-scale corporate miners from abroad and artisanal and small-scale miners from Tanzania, in which the latter felt distinctly disadvantaged. As one miner put it, "They came here with their briefcases but today they own huge gold mines . . . If this is what globalization is about, then most of us won't survive."[5]

The sale of mineral assets to foreign firms incurred the wrath of Tanzanians because locals saw few benefits from the huge revenues generated in the sector. While mineral exports from the country rose from US$16 million in 1997 to US$790 million by 2006, the contributions from mining to GDP remained relatively low, rising from a negligible sum in 1997 to only 3.8 percent of GDP in 2006.[6] The commonly held impression was that the majority of the profits gleaned from mining were being taken offshore. As one columnist put it, "the gold exported from Tanzania is 'Tanzanian' only to the extent that it is extracted from Tanzanian soil. But the exports—and, therefore, the sales proceeds—are not truly Tanzanian. The [largest] proportion remains abroad" (Lyimo 2006a, 15). Locals focused their attention on royalty payments assessed against miners. By statute, miners were required to pay royalties equivalent to 3 percent of gross revenues for gold and 5 percent for unprocessed gemstones, rates that were deemed outrageously low by Tanzanians.[7] The prevailing sentiment was captured on a placard carried by small-scale gold miners during a May Day workers' rally in 2005, which read, "3% for us, 97% for them. We might as well give them the whole country!"[8]

At the same time, the major mining firms were granted numerous tax exemptions.[9] To the astonishment and deep skepticism of Tanzanian observers, these loopholes allowed the firms to report net operating *losses* from their mines. After extracting some 20 million carats of high-value diamonds from its Mwadui operations over a fifteen-year period, De Beers never posted a profit and paid no corporate taxes.[10] Similarly, despite removing 3 million ounces of gold worth an estimated US$1.143 billion in just five years from its Geita holdings, AngloGold Ashanti completely avoided paying corporate taxes during this period. Indeed, when Tanzanite One made a corporate tax payment of roughly US$2 million [TSh2.4 billion] in 2006, press reports indicated that this was the first payment of corporate taxes by *any* foreign mining company in twenty years.[11]

As this story broke, newspapers were full of innuendo that gold miners were "swindling" the government out of tax revenues via accounting sleight of hand (Abdul-Aziz 2006, 1). Press accounts estimated that the country had suffered revenue losses totaling US$1.04 billion since the initial investments of mining capital in the mid-1990s (Shekighenda 2007). One analyst concluded that Tanzania would lose nearly a quarter of its potential tax revenues due to fraud and/or statutory exemptions in the mining sector in 2006, "an amount that would otherwise finance at least seven ministries for a year" (Kamndaya 2006c, 6). And the Tanzanian Revenue Authority commissioner himself was quoted as saying that "under-declaration of profits" by mining firms cost Tanzania US$207 million in 2007 alone.[12]

The country's endowment of billions of dollars' worth of precious metals and gemstones represented a potentially instant source of revenue for a population beset by desperate poverty.[13] The impression that valuable resources were being extracted "tax-free" by foreigners instead of meeting the basic livelihood needs of locals was widespread.[14] Public relations officers for the mining firms sought to counter this impression by highlighting the firms' contributions to rural development projects, but these were derided in the press as self-serving publicity stunts:

> We are reminded ad infinitum, ad nauseam that the mining companies—
> through what is fashionably described as "corporate social responsibility" or
> some such legerdemain—build primary schools, health centres, police posts,
> access roads, and water supplies. What we are not told is that these facilities
> also serve the mining companies and their people. And that they are ephemer-
> al. Soon after the mines are exhausted and the owners decamp for other golden
> pastures, the facilities are bound to collapse for lack of maintenance, repair
> and operating costs. (Lyimo 2006a, 15)

Indeed, despite the corporations' own accounting of their community development activities, it took pressure from the Ministry of Energy and Minerals and members of Parliament to force the firms to live up to their statutory obligation to pay local district councils an annual fee of US$200,000 for local development purposes. Kanyabwoya reports that the day after members of Parliament brought this issue to the floor in the National Assembly in 2006, four district councils, including Geita District where AngloGold Ashanti is based, received payments of US$200,000 each from mining corporations operating in their territories (Kanyabwoya 2006).

To add insult to injury, mining executives were perceived to be living lavish lifestyles. Rumors that executives were commuting by air back and forth from their homes in Dar es Salaam to the mining districts near Lake Victoria on a *daily* basis provoked an outraged response in the op-ed pages of the local newspapers: "Investors can only do that where costs are extremely low, yields exceedingly high and profits nothing but pure obscenity. So even the deliberately blind can see and tell that mining in this country is shameless plunder and looting of a poor people's natural wealth at a magnitude unimaginable even under the most primitive conditions" (Munyaga 2006, 3).

Faced with this public backlash, the government sought to counter what they saw as a series of gross misapprehensions on the part of Tanzanian citizens. President Mkapa was paraphrased in boldface headlines as saying that mining investors were "not thieves" and that the criticism of their activities in Tanzania was "counterproductive and stupid jealousy."[15] The Ministry of Energy and Minerals argued that the royalty payments paid by foreign miners were on par with those in other countries (cf. Madatta 2005, 1–2). And the private sector's Tanzania Chamber of Minerals and Energy reported that even though foreign miners had not paid the highest tax rate of 30 percent, which applied to corporate profits, they had in fact contributed a total of over US$250 million in the form of statutory taxes and other contributions from 1997 to 2005. It also provided an itemized list of the costs of gold exploration, which ranged from US$50 to US$100 per ounce of gold, in an effort to challenge the notion that foreign miners were profiting unfairly from their operations in the country.[16]

The head of Geita Gold Mine, South Africa's largest mineral holding in the country, spoke out on behalf of the mining firms, arguing that royalty payments in Tanzania could not be levied at rates as high as those miners were required to pay in South Africa. Unlike in South Africa, he maintained, firms in Tanzania also had to provide their own roads, water supply, and other infrastructure in order to operate. Royalty payments, he suggested, needed to be adjusted accordingly (Madatta 2006, 1). Gold miners also made public a more detailed accounting of their operating costs, indicating that their expenses included routine production costs (57 percent), taxes and royalties (15 percent), dividends to shareholders (13 percent), interest payments on debt (10 percent) and capital reinvestment (5 percent). As far as another Geita mining official was concerned, the bottom line was all that mattered: "People should know that we are here to do business not to run charity organizations."[17]

This additional information on mining costs did little to dampen the public criticism of the sector, however, especially in light of repeated reports of violence in and around the mines. In 1996, for example, allegations were raised that more than fifty artisanal gold miners were buried alive when a foreign corporate miner, acting with government blessing, bulldozed dozens of small-scale mining pits to prevent illegal miners from operating in the area (Mines and Communities 2001). The fact that the firm implicated in this instance was Canadian rather than South African was of little consequence to locals who tended to associate mine violence with South Africans wherever it occurred. As the political affairs officer at the South African High Commission explained, "It is unfortunate that the color of our people unfortunately carries even some of the problems that are not of South Africans [*sic*]. So we have Canadians [in the mining industry], we have Australians, you know, and so on. An incident that would happen in the mines, as long as that person is white, then it is [assumed to be a] South African. That is a very unfortunate situation."[18]

What the SAHC representative failed to acknowledge, however, is that South Africans earned this reputation, largely as a consequence of violence surrounding tanzanite mines.

Tanzanite Nationalism and Foreign Corporate Control

Even in the rarified world of international gemstone trading, tanzanite stood out as something unique. To begin with, the deep blue-violet stone, which is technically known as blue zoicyte, was only found in one location in the world, the twelve-square-kilometer enclave I visited in the foothills south of Mount Kilimanjaro. This distinctive geological provenance was, of course, a gemstone marketer's dream, and the oft-repeated claim that tanzanite is "1,000 times rarer than diamonds" helped generate an estimated $300–500 million in annual sales worldwide.[19]

The gem also benefited from the cachet of a unique association with the world renowned jewelry outlet Tiffany and Company. In the version of the tanzanite discovery myth featured in corporate promotions, the "mysterious" blue stones were originally found by a Maasai "tribesman." They were eventually taken to geologists, who showed them to Tiffany's representative, Henry Platt. He proclaimed tanzanite the "most beautiful blue stone discovered in two thousand years" and launched a major marketing campaign declaring that "tanzanite could only be found in two places on earth—Tanzania and Tiffany's." Fearing that the genteel gem-buying public might shy away from a stone whose geological designation, blue zoicyte, sounded so much like "suicide," Platt chose to rename the gem "tanzanite" after its country of origin. The gem's name, its exclusive location within Tanzanian national borders, and its distinctive geological history all subsequently ensured that it would come to serve as a potent national symbol. The tanzanite mining sector accordingly became a primary site for the assertion of Tanzanian national identity.[20]

The Tanzanian government's policies toward its distinctive gemstone resource underwent a number of radical changes in the four and a half decades following its discovery. In the original gem rush, the government allowed prospectors to stake individual claims to mine shafts on an open access basis. Then, in 1971, the Nyerere government nationalized the tanzanite mines, and production on the site was put under the control of the parastatal State Mining Corporation (STAMICO) and its subsidiary, the Tanzania Gemstone Industries (TGI), for the better part of a decade. This arrangement proved unwieldy and unprofitable, and the state once again elected to recognize the mining rights of individual artisanal and small-scale miners as part of a new national mining policy (URT 1979). By 1989, an estimated 30,000 ASM miners, most working as laborers for absentee claim holders, were active in the area.[21]

In 1990, the government, already deep into its economic reform program, took a series of steps to curtail artisanal tanzanite mining in favor of private corporate investors. The tanzanite mining area was divided into four zones, which were designated Blocks A, B, C, and D. All ASM miners working in the area were forcibly removed as the blocks were allocated to small mining firms (Chachage 1995, 84–86). Blocks B and D were eventually reallocated to ASM miners, and Block C, which represented the core of the enclave, was put up for sale to an international investor. Rights to Block C were initially acquired by a British-owned firm known as Graphtan, which primarily mined graphite. In 1996, Graphtan's assets were acquired by the South African firm African Gemstone Ltd., or Afgem, which concentrated its efforts on mining tanzanite. Eight years later, in 2004, Afgem restructured itself and sold its assets to a new corporate entity run by former Afgem board members known as Tanzanite One.[22]

Within Tanzania, the terms of these transfers were viewed with intense skepticism, largely because they were so "intransparent."[23] Critics questioned why a firm that mined graphite chose to site itself directly on top of the most lucrative vein of tanzanite in the country and argued that the graphite mining venture was little more than a Trojan horse granting South Africans a foothold in the country's lucrative gemstone industry. When the mine was transferred to Afgem as a tanzanite mine, locals felt their suspicions were confirmed.[24]

The acquisition of Afgem's assets by Tanzanite One was cause for similar skepticism. Local observers noted that several members of the Afgem board of directors— including the CEO and the chief operating officer, as well as most of the mine's senior on-site personnel including geologists, engineers, security officers, and marketing specialists—were "transferred" to Tanzanite One along with Afgem's mining and prospecting rights. The restructuring that led to the creation of Tanzanite One was seen as a shell game designed to allow the firm's principal stakeholders to take advantage of a tax holiday on offer to new corporate investors. The member of Parliament representing the Mererani area explained the prevailing view: "We have seen many such foreign owned firms, changing ownership or names thus earning themselves another tax relief holiday, while other businesses keep staggering under the weight of taxation being imposed on them."[25] As if to underscore the point, locals used the terms Afgem and Tanzanite One interchangeably when referring to the firm.[26]

Within the corporate mining world, Afgem/Tanzanite One enjoyed a positive reputation. Modeled after De Beers, the firm was praised by industry observers for technological innovation, especially in the design of optical scanners for gem sorting; shrewd marketing efforts that linked the firm's gems to iconic images of Maasai warriors and the majestic Mount Kilimanjaro; its successful strategy to recapitalize the firm by shifting its stock listing from South Africa to London's Alternate Investment Market; and above all, for the critical role it played in promoting tanzanite on the global market.[27] These industry accolades notwithstanding, the mine operators' South African national identity continued to attract a great deal of controversy within Tanzania.[28]

Corporate officers were well aware of these public relations difficulties, and they used a number of strategies to try and blunt their effects. When Afgem first launched its tanzanite operations, for example, it set up a local subsidiary, Merelani Mining, Ltd., which was run by Tanzania's first ambassador to South Africa, Ami Mpungwe.[29] Mpungwe aggressively defended Afgem against its critics, employing the by-now standard technique of denigrating Tanzanians while simultaneously extolling the virtues of South Africans (see chapter 3):

> AFGEM's operations at Merelani are managed as a *Tanzanian* company,
> with *Tanzanian* shareholders, *Tanzanian* directors and myself as chairman.
> AFGEM, at the invitation of the Tanzanian government, is providing the
> necessary capital, technology, and expertise to develop tanzanite mining in
> Tanzania—something we, as Tanzanians, have been unable to do for the past
> 33 years (Kondo 2001b, original emphasis).

Afgem/Tanzanite One representatives also argued that they were not in direct competition with small-scale miners.[30] To the contrary, they maintained that the firm's efforts were instrumental in expanding the market for tanzanite worldwide.[31] Illustrating the point, Afgem/Tanzanite One officials noted that only 4 percent of South Africans had heard of tanzanite in 2001. Five years after a concerted marketing effort, 70 percent of survey respondents were familiar with it.[32] Such growth in recognition, they suggested, clearly redounded to the benefit of all tanzanite miners and mineral dealers.

Tanzanite One's executives also sought to extol their efforts in the realm of good corporate citizenship. When Tanzanite One's chief operating officer was interviewed in the local business press to mark the end of the 2005 fiscal year, for example, he called attention to the firm's corporate tax payment that year, which he described as "undoubtedly the most significant tax payment received by the government of Tanzania from the mining sector in its entire history."[33] By citing its dutiful tax payments, Tanzanite One distinguished itself from its counterparts in the gold mining industry, where non-payment of corporate tax had been the norm for years. In both absolute and relative terms, then, Tanzanite One used the tax issue to burnish its credentials as a model corporate citizen.

This sort of argument was lost on local critics, however. Instead, they lamented the fact that the bulk of the rough (uncut, unpolished) tanzanite mined by Afgem/ Tanzanite One was being shipped directly to South Africa, where it was sold to wholesale buyers and then redistributed to a number of offshore processing plants. This practice was undoubtedly the source of sensational rumors making the rounds in northern Tanzania in 2005, according to which South Africans had taken a cache of rough tanzanite specimens to South Africa where they had "spread them around underground" so they could be "discovered" by local miners.[34] This ruse supposedly gave Tanzanite One a conduit for smuggling uncut gems out of the country to be processed abroad without paying royalties or taxes in Tanzania.

A news article that appeared in the Tanzanian press in 2005 under the headline "Controversy over 'Tanzanite' Origins in SA" amplified these sensitivities. The journalist who filed the report noticed during a trip to South Africa that in-flight magazines for local airlines had identified tanzanite as found "only in Africa," rather than clarifying the gem's exclusive Tanzanian origins.[35] This oversight was seen as a deliberate attempt on the part of South Africans to usurp Tanzania's national heritage.

Other controversial symbolic slights were attributed to an entity known as the Tanzanite Foundation. Established in 2000 with a $3 million budget, this unit was launched to design and implement development projects benefiting communities affected by the firm's mining operations, manage public relations related to these initiatives, and devise a standardized system for branding and marketing the gem.[36] The foundation was conceived in part as a preemptive response to a growing controversy that was brewing in the gemstone industry. So-called blood diamonds had been implicated as a partial cause of, and source of funding for, brutal civil wars in Sierra Leone, Liberia, Angola, and the Democratic Republic of the Congo.[37] According to one source, Afgem's managers saw early on how prominent American politicians were "jumping on the conflict diamond band wagon," and how the diamond industry was "taking a hammering" as a consequence. They accordingly took several steps to prevent this issue from spilling over into the tanzanite industry.[38]

The key initiative was to certify in writing that select high-value tanzanite specimens had been legally mined and marketed under secure conditions.[39] These stones were then laser-inscribed with a serial number and a microscopic logo known as the "Mark of Rarity," which was meant to assuage fears that the gems were associated with conflict in any way. The implication, however, that stones *without* the firm's imprimatur had illegal or unethical origins was infuriating to ASM miners and traders. In their view, the "Mark of Rarity" was a sinister design on the part of the *makaburu,* a blatant attempt to convert tanzanite into a South African brand that was purposely "aimed at wiping out small-scale tanzanite miners on the international market."[40]

The negative response to the "Mark of Rarity" eventually led the firm to stop laser inscribing its gems. It nonetheless continued to highlight the gem's rarity in a series of remarkable advertisements. A particularly cynical example in Tanzanite One's 2004 annual report sought to instill a sense of guilty pleasure in gemstone buyers: "At last it's acceptable to wear something on the endangered list—tanzanite, a thousand times rarer than diamonds" (Tanzanite One 2004). Similarly, the Tanzanite Sales Training Manual, which the Tanzanite Foundation circulated to the proprietors of retail outlets, smugly promoted the gem as an "heirloom stone" with the tagline, "Some things you can teach, some things you can learn, some things you can only inherit."[41]

Corporate Social Responsibility, Revenue Sharing, and the Mine-Based Livelihood System

To help bolster its public image as a "socially responsible" corporate citizen, the Tanzanite Foundation launched a number of community development initiatives on behalf of Afgem/Tanzanite One. Among other projects, it supported school construction, a livestock watering hole, stand pipes for domestic water consumption, road improvements, a church building and a health clinic.[42] The firm also hired local residents for largely menial jobs at the mine site, and allowed local women to re-mine tailings piles left at the end of the corporate mine's ore crushing and sorting process. Photos and descriptions of these projects were prominently featured in corporate and foundation websites, the firm's financial reports, and the trade literature, where they attested to the firm's commitment to community development (Genis 2006).

There was one catch, however: nearly all of these projects were confined to a single small section of Mererani. The mining boom town is divided into several sections or wards. The most populated of these, an urban settlement also known as Mererani, is where most ASM miners and their families live. The area where the tanzanite mines are located, however, is part of a less densely populated ward known as Naisinyai, where the residents are primarily Maasai agropastoralists, a group that is more heavily involved in gemstone brokering (wholesale buying and selling) than mining per se.[43] Since the residents of Naisinyai retain residual surface rights to the entire territory currently under excavation by tanzanite miners, they were targeted by Afgem/Tanzanite One to receive the development benefits distributed by the firm.[44]

Critics disputed the idea that these projects represented a genuine commitment to distributive justice concerns or better development standards by the firm. Instead they saw these efforts as attempts to manipulate public opinion:

It's like when you have a small child who has got their hands on something very valuable and you want to take it away from them so it doesn't break. So you give the child a piece of candy so they'll give up the valuable item. The donations Tanzanite One have given to Naisinyai are like that piece of candy; this is how they manage to take away the land rights that belong to the residents.[45]

The selection of Naisinyai to receive the corporate largesse drew criticism from miners based in the nearby ward of Mererani in particular. Many ASM miners living in Mererani were displaced when Block C was privatized, and they felt that they, too, should be compensated for their losses by the firm. However, Mererani ward received few tangible benefits from the firm.[46] A 2005 newspaper article played up this fact:

The Mererani township, despite being the source of the world's only blue gems, is in pathetic condition with most of its building in poor state [sic] and in fact the entire area with the exception of a few structures is a slum township, all these being attributed to the fact that most of the revenue earned from Tanzanite does not benefit the area of origin. Mererani area lacks basic community services such as a public hospital and as a result, the area is now depending on private health facilities. . . . The mining ward depends on two Primary Schools . . . with a total of 2400 pupils between them. These are heavily congested since a single classroom has up to 130 pupils.[47]

One miner stressed that he could see no evidence whatsoever of Afgem/Tanzanite One's impact on livelihoods in the ASM mining community, and argued that what Afgem/Tanzanite One was doing should be called "looting" rather than "investing"; that was a more accurate way of describing their actions in the country.[48] A local mineral dealer was even more caustic:

How long have the South Africans been in the country? And what have they done for Tanzanians? They earn 200 million dollars and what have they done with it? The Tanzanite Foundation is not a *charity* [voice dripping with sarcasm]; it is not a foundation like that. These people are *businessmen*. They repaired the road *once;* they built a dispensary *once;* they built a school block *once*. What is that when you have taken millions of dollars of profits out of the country?[49]

ASM advocates pointed to the corporation's road construction project as a particularly apt illustration of the limited impact of corporate gift giving. The 14-kilometer section of the road that was "improved" by the Tanzanite Foundation passes directly through Naisinyai ward (the easternmost section of Mererani), but then stops at the entrance to the Tanzanite One mine offices. The remaining five-kilometer stretch of road between the corporate entrance and the far western sections of Mererani where most of the ASM mining population is located saw little or no improvement at all. To many, the break in the improved road between the mine entrance and Mererani proper symbolized the gap between the corporation's public relations claims and the ASM miners' own bleak lived realities.

ASM miners sought to undermine the corporate miners' position further by advancing a moral economic argument on their own behalf. In their view, the economy of the whole of northern Tanzania was driven by multiplier effects associated with tanzanite incomes. One activist asserted, for example, that for every mine claim holder working in Mererani, another 300 individuals earned a livelihood either directly or indirectly. He enumerated the negative consequences of foreign control over the mine:

> So that means whatever tanzanite is going to come from Mererani is going to go through a set arrangement, making its way through the company's offices and through South Africa. This directly cuts off the Mererani village, and the villages that surround Mererani that depend directly on the mining. Because these minerals will not go through the village; will not pass through the hands of the local buyers, the broker/dealers; will not come to Arusha, where hundreds, thousands of people are making livelihoods out of it; will not go to [residents of other provinces], who depend on their sons, fathers, uncles, who are also mining. So it means that the livelihood capabilities will be destroyed. Who will get the benefit? The South Africans.[50]

The social benefits associated with ASM mining alone, he argued, were enough to warrant protecting the ASM sector at all costs.

Mining Ethics after 9/11

Two months after the 11 September 2001 attacks on New York City's World Trade Center and the U.S. military's Pentagon headquarters, the *Wall Street Journal* published an article that claimed to have uncovered an important money-laundering operation used by al-Qaeda, the group claiming responsibility for the attacks:

> In the shadow of Mount Kilimanjaro, miners with flashlights tied to their heads crawl hundreds of feet beneath the East African plain, searching for a purple-brown crystal that will turn into a blue gem called tanzanite. Many of the rare stones . . . find their way to display cases at Zales, QVC or Tiffany. But it's a long way from these dusty plains to U.S. jewelry stores, and the stones pass through many hands on their journey. Some of those hands, it is increasingly clear, belong to active supporters of Osama bin Laden. (Block and Pearl 2001)

Citing sources in Mererani, the authors of this piece alleged that al Qaeda sympathizers were using tanzanite to raise funds for terrorist activities. In the emotionally charged aftermath of 9/11, these claims could not have been more inflammatory.

Reacting to the *Wall Street Journal* report, retail outlets in North America, which accounted for roughly 70 percent of annual tanzanite sales worldwide, immediately stopped selling tanzanite, and family members of 9/11 victims mounted a lawsuit demanding $1 billion in compensatory damages against tanzanite industry stakeholders (Weldon and Donahue 2002). When al-Qaeda ties were disavowed by the U.S. State Department, the lawsuit was dismissed and sales of tanzanite resumed (Stauffer 2002). Still, the damage to the gemstone's reputation was significant, and Afgem's public relations apparatus was forced into high gear.[51]

The new promotional strategy began with a statement by Afgem spokesperson Joanne Herbstein, who said in the trade press, "It is most distressing that the tanzanite trade, like so many other industries, has been implicated with the al Qaeda network. . . . The tanzanite industry has been unregulated and informal, with little control of the channel through which tanzanite exits Tanzania. With this historic lack of regulation, illegality was bound to prevail." Herbstein continued by taking a swipe at ASM miners: "Tanzanite has been mined on an informal basis by small-scale miners that typically have neither the capital nor the technology to employ safe mining methods. This has resulted in many tragic fatalities and has opened the market to the exploitation of child labor, much to the disdain and concern of international labor bodies and the Tanzanian government." And she concluded by highlighting the conflict-free chain of custody certified by the "Mark of Rarity" brand: "Our Tanzanite Foundation brand will further ensure the socially-aware consumer of the origin, mining methods and export channels of their purchase."[52]

The "Mark of Rarity" was relaunched "as an icon synonymous with absolute assurance of the quality, grade, source and *ethical provenance* of tanzanite and tanzanite jewelry" (Tanzanite Foundation 2005b; emphasis added). Buyers could rest assured that their purchase of branded tanzanite carried with it "an ethical guarantee which ensures that the gem has gone from mine to market with complete integrity. In other words, that it was legally exported" (Rutter 2004). The foundation also promoted specially designed jewelry that would appeal to prospective buyers "who have a passion for ethics as well as for aesthetics" (Tanzanite Foundation 2006).

The new tanzanite brand was widely publicized in gemstone trade publications and was used by the firm to differentiate corporate gems from those entering the market through the artisanal sector. Ad copy in a prominent trade magazine played on the insecurities of prospective gemstone buyers to maximum effect, notably drawing on a bit of sexual innuendo:

> *Is she really who she says she is?* With just a single source in the foothills of
> Mount Kilimanjaro, and no more than a decade or so of supply left, few indi-
> viduals will ever own a tanzanite. If you are fortunate enough to possess one of
> these most exquisite and beautiful blue violet gems, you will want to know that
> your investment is guaranteed, now and always. The Tanzanite Foundation
> exists to guide your investment. Look for the Tanzanite Foundation's Mark of

Rarity™ which serves to guarantee that your tanzanite is genuine and has been expertly graded according to the industry standard. Also that it has followed an ethical route to market and that your jeweler is of the highest repute. Rest assured and know what you are getting. Insist on a Tanzanite Foundation certificate, the Tanzanite Foundation's microscopic Mark of Rarity™, which can only be identified through a special Tanzanite Foundation Viewer and the Tanzanite Foundation's jewelry tag, because, if it's not Tanzanite Foundation, is it really tanzanite?[53]

The idea that only Afgem/Tanzanite One practiced "ethical" mining and that all other tanzanite production was illegitimate infuriated ASM miners and mineral dealers not associated with the firm.

Mine Violence

The years between the initial Afgem acquisition in 1997 and the launch of full-scale tanzanite mining in 2000 saw repeated "invasions" of the Afgem/Tanzanite One mining enclave in Block C by ASM miners protesting South African control. The situation underground was equally unstable. Successive waves of mine development on the site left behind a warren of active and obsolete mine shafts, several of which cut across the boundaries between Blocks C and surrounding areas held by ASM miners.[54] Confrontations between corporate security guards and "trespassers" allegedly violating corporate boundaries became so common in the contested zone between mining blocks that locals jokingly referred to the area as "Gaza."[55]

Block C was surrounded by a razor-wire fence and was regularly patrolled by specially trained guard dogs imported from South Africa. These dogs were implicated in an incident in 2000 which dramatically framed South African involvement in the tanzanite industry in racial terms. Press accounts quoted one of the victims who said that six miners were attacked by guard dogs and "accosted" by the firm's security officers at gunpoint while waiting for a bus (Muindi and Majtenyi 2001). While Afgem officials maintained that the miners detained in the incident were illegally mining in their area, the image of dogs being sicced on Tanzanian citizens seared the national psyche.

As the firm ramped up production, the number of violent incidents along the Block C boundary mounted. Seven ASM miners were killed and dozens others wounded during a demonstration on the Afgem site in September 2000, the same month that the alleged "dog maulings" occurred. In April 2001, ASM miners threw a petrol bomb into the mining complex, and two weeks later a seventeen-year-old boy named Emmanuel Obed was shot and killed during an anti-Afgem demonstration. To protest the killing, Obed's corpse was paraded around Mererani township by a large group of ASM miners in an eerie reenactment of scenes following police actions in South African townships under apartheid. A few weeks later, dozens of miners were injured after a major invasion in Block C. In early May 2003, twenty-three-year-old Emmanuel Pallangyo was shot in the jaw, allegedly by a South African security guard at the mine. In November that same year, twenty-five-year-old Nilis Stephano died instantly after being shot in the chest, allegedly by an Afgem employee. In 2004, Emmanuel Urassa was shot in the legs, allegedly by Afgem's general manager. In February 2006, thirty-two-year-old Innocent Thobias was shot in the back by a shotgun allegedly wielded by a Tanzanite One guard. Three other ASM miners were also wounded in the incident. And two months later, an ASM miner known only as Issah was shot dead underground when he and several colleagues sought to force their way into the Tanzanite One mining zone.[56]

A steady stream of such incidents kept the issue of violence directed at Tanzanian citizens alive in the ongoing national debate over South African investment in Tanzania. Members of the national press corps repeatedly called upon the government to intervene to address the untenable circumstances in the small-scale mining sector. One editorial writer opined,

> As concerns mining activities in Tanzania, there seems to be a problem. We keep getting reports from different mining areas of local people being targeted by trigger-happy security guards. In a number of incidents Tanzanians have lost their lives in Mererani where a company is mining tanzanite. . . . One wonders how a company can operate with impunity in disregard of the laws of the land governing exploitation of natural resources. These companies should be able to co-exist in peace and harmony with the local people. . . . The mining companies should not reduce nationals in the areas they operate into refugees in their own country or subject them to inhumane treatment.[57]

Another contributor to the op-ed page added,

> In Arusha, for example, the authorities have miserably failed to end conflicts between local miners and foreign investors fighting for mining rights in Mererani, as exemplified by the constant fighting between guards employed by Tanzanite One (previously known as AFGEM) and the local residents, small miners and labourers. Local miners want Tanzanite One, which has been given a 30-year lease to conduct mining operations in the area, to be kicked out of the country. They accuse the company of setting their security dogs to attack locals passing in the neighbourhood of the company premises. The locals argue that this is reminiscent of the atrocities in apartheid South Africa before 1994, further claiming that the company's managers are racists bent on plundering Tanzania's resources . . . Locals still claim that the company's managers are treating them as sub-humans. Often, the locals feel humiliated by foreign investors for investing heavily in various sectors and sometimes driving the

locals out of business. The sentiments have reached boiling point and things may soon get out of hand if no bold intervention is forthcoming. Not surprisingly, some locals regard the invitation of foreign investors as being equal to bringing back colonialists to harvest our resources as was the case before independence . . . Tanzanians lack capital and the technological cutting edge with which to make a real economic take off . . . However, that does not mean that we should forget about economic nationalism altogether. It is crucial that the locals continue to be protected. (Mlangila 2005, 6)

Advocating on the firm's behalf, representatives argued that outsiders frequently trespassed on corporate property and that violent incidents were rare. In April 2006, for example, Tanzanite One claimed that the victim in a fatal shooting incident was roughly the hundredth artisanal miner to breach Block C boundaries since that year began; company officials asserted that roughly 400 incidents of trespass had occurred the previous year (Nkwame 2006). The firm insisted that its security personnel only used force in self-defense and as a last resort when confronted by armed intruders.[58]

ASM advocates acknowledged that miners sometimes accidentally trespassed on corporate territory due to the disorientating effects of the steeply pitched mine shafts and that individual ASM miners occasionally entered the corporate mining zone with the deliberate intent to steal tanzanite. They argued, however, that the heavy-handed response by corporate security guards was unwarranted. They pointed out that when trespass disputes occurred among small-scale miners, they were referred to the elected representatives of their "peace and security" committees for mediation and resolution (Saramba 2004). By contrast, whenever anyone was caught trespassing in the corporate zone, there was an immediate presumption of guilt and violators were routinely subjected to the use of lethal force. As one activist explained,

I asked [the firm's general manager], "So what is your position at the moment?" He said that "as a mining engineer, and not very conversant with the other parts of development thinking, but as a mining engineer, let me tell you: I will make sure that my staff is protected. No matter how much strength of force I use to protect them, I will do that." So I told him, "The impression I am getting is that you are doing the shooting to kill. . . . Why is it that every time you shoot at somebody, you end up killing him? And why is it that every time you go to shoot at these people, when you go to see the postmortem reports, it's around the chest or the head?"[59]

ASM miners bitterly noted that if their peers managed to invade the corporate mine headquarters, the Tanzanian army itself would show up to protect the firm. If, on the other hand, small-scale miners were shot at by mine security officers, they would be left to protect their rights on their own.[60] Lawyers and activists representing ASM miners in a number of court cases noted that, despite the gravity of the legal issues raised by shootings and other allegations of violence, the Tanzanian government was either unable or unwilling to aggressively pursue legal action against South African perpetrators. Indeed, they argued that legal proceedings involving corporate defendants had a tendency to get lost in the courts for years at a time.

By contrast, they pointed to cases involving Tanzanian defendants where justice had been relatively swift and painful. The crime reporter for the local newspaper, the *Arusha Times,* reported in 2003, for example, on the case of an Afgem *employee* who was arrested for "insolence" and held until a bond of roughly $1,000 was paid to secure his release (Lazaro 2003). That case prompted the following letter to the editor:

> I am reading the story about the employee at the South African gemstone mine. I am absolutely astounded to learn that "insolence" is grounds for arrest and judgment. And one million shillings set as bond? Perhaps this was so in South Africa during apartheid, but in modern day Tanzania? Is my favorite country going backwards? Unless your article failed to tell of any bodily harm inflicted on the accused's superior, I cannot even imagine such a horrendous misapplication of "justice." Shame, shame. (Bullas 2003)

A similar sense of disquiet was voiced following reportage on a case involving a Tanzanian national accused of attacking one of the Tanzanite One guard dogs with a machete. While this was obviously a valuable animal, the penalty assessed by the court struck some as being unusually stiff. The veterinarian who treated the dog for injuries to its right eye and legs recommended that it "be given a week off to heal the wounds." The perpetrator, on the advice of prosecutors that a clear signal be sent to "his ilk," was sentenced to eighteen months in jail (Masayanyika 2006, 2).

In this context, the Tanzanite Foundation's claim that the firm's production system was characterized by "integrity" and "peace" seemed laughable to the firm's critics. A Tanzanian mineral dealer scoffed at the notion that the corporation was engaged in "ethical" mining:

> What, are they trying to tell the world that *they* are the only ones practicing ethical mining? . . . Shooting the small-scale miners, is that ethical mining? We need to hold a symposium so we can show the bloodshed brought about by [the corporate investors]—how they have killed the market and how they are killing the miners. These [ASM miners] are people who are trying to feed their families, who have thousands of dependents, who take the money they earn from tanzanite and reinvest it in tourism, in agriculture. If you establish a monopoly and remove this opportunity from small-scale miners, that will bring about the killing of an entire nation.[61]

A mining activist who has followed developments in the tanzanite industry since the mines were first privatized brought the discussion back to the broader issue of South African presence. The fact that so many of these incidents involved white security guards detaining and/or shooting Tanzanian small-scale miners led him to the conclusion that the violence was racially motivated:

To locals [Maasai residents of Naisinyai], it doesn't matter if it is South African or not. It doesn't. I mean for them it is an economic crisis, forfeiture of land rights, forfeiture of their cultural rights, and that's it. But at the same time, to the older generation [of miners] who have been living longer than I, who've been living in ujamaa, etc., who've been involved in anti-apartheid, who've been experiencing anti-apartheid things, to them it means a lot. A lot! . . . The South African connotation is just terrible. And every time [the firm does] these acts, the dog mauling, and the use of chains [to detain trespassers] . . . they just link these things to apartheid. And I also have a report from one of these committees that was launched by the Ministry [of Energy and Mineral Resources] to investigate these things. They issued a report, and the minister, upon receiving the report and our recommendations, called the stakeholders to a meeting and said the proprietors of Afgem should stop these apartheid acts. Because it reminds Tanzanians of what their [South African] brothers went through . . . And even if you should go to Mererani at the moment and ask anybody about Afgem, the name they use is *kaburu*. The fact is they will use *kaburu*, and *kaburu* is a name we used . . . during the apartheid regime. So we don't regard it as the new South Africa; we regard it as the old *kaburu* regime.[62]

A local pastoralist leader echoed and extended these sentiments in his assessment of what South Africans gained from their involvement in gemstone mining in Tanzania:

For me, South Africans are here . . . for strategic reasons . . . Mererani is one good place for them because it has natural resources in the form of gemstones that you can't get anywhere else that will make them not only rich but powerful socially, economically, and politically. They can shut any door and open another. They can influence the decision of the government of Tanzania. They can do anything they want with the money they have. They can invest, they can feel good. It's about power . . . it's putting yourself in a powerful position to be able to decide to drive the world the way you want and to feel happy, I think. Ultimately it's about that level of satisfaction. This is what I think for South Africa. . . . Profit, money, power, decide, drive, be on top of it, full stop. That's how I see it. Yes. So they're part of the drivers of the world. . . . And I think there's nothing sweeter. . . . The power to put everybody below you is always a sweet one.[63]

Conclusion

A Dar es Salaam lawyer who built her business around major contracts with South African firms invested in Tanzania, including several in the mining industry, had a revealing take on the violence that permeated the tanzanite mining sector in the early 2000s. In her view, the corporate miners of Afgem/Tanzanite One were fully within their rights to use force in defense of their private property rights. "That is the reality of private property," she explained. "If you have private property you must protect it against incursion from other people." She noted that the rights of private property were enshrined in the Tanzanian constitution and concluded by reiterating her justification for the firm's use of force in the mines: "So when I have private property and you get on it, of course you'll have dogs on you!"

The lawyer might well have expanded her argument because the exclusive property rights enjoyed by Tanzanite One were not just a matter of constitutional legal principles. They were also reinforced by the Tanzanian government, which deployed its police powers on behalf of the firm, and were backed by the World Bank's Multilateral Investment Guarantee Agency, which shielded the international investors from the risks associated with investing in Tanzania's risky "emerging" market. Under these circumstances, the corporation's rights to exclude others from using the tanzanite deposits in Block C could hardly have been more secure.

This lawyer's line of analysis provided a prime example of the ideological rationale that is often used to support neoliberal economic reforms. As such, it displayed a number of flaws that typically underpin such thinking. First, the lawyer's argument obscured the fact that the corporation's private property rights to tanzanite deposits rested on remarkably shallow historical precedent. Almost the entire hillside where the corporate tanzanite mine was established in 1996 had been controlled by artisanal and small-scale mine operators less than a decade earlier. And little more than two decades before that, the area was a commonly held pastureland used for livestock grazing by Maasai. Both of these land-use systems were replaced with little or no compensation by an arbitrarily designated set of territorial "blocks" whose boundaries cut across preexisting ASM mine shafts and disrupted livestock keepers' rights of way. Maasai land rights were obliquely recognized by the firm through its corporate gift giving to the Naisinyai community, but neither the ASM miners nor the pastoralist groups were given the opportunity to assert their own priorities with respect to land use and subsurface mining rights in the area. The act of privatization that produced this outcome was thus premised on a combination of historical amnesia—yet another act of "forgetting from above" (Pitcher 2006)—and spatial myopia. The net effect was to naturalize private property claims, that is, to treat them as givens, rather than lay bare the arbitrary and capricious governmental decisions that created them in the first place.

The lawyer's analysis of the corporate miners' private property rights illustrated a second major fallacy of neoliberal thinking in its fetishization of legality. That is, the proponents of privatization gave a disproportionate weight to private property claims by virtue of the fact that they were legal. But just because a particular action or condition is legal does not make it morally acceptable or justifiable. The apartheid system itself was legal, but nothing could have been more immoral. The act of selling off prized national assets such as the tanzanite deposits, while legal in the strictest sense, was widely seen as being immoral and unjust by those most directly affected by the sale. And it was an especially bitter pill to swallow when the firm buying the mine was run by white South Africans.

Many, if not most, of the miners and gemstone brokers who found work in the ASM side of the tanzanite industry in the 1980s and 1990s did so primarily out of desperation. Some had lost their civil service jobs in the wave of retrenchments mandated by the World Bank and IMF or otherwise initiated by new employers under the privatization program. Others had either seen their crops fail or their cattle die due to recurrent drought and the shrinkage of government services under structural adjustment constraints (Sachedina and Trench 2009, 264). The mines were accordingly a last resort. Some were fortunate enough to make it, especially in the early years. The "lucky people who slept like paupers and woke up millionaires" found quick money through tanzanite sales and plowed it back into real estate ventures, livestock herds, nightclubs, and tourism operations (Matinyi 2006, 21). When the core of the tanzanite mining district was privatized, however, the size of the area allocated to small-scale miners was reduced by more than half. With the number of would-be miners flooding into the area increasing on a daily basis, the odds of success in the artisanal and small-scale mining sector narrowed considerably. Thus, for the vast majority of ASM miners, the tanzanite dream never materialized.

It is in this distinctly *moral* economic sense, then, that the position adopted by artisanal miners and their proponents was thrown into stark relief (cf. Ferguson 2006a). The critics of Afgem/Tanzanite One took exception to instances of both material and symbolic violence initiated by the firm and its backers in government. They decried the corporation's "branding" of prized tanzanite specimens and vague references in advertisements characterizing the "mysterious" blue stone as being found "only in Africa." They scoffed at the notion that the firm's humanitarian contributions to one ward of one community effectively discharged its responsibility for sharing the wealth generated through the extraction of one of Tanzania's most valuable natural resources. They stressed that the firm was run by South Africans, *makaburu* miners who, in their view, allegedly shot Tanzanians with impunity and treated their dogs better than their "insolent" employees. These "apartheid acts" could not go unchallenged. Nor could the corporation's domination of the industry, which, they argued, threatened to choke off a complex and vital livelihood system that generated jobs and incomes for tens of thousands of Tanzanians.

5

Bye, the Beloved Country

On 11 November 1998, a political cartoon published in *Die Burger,* one of South Africa's leading Afrikaans-language newspapers, depicted Anne Paton, the widow of the late South African author Alan Paton.[1] Shown pushing a luggage cart towards an exit sign, Paton speaks the words, "'Bye, the beloved country." Under her arm is a photo of her husband and in the basket of her luggage cart is a copy of his famous novel, *Cry, the Beloved Country,* to which her ascribed parting message is an obvious and ironic allusion (Paton 1976).

Written in 1948 as South Africa's National Party was coming to power, Alan Paton's novel provided a vivid, critical account of the system of racial oppression that was to be legally enshrined as apartheid. Given her husband's fame as an early and forceful critic of racial oppression in South Africa, Anne Paton's decision to leave the country so soon after it had finally achieved the goal of a democratically elected government was a symbolic blow to its leaders. Indeed, to say that her departure touched a nerve with South Africans would be an understatement.

When Paton published the reasons for her departure in an open letter to the *London Sunday Times,* it quickly circulated among South Africans living overseas. Appearing under the heading, "'Why I'm fleeing South Africa,' by Anne Paton (widow of Alan Paton)," the letter poignantly invoked Alan Paton's memory: "I was so sorry he did not witness the euphoria and love at the time of the election in 1994. But I am glad he is not alive now. He would have been so distressed to see what has happened to his beloved country." Paton explained that she had survived an armed car-jacking and repeated attacks on her home, and was returning to her birthplace in England because it had become too dangerous for her to live comfortably in South Africa any longer. "There is now more racial tension in this country than I have ever known."[2]

Paton's departure came at a moment of tremendous upheaval in South Africa. Nelson Mandela's ANC government had not yet consolidated its hold on power. Heightened expectations on the part of the non-white majority for immediate resolution of such intractable problems as an acute housing shortage, widespread unemployment, and lack of safe drinking water and electricity were proving nearly impossible to meet. There was a surge in violent crime, with whites, the custodians of most of the nation's wealth, often deliberately targeted. The politically charged Truth and Reconciliation Commission hearings were generating sensational revelations concerning government-sponsored racial violence under apartheid. New policies were implemented that required white-held firms to divest their holdings in the interest of "Black Economic Empowerment," and far-reaching affirmative action programs designed to move non-whites into more senior positions within the government were dramatically reshaping the job market.

For many whites, it seemed that the time of reckoning for apartheid's crimes was finally at hand. Whether they had been active supporters of apartheid, passive beneficiaries of white privilege, or even critics and opponents of the system, their direct and indirect complicity as whites in a segregated society left them increasingly vulnerable to attack. Many questioned whether South Africa held a place for them any longer given its rapidly changing social and political-economic landscape (Steyn 2001). Rather than subject themselves and their families to ongoing insecurity, they followed the path taken by Anne Paton out of the country. Most who left during this difficult transition period fled to Europe, North America, Australia, or New Zealand. Significant numbers, however, opted to remain in Africa where they set out in search of new economic opportunities. This chapter features the personal stories of those who ultimately relocated to Tanzania. Drawing on oral histories conducted in 2005 and 2006, it explores in depth the reasons they opted to stay in Africa, why they chose Tanzania as an end destination, and how they viewed their new lives in East Africa.

The image that emerges from this analysis is complex. First, the South African community that moved to Tanzania in the 1990s and 2000s was quite diverse in terms of linguistic and ethnic background, geographical origins within South Africa, and prior work and social experiences. Recognition of this diversity challenges the one-dimensional stereotype that is attached to *makaburu* in popular discourse in Tanzania (a tendency that I have no doubt reproduced in this book). It also helps account for the sometimes sharply divergent political, cultural, and social attitudes that were reflected in the internal debate Tanzania's South African community held with respect to racial and national identity, and their country's role in reshaping the region's economic geography.

Second, many South Africans living in Tanzania occupied contradictory social locations. Members of this arbitrarily constructed group identified in different ways and to varying degrees with other South Africans, other Africans, and other whites (cf. Brubaker and Cooper 2000). The extent to which they claimed to share any of the attributes commonly ascribed to South African national identity varied widely. Indeed, their transnational status as South African expatriates living abroad undermined any firm sense of having a homeland: in some cases, informants expressed a dual sense of "home"; in others, allegiances had shifted away from South Africa and toward Tanzania. Several of my informants had also recently experienced either upward or downward pressures on their relative economic status, and this, too, influenced their sense of attachment to place.

Finally, my informants did not bear the burden of their past lightly. Whether individuals were callous and defensive or thoughtful and open-minded in discussing the past, both the experience and the legacy of apartheid reverberated strongly in their dealings with Tanzanians in the post-apartheid period. In contrast to other expatriate groups, most South Africans came to Tanzania with a fairly acute sense of their own whiteness. They initially felt themselves to be on uncertain footing as far as living and working with Tanzanian nationals was concerned and expressed fears that they might be subject to some sort of reprisal for the sins of apartheid. Over time, however, most came to view their lives in Tanzania as an opportunity to leave behind the stigma of apartheid and take advantage of a rare opportunity to rebuild their lives in a new setting.

The Trek to Tanzania

Both in the run-up to the end of apartheid and in its immediate aftermath, hundreds of thousands of South African nationals left their homeland to take up residence elsewhere. Perhaps a quarter million people fled the country between 1989 and 1997.[3] These emigrants were motivated in part by a desire to escape the growing incidence of violent crime in South Africa, by fears that the country was about to descend into social and economic chaos, and by rapidly declining professional opportunities under de facto and de jure affirmative action hiring and black empowerment initiatives.[4] They also emigrated in search of economic opportunities. Throughout the early 1990s, the value of the South African rand currency was extremely low, and the prospect of living as an expatriate and earning a dollar-denominated salary proved extremely enticing for many.

Most who left in the early waves of emigration ended up in the United Kingdom, Australia, New Zealand, the United States or Canada, English-speaking countries with advanced industrial economies (Brown et al. 2002; van Rooyen 2000). The much smaller contingent that left South Africa but deliberately chose to relocate in other African countries was thus a distinctive lot. As I demonstrate below, many of these latter-day African trekkers strongly identified *as* African and could not see living anywhere else in the world. Some of these emigrants moved temporarily to the nearby countries of Namibia, Zimbabwe, and Botswana and eventually repatriated to South Africa. But others went further afield, seeking adventure and bolstered by increasingly generous rules governing the amount of money they were allowed to take with them and invest abroad (Miller, Oloyede, and Saunders 2008; van Rooyen 2000, 60–62).

As a group, the South Africans living and working in Tanzania between 1997 and 2011, when my own research was conducted, were virtually all white, and of both English and Afrikaner origins. Occupationally, this contingent consisted of relatively senior-level managers and their families, on the one hand, and a large group of much younger technicians and fieldworkers, on the other. Both of these groups were overwhelmingly male, reflecting the social makeup of the workforce in the mining and safari industries in particular, where South African capital was disproportionately concentrated. Many of the male executives originally came to Tanzania on their own, sometimes commuting between Tanzania and South Africa for lengthy periods before satisfying themselves that it was safe to bring their families to join them in Tanzania.

While the numbers of South Africans living and working in Tanzania increased substantially throughout this period as the scope of South African investment expanded, it was difficult to obtain reliable figures on the actual size of the South African contingent. Anecdotally, members of this community estimated that there were as many as 6,000 South Africans living in Tanzania in 2006. Since many of these newcomers were either not officially registered or lacked the requisite work permits, however, not even representatives of the South African High Commission could give a more precise estimate.[5] The paucity of hard data notwithstanding, by 2003, the deputy minister for Foreign Affairs and International Cooperation said that South Africans had become the largest group of foreign nationals in the country.[6]

South African Stories

In order to better understand the social dynamics that emerged in Tanzania following the rapid influx of South Africans in the late 1990s, I conducted a series of oral histories with South Africans active in different sectors of the Tanzanian economy. I have chosen eight people, six men and two women (including one married couple), to represent the range of life experiences South Africans brought to Tanzania and the variety of opinions they developed concerning their new lives "in Africa." While this is not in any sense a random sample, the stories told here reflect a number of recurrent general themes.

Piet van R.:
"Coming here . . . has given us the freedom to forget"

Piet van R. relocated to Tanzania from a small town in South Africa in 2003 when the international financial services firm he worked for abruptly closed.[7] He was hired for his current position by an executive who flew down from Tanzania for the explicit purpose of recruiting South Africans for his post. He had traveled previously in West Africa, which he described as an eye-opening experience, but had never set foot in Tanzania before. As he explained,

> In the end we saw it as a great opportunity. We were both fairly young [he and his wife were in their late thirties at the time] and it was clearly something of an adventure and a risk, but we thought, what's the worst that could happen? We could go, give it a few months, and if need be, come back to SA and start over looking for work then. So I . . . arrived in Tanzania, and I could immediately see that this was civilization compared to [West Africa]. Three months later, I went back to South Africa to collect my family and finalize the sale of our house . . . So it's not like we were fleeing from the current political situation in SA or anything. We looked at this whole thing as a great opportunity for our children and for us to experience another culture.

As a middle-aged white male, his fortunes in South Africa appeared bleak at the time he chose to leave the country:

> I'd say that it was sort of a way of getting even after the war: the white male has no role to play. Only a handful of white males have really gotten rich in the decade since 1994. Otherwise, it's people like Cyril Ramaphosa and Tokyo Sexwale who have gotten fantastically rich since the end of apartheid. It's not really revenge [against the white males], it's just balancing the scales again—and actually, women are seen as one of the minority groups. The old government started to appoint women to government posts and pointed at them, "Look, we're appointing minorities."[8]

Immediately upon arriving in Tanzania, Piet and his family had to deal with the language and cultural barriers posed by his Afrikaner heritage:

> We arrived in Tanzania as a family on a Monday, and on Wednesday, my oldest son [started school]. He had been in an Afrikaans-speaking crèche, and now he was in a full English-language-speaking school. In South Africa, year one in school doesn't begin until age seven. Here, my son was thrust immediately into a full formal school year, speaking English, which he only knew a few words of from watching television . . . The school put my son in a remedial program so he could catch up in writing. And by mid-year, they told us he didn't need the extra training any more, that he had caught up. And by the end of the year, he had made very good marks. I was extremely proud of my son because of what he was able to accomplish during that one year. Now, it's like the pendulum has swung in the other direction, and he speaks Afrikaans with an English accent. So we've been introducing Afrikaans books to him, books geared towards five-year-olds in Afrikaans, because we don't want him to lose his culture. It is important to us that we teach him his traditions and his lan-

guage. Otherwise we're just going to become an entity, or a plant without roots
. . . We don't want to take away [our sons'] own history from them.

Piet was clearly intent on protecting his family's Afrikaner heritage, but at the
same time, he did not feel bound by it. He explained, for example, that while there
were a few other Afrikaans-speaking families living nearby, he and his family rarely
socialized with them.

We know one another, but it's not like we all get together like some sort of
Afrikaner club. If we wanted that sort of thing, we would have stayed in South
Africa. Unfortunately, there's a very negative image of Afrikaners, but just
because I'm a white Afrikaans speaker doesn't mean that I'm a monster. [In
my son's school] there's probably three other white kids in his class, and the
rest are either Indian or black African. It's not like he just plays with the other
white kids. One of them he can't stand, and the others are not particularly special friends. His best friend is a little black boy, and he couldn't care whether
he is black or white—he's just Amani [the boy's name]. I consider it a real
privilege to be able to raise my children here in an environment that's free of
the tensions in South Africa, in an environment where you can do it. It's really
nice to see it working out in practice. And that's really a credit to Tanzanians.

This thought prompted an extended discussion of the differences Piet perceived
between black Tanzanians and black South Africans:

The local people here are very different from South African blacks. They
[Tanzanians] are friendly, patient, and helpful, people who you can actually do
work with. The black men in South Africa tend to be aggressive, angry, chip-
on-the-shoulder type of people. When I go back home [to SA], I step off the
plane, and not even through the passport control for ten minutes, and I'm irritated with the way people are treating me. [By contrast] I land at Kilimanjaro
[the airport serving northern Tanzania], out in the middle of nowhere, and I
immediately feel like [raises his arms over his head in a gesture of release and
freedom] I am at home. It's very hard to explain to people back home in South
Africa what that feels like. Tanzania's been a very different experience for me.
I can go a very long way living and working with the Tanzanian people . . . You
can see it in the way they treat children. There's not a snowball's chance in hell
that I would ever leave my children with black South Africans unattended, but
Tanzanians are completely different. You know back home in South Africa
there's this thing with kids going barefoot all the time. Here, Tanzanians will
say, "You should have your children wear shoes." They have even offered to buy
them for them. And you don't dare give your kid a hiding in public because
they'll try and stop you. That says a lot about who Tanzanians are.

Like other South Africans I interviewed, Piet had a keen sense of the unique
position of his age cohort within the sweep of recent South African history:

It's a difficult position to be in . . . The fathers of apartheid were our parents, but we were the ones who had to fight the war to defend the system. I was in the army from the ages of eighteen to twenty-one. You fought in the war, but then you want to know whether it was all worth fighting for. I lost some good friends who were killed in the war. What was it actually we were defending? I can remember the day Mandela got released from prison, and I thought, "What was it we were bloody fighting for?" Now after a few years, I have a bit of a different perspective, but at the time, I was very bitter. Many of us grew up on farms, and our best mates were the African kids who were sons of the farm workers. And then when we turned ten, twelve, thirteen, we were told it was no longer okay to play with them, and then three, four years later, we are facing them across a fence, both of us holding a gun [mimes holding a gun]. In that sense, we were a generation in between: we didn't create apartheid, but we're now old enough to be blamed for it and to be asked to fix things. They aren't going to blame my sons—they're too young to have been responsible for anything—but they *are* blaming me. And it's that middle generation that has left the country looking to start over someplace else.

He bristled at the idea that his identity as a white "southerner" should set him-self apart from other white expatriates, however, especially white Kenyans:

To tell you the truth, I think that nine out of ten Tanzanians actually prefer the "southerners," because north of the border [that is, in Kenya] you also have this colonial mentality. . . . They're the people who have ten nannies in their house but still have this superior attitude . . . As far as this anti-southerner thing is concerned, they see us as a threat. Sometimes, when I get a chance, I try to rub it in a bit, to get a stab in here and there. And it is unfortunate that it is the white Kenyans who have to be the prey. I see [Kenyans' attitudes towards "southerners"] as discrimination. Don't we see that as a form of discrimina-tion? Isn't *any* form of discrimination wrong? Is it only discrimination when it is *race* involved? What gives him the right to question the process that took place in South Africa a long time ago? He is just being a hypocrite. In 1994, did the clock stand still, did the earth stop spinning? No! We've all moved on. Now I can't say it was the right thing to do. It could have been done in a different way. Apartheid was wrong. But it's done; it's history. Is for ever and ever the "southerner" going to be the big bad wolf? We're not going to lose sleep over white Kenyans' [claims of superiority given their] colonial past.

I asked Piet to compare Tanzania and South Africa in terms of quality of life. I wondered what it was like for him when he went back home, for example. Posing the question, I caught myself, acknowledging that I did not know which country he now considered home. And he replied: "Yeah, I'm not sure either." He continued,

Well there is the "nice to have" stuff. The first time we went home, we stocked up on all kinds of things and ended up having to buy two extra suitcases when we came back to Tanzania. But all the essentials are here. The second year we went back [to SA], it was less. There's not really anything specific that we needed. After a while, it got so I didn't buy any more there than I would have here. It's expensive, for one thing. So I don't get very extravagant.

He acknowledged that life in Tanzania was "physically harder . . . not a stroll through the mall," but kept returning to the notion of freedom and what a great opportunity it was to be able to raise his family in Tanzania rather than South Africa:

The other thing about living here is that it's a great environment to bring my kids up in. It's healthier and safer. And it goes beyond just not having to worry about them being kidnapped. It's a carefree lifestyle for the kids. I'll give you an example: my older son came home from school the other day, and my wife wasn't home yet. And he simply wrote her a note and left it on the refrigerator to say that he was going to a friend's house. Now he could never have done that in South Africa. He never would have had the freedom to just go off on his own there. But here he can.

The last time we were home on leave, we rented a car . . . We were driving through Jo'burg, and my littlest son rolled down the window in the back like they do all the time here in Tanzania. And my wife said to him, "Be careful, son. You need to roll up the window because they're going to come steal you. A robber is going to come and kidnap you." And our son said, "I'm not afraid of any robbers and thieves. I am only scared of a lion." And when we heard that, we knew that we had done the right thing by coming here. It has given us the freedom to forget. So, yes, maybe South Africa is more civilized—well, not civilized, more *developed*—but we have the privilege of raising our kids here . . . It's that sense of freedom that makes living here so great.

He explained that his family would soon be faced with a difficult choice:

The next decision point will come in four or five years, when it will be time for my oldest son to go to high school. So now we try to save as much as possible, to keep our options open. But eventually we're going to have to decide whether we pack up our tents and move back to South Africa or somewhere else, or to stay here and send our sons to boarding school.

At that point, I will be a [middle-aged] Afrikaans-speaking white male, and it will be extremely difficult in the current climate in South Africa for me to find work. Not at my current package [salary, etc.]. So do you try and start up a little something of your own, that takeaway shop that you've always wanted to try? There is a great deal of white redundancy in South Africa now. Many of those who have been laid off have tried to start their own businesses. And if you look at the statistics, a huge percentage of the failed businesses right now are those that were owned by whites who have tried to go it on their own and failed. So there you run the risk of not just losing your income, but also your house, and your children's chance at a good education.

Last year we visited a boarding school [names the school] which has a very good academic reputation, and very good sports as well. My son is a rugby fanatic, and one of his rugby heroes who plays for the national side came from [that school]. So he's enthusiastic about going there now. We asked the administrators at [the school] how they handle adjustment for children such as ours who come from outside the country, what they do to help the children. And we came away quite impressed. Now our son can see the future for himself.

Marie J.:
"The biggest relief is . . . nobody really views you as an enemy."

The South African contingent in Tanzania in the mid 2000s included relatively few young, single women. In this sense, Marie was atypical.[9] She was attracted by the prospect of working in Tanzania originally because she was a staunch wildlife enthusiast and knew that Tanzania offered some of the most spectacular game viewing opportunities in the world. Marie worked for an international medical insurance company that had a regional hub in South Africa and branch offices in Tanzania. Her job entailed traveling back and forth between Dar es Salaam and a number of outlying cities where several of her South African corporate clients were based. Professionally, her clientele included a disproportionately large share of South Africans.

It just makes logical sense that that would happen. For example, why do I stay in the Holiday Inn [a South African–managed franchise in Dar es Salaam]? The truth is, I know the brand. I know the brand from South Africa. I've stayed there before. I know it's comfortable, clean, you know, safe (see chapter 6). So I guess it's something that would clearly happen. And if I think of my own profession, I know that South Africans enjoy dealing with [South African insurance agents]. So some of my large clients—the high-level person that you deal with are South Africans, so it's almost, it's *easy* for me to set up an insurance package for them. Like [she names a firm], a huge firm. You know, there's a *connection*. So, yes, there's definitely that pattern. Because you speak the same language. On the same wavelength. So, yes, definitely. It helps! It helps communications, and all that. Another thing is, if the head company is insured by my firm in SA, its subsidiary in Tanzania will also be insured by us. It's logical that that would happen. Because it's all about relationships at the end of the day.

Being posted in her firm's Tanzania office involved a lateral career move for Marie, but she took it because she thought it would give her an opportunity to add certain kinds of administrative experience to her existing technical skills. When she arrived, she found her job extremely fulfilling because it gave her the opportunity to do everything "from chief cook to bottle washer." She was, however, unprepared for the possibility that she might acquire new skills and insights on the job in Tanzania by observing and interacting with her professional colleagues, almost all of whom were Tanzanian nationals. As she somewhat haltingly explained,

> I came here with a bit of an expectation. I came here with the feeling that [pauses] . . . Coming from South Africa, you almost feel that you are part of [pauses] . . . South Africans often have the feeling that we are superior to the rest of Africa. Because I think we are just more developed. And I, just coming out, was definitely thinking that technically and so forth, *professionally,* I would be able to really come in and pass on skills. Because there *were* no skills here. But actually after I arrived here, I found that, indeed, I had technical skills that I was able to bring to the table, but certainly there were a huge amount of skills that I was able to pick up here. So I was very, very surprised at how this office, at how up to date they are . . . Up to date with all the latest training standards, all the latest developments. I guess it's because they are part of a worldwide network. They are really very progressive.

Like Piet, Marie, too, felt a remarkable sense of personal freedom in Tanzania, which stood in sharp contrast to her experiences back home in South Africa. She chose her words carefully, though, as she tried to articulate her social position within both her firm and Tanzania more generally:

> It's quite a change from South Africa from a political point [of view], because in South Africa, there's still quite a number of years for the effects of apartheid to be washed out. Because there's still a generation that's still bearing the scars. So the relationship between the different, um, cultures, ethnic races [*sic*], is still quite strained. And it's improving, yes. The government's given a lot of attention to this. So for a South African coming here, the biggest relief is you're treated as . . . you're not immediately looked upon with distrust. I mean nobody really views you as an enemy [laughs nervously]. In South Africa, you find that when you meet people, they really psych you out. Especially black people, because you are of the, uh, you know, the previous oppressors. So that was the first thing. It's just that I feel the . . . much more open . . . spirit? I don't know if I can use that word. Or, um, when you're dealing with people, it's almost on the merits of who you are. You are not prejudged . . . which has been very refreshing. You don't always have to feel that you're proving to someone that you're actually a nice person and not a racist [chuckles].

She continued, sharing additional thoughts on her status as a foreign businesswoman:

> I think that as a *mzungu* [Kiswahili; white person or European], in this country, *mzungus* get away with murder. Not, um, not literally of course . . . But I feel that, I guess it's because a lot of *mzungus* have brought in skills, and

a lot are brought in at higher-level jobs. Because they're coming in with skills. And they're coming in with experience. I think often you get used to being of a certain caliber and status, that you have a particular status *because* you're white. And that's not always right in my opinion. I mean as a *woman* there are definitely occasions where, being a woman, you don't get taken as seriously. Because of the culture of the country. I think it's just the culture of the local Tanzanians. I think if you look at the Maasai culture, I mean women basically come after cattle [in a social hierarchy]. So, you know, there are definitely times where I've picked up that I'm not getting the same respect as that. But it is something that is manageable. Because I think for someone coming from South Africa . . . living here is really not that difficult to deal with. And you don't have to deal with people's *pre*-judgments. Whereas women from other parts of the world will arrive here, and they will actually be insulted, and feel . . . you know, take things to heart . . .

But then again, you must remember: my work is in quite a professional environment. So from a professional point of view, I am usually dealing with either expatriates, or local Tanzanians, black Tanzanians, Indian Tanzanians, or whoever . . . I am dealing with people who are at quite a senior level, and quite professional. So I guess you could say that those [negative] experiences are a lot more limited for me. I'm quite, I guess you could say, protected and sheltered from that. I mean they have to be nice to me if they want me to insure them! [laughs]

Marie's social life was limited by her work hours but involved a great deal of contact with other South Africans. She saw a significant difference between the South African community in Dar es Salaam and South Africans who lived in Arusha. In Dar where the contingent was much larger and consisted of dozens of corporate executives and their families, "you find these little bits of South Africa," social groups that "do everything together." By contrast, in Arusha, South Africans were much more completely integrated into the wider white expatriate community. She herself had a best female friend from South Africa, but the rest of her female friends were from other countries. Among her male friends, she estimated that about half were South African. She also described herself as "an absolute rugby fanatic," and her social life often revolved around rugby viewing:

And I guess that is really a link to back home. You know, everyone getting together in your South African Springbok rugby jerseys and watching rugby together. It's a unique thing here: you know you have a lot of different people here from different cultures and backgrounds, and different countries. But there's always a special link you have with people from your own country. I mean you can know someone for three or four months . . . and the day you meet someone from South Africa, you just have a rapport, which you'll find as deep as that with any other friends you might have. Because of the common background.

Koos P.:
"Haraka! Haraka!"

Koos P. was a miner in his late twenties who came from a small farming town in South Africa.[10] Like many of the hundreds of young, single men who came to Tanzania in the post-apartheid period, Koos saw Tanzania as having given him a chance to "experience life" like he never could have done in his hometown. In this sense, his time in Tanzania dramatically expanded his horizons. Koos's closest friends were South African, but he socialized with a group of men and women from a half a dozen different countries: "I've met more people here than I met in my whole life in South Africa, different cultures, different types of people." Koos and his friends frequented sports bars, restaurants, and night clubs where white expatriates gathered on a nightly basis. A hard-drinking crew, their attitudes and practices alienated some of their compatriots. As one South African informant commented with respect to Koos in particular, "The way I look at it is that if we were in South Africa, he would never be allowed in my house. So why should I treat him any differently just because we're South Africans living in Tanzania? Why should my house become some sort of sanctuary for him just because we are South Africans? I don't care if you're Chinese or English or South African or what have you, if you are not a good person, you will never darken my doorstep."[11]

Like many members of his age cohort, Koos originally came to Tanzania on a short-term contract and stayed on when he found both his professional options and the social setting to his liking. This was partially due to the presence of large numbers of other South Africans in the area:

> When you first come here, everybody comes with a sense of coming here for, first of all, for money . . . That's why you work outside . . . After two years you must either decide you're gonna stay or you're gonna go. And you know, usually guys come here two years to work. Doesn't get out at all [sic], just goes to the mine, and that's it. Works for two years, doesn't get out, doesn't go into [the city], doesn't learn anything about the culture, maybe once or twice [he] went to the coast. Saves up his money, went back and start his family [sic]. You know there's not always opportunity for that in South Africa.
>
> And then you get those who come here, they don't think a lot of the place. They don't think there's going to be a lot here to do. They go two years, they go three years, they go four years . . . Like myself, I've been here five years now. And a lot of the guys at the mine have been here five, six years now. We're like a group that's been sticking it out. I don't know. I used to work at the mine; I was at the mine for about three and a half years. I'm in [the city] right here

now because we opened [an office] here to work in relation to the mine. And I mean I had no problems since day one. To me . . . your environment and stuff is not a lot different from South Africa . . . There's all these South African companies in Tanzania which feels like you're at home. I mean especially there's [a recently refurbished hotel]. When it opened, you know, the first impression is that it's South African–based. I mean it's got that look like it's been built by a South African company, or a guy designed it that maybe is a South African. Which makes it a lot, a "feel at home" type of place . . . I mean it's just the look that it gives you, it gives you the sense that it is South African, that it's got to be.

The presence of so many South African firms with significant numbers of South African personnel obviously made life comfortable and familiar enough to entice Koos to stay beyond his original two-year contract. He acknowledged, though, that South Africa's presence was not universally appreciated in Tanzania:

I mean it's not fair to Tanzania, as well, I think. Everybody's just fighting for his own pocket. Nobody is giving back to the country. That's why a country can't go forward, 'cause everybody is just fighting for himself. But again it's difficult, because, you know, it's Africa. People are not happy; people are not that rich, or educated, whatever. And I think when you get back to South African companies being *in* Africa, I think that is the whole point at the end of the day. Trying to teach people, to give them more education, in order to save their own country. And they don't see it like that. They think we're coming to take the money and run away, [that] that's the whole idea behind it.

When Koos spoke to other South Africans in his office, or to friends on the phone, he often used Afrikaans, his first language. Having lived in Tanzania for five years had nonetheless convinced him of the need for local language training:

[Another firm that employs a large number of South African employees] has done a great thing by not forcing, but getting their staff and management to learn to speak Swahili. But we don't do it as much. I think that is our biggest problem at the end of the day. I mean we've got, we've got Tanzanian inner management to help us with our business stuff. By the end of the day, the thing is it stops me from doing business, because I can't speak Swahili properly. And yeah, sure, it shows that you have respect for Tanzania, and to a Tanzanian, they would like you to learn.

This theme of respect was one that Koos returned to repeatedly in our discussion:

And then you get your old South Africans who'll say, you know, they just can go back to the way it used to be. A lot of people say that. It doesn't matter which color you are. And I think it's true as well. Not to go back as much to apartheid, and all of that, but just to go back to a basic way of respect. Me, I have a problem with [people who don't show proper] respect. I've got a big problem with [that]. A lot of, a lot of people, *young* people can't show respect to older people. And for people like me, it's a big problem. Probably because I've been brought up in a small countryside rural village. But you've got respect for older people . . . You know . . . if you think he's older, then show respect. And if you can't show respect . . . you get a hiding. And for me that is the right way of doing things . . . I mean why do you spank a dog when it craps in the house, because it must learn. And that's the whole thing. To me a big thing is respect. Tanzanians have got respect for you, so why can't you have respect for them? That's another thing to look into.

Watching Koos carry out his business on a day-to-day basis, I saw little evidence of the respectful attitude he described in our interview, however. Twice I saw him treat Tanzanian staff roughly. In the first instance, he asked a young woman in his office to make a "photostat" of a document for him. When she misunderstood what he meant, he raised his voice: "A photostat, a photocopy! Go and make a copy of this and bring it back to me." Then, rudely, in Kiswahili: "Haraka, haraka!" (Literally, "Hurry up! Hurry up!" Or, in the vernacular, "Chop! Chop!") At another point, Koos waved a Tanzanian work foreman into his office and said, "Speak to me." The supervisor explained that a mason was ready to begin a small repair project on some steps. After reviewing the repair plan, Koos told the man to let him know right away when the work would start. "Just shoot me an SMS and let me know, even if it's just to say, 'The work is not starting today,' so I know what to expect." He continued, "And make sure it goes according to plan, or I may have to get out my new stick." At this point, Koos reached behind him and took out a taser gun, brandishing it in the direction of his employee. While this gesture was certainly made in jest, the use of a taser gun to make his point seemed gratuitous and needlessly callous, especially in light of repeated incidents of violence involving corporate security forces in the mining industry (see chapter 4).

Zoe and Martin M.:
"We're all tarred and feathered with the same negative brush."

Zoe and Martin M.[12] worked off and on in Tanzania's tourism industry since the mid-1990s. Initially responsible for setting up a safari camp for a South African tourism firm in central Tanzania, they subsequently relocated to Zanzibar with their children, Jonathan and Sophie, where I encountered them in 2005. The fact that their first posting was in an isolated location on the mainland raised a number of professional difficulties for the young couple.

ZOE M.: We used to be the mercy mission.

MARTIN M.: I can remember one time, it was the chief's father, and he had a
    raging case of TB, and we took him in the car, and he was coughing in the

back seat directly on Zoe, who was pregnant at the time, and I'm thinking, "This is not the way it's meant to be!" But you either become part of the community or you don't.

ZOE M.: [Our employers] had told us to stay out of the community, don't get involved. But that's not our way. There was a [local] guy—we'd only been there for two weeks at the time—and he got hit by a buffalo. So we stepped in and rushed him to the hospital, and from that point on we were deeply involved. Martin became the local doctor, and every day, for one and a half hours in the morning, people would line up outside the door of the lodge, and Martin would dispense aspirins, and malaria pills, and whatever else we could, because there was no other option. We eventually got the [government] to establish a clinic . . .

MARTIN M.: It was a difficult situation. The previous [managers] had been hunting for staff rations. Shooting game for the meat to feed the staff. When we got there, we went to total non-consumptive policy. We stopped the hunting practice because it just confused the issue [of promoting non-consumptive tourism]. Eventually, we started buying meat from the village . . .

ZOE M.: In South Africa, things sort of went ten-ten-ten [gestures with her hand to indicate things lined up in order, one after the other], but we quickly learned that it doesn't work that way here . . . We realized that we were not getting anywhere, that we were actually going backwards. So we very quickly threw the company policies and procedures out the window . . . When we were there we had probably four people hired from the outside, and they would have been difficult to get rid of because they had been there for so long. Otherwise we hired locals. That was a huge amount of work training them. A staff person pours red wine into a white wine glass—all he sees is an empty glass that needs filling. He doesn't know the difference.

Raising children under these circumstances was especially challenging:

MARTIN M.: Our children were basically raised by [locals]. They spoke better Kiswahili than they did English . . . They were totally into Tanzanian culture.

ZOE M.: It was actually kind of embarrassing. Martin spoke the textbook Swahili, and I spoke a few words—enough to get by around the office—but Jonathan and Sophie were fluent in the sort of "kitchen Swahili" that was spoken by our staff. There were times when we couldn't understand what [the kids] were saying, and we would have to ask people to tell us.

MARTIN M.: In [the camp], [Jonathan and Sophie] would eat what the staff would eat . . . They'd go around the table chewing on bones that other staff members had left behind. And I'm thinking, "This is so unhealthy." But that was the way we were living at the time.

Eventually Zoe and Martin resolved that they needed to get their kids back to "civilization," and moved their family back to South Africa. Their time there was not everything they imagined it would be, however, and they returned Tanzania again less than a year later:

> MARTIN M.: We couldn't stand it in Pretoria. Our son who absolutely loves the outdoors kept asking when we were going to go back home. After ten months, we had to come back home to Tanzania.

> ZOE M.: We also came back because of [the kids' international school]. Last year my son had eighteen children in his classroom. And out of those eighteen children, there were seventeen different nationalities. There's no way he would have gotten that kind of experience if he lived in South Africa. He's just so open minded compared to South African kids his age. He knows so much more about the world than we did as kids growing up under apartheid [mimes putting blinders around her eyes]. He's being exposed to so much more cultural difference than we ever were. . . .

> MARTIN M.: We still go to South Africa once or twice a year—not to be left behind, so that Jonathan and Sophie can get the exposure, so they are comfortable walking into a shopping mall and have that experience of modernization. Then they can choose. We want them to have a choice in what they do with their lives.

I asked Martin and Zoe about the negative reputation that South Africans have in Tanzania and whether they thought this was justified. Martin responded at length:

> MARTIN M.: [The first firm we worked for] was not our proudest investment in Tanzania as South Africans. Their sole purpose in investing in Tanzania was to move their investment capital out of SA because they were worried about what might happen to their holdings in the post-1994 era. So that is the reason they came out here. Then when things stabilized in SA, they just liquidated their assets here and let them go. [That firm] deserves all the bad press they got for all their bad dealings in Tanzania. Their managers abandoned their South African staff on the ground here. The former manager still has several civil suits pending against him if he ever sets foot in Tanzania again. . . .
>
> [Still] I feel aggrieved that we're all tarred and feathered with the same negative brush. South Africans have brought in new standards, new equipment, they raised the bar in the hotel industry. We came in and . . . said, "We'll import from South Africa. We're not going to import from Europe. We're going to bring it up from SA ourselves." In the end of the

day, you're going to step on the toes of the guy who had been importing from Europe for years. The same is true if you start buying more locally. But how else are you going to develop the local community?

The old colonials from Kenya complained that we would come up here and work for less—for dollars [his face lights up]. We worked for less than they would ever to agree to work for, but we were happy because we were paid in dollars, and you could take them back home to South Africa and that way you could make a fairly good living. The old Kenyan colonials resented the fact that you were taking "their" jobs from them.

You don't just fit into the old colonial crowd, particularly if you don't have horses, and you don't play polo, and if you're not a member of all the old clubs. It takes a long time to break in. From their perspective, we were just here to work our two-year contracts and leave. And to a certain extent early on that was true. I can remember a trip we took a few years ago to [a beach resort area] and it was mostly South Africans who went on the trip. There were nineteen of us—a year later, there were only five of us left, and now there are only three. But we're here now, and we are considering buying land and settling. We couldn't do that before.

Zoe intervened at this point to share a story about the tension between South Africans and white Kenyans, which flared a couple years ago. A group of white expatriates was watching a rugby match between South Africa and Australia at a local South African–run sports bar (see chapter 6). Everyone placed a wager on the final score of the match, and Martin won the bet. He used his winnings to buy a round for everyone present. Rather than gracefully accept this gesture, however, the "old colonials" walked away without taking their drinks. After listening to Zoe recount this tale, Martin responded thoughtfully:

MARTIN M.: It's funny. We're African. We would always shout for the African team. If Kenya is playing Britain in cricket, we'd be for Kenya, and the old colonials would root for Britain. And I can't figure that out. It's like for us, when we think about where we're from, we're African, whereas for the old colonials, even those who have been here much longer than we have, they still think of themselves as British. I mean we've been in Africa for five or six generations, and now we *think* of ourselves as Africans. We could live anywhere in Africa, whether Zimbabwe, or Zambia, or South Africa, or Tanzania, but we could never see ourselves living in Europe. We've always been pioneering in nature. The ending of apartheid has allowed South Africans to do what they probably would have done fifty years ago if it hadn't been for apartheid. South Africans like that feel: they're Africans. They're very patriotic towards Africa.

As for the connection to the old South Africa and its apartheid ways, Zoe left no doubt that her family had decisively turned a corner:

ZOE M.: Last night we went [out] with another South African, three Australians, and ourselves. And they got involved in a racist conversation. Somehow the topic turned to some effort in the past to put down a riot in South
Africa. And they were commenting on the fact that over 200 people were
controlled with just fifteen dogs, marveling at the fact that the Africans'
minds were "so slow" that they couldn't figure out a way to subdue the dogs
with their superior numbers. We couldn't stand to listen to it. They told us
we had gotten too sensitive to race. That the pendulum had swung too far
in the other direction. But we've really moved on. We don't think that way
anymore—and I certainly don't want to expose my kids to it.

What people sometimes forget is that it's our generation [both are
now in their mid-thirties] that changed [the apartheid system]. We *chose*
it. There was a referendum, and it was our generation that swung the vote.
It certainly wasn't our parents who swung the vote [laughs at the absurdity of the thought]. *We* made that choice.

Trevor H.:
"For the kids . . . at least they go back with a purged mind"

Trevor H.[13] is a senior executive managing a restaurant chain for a South African corporation in Dar es Salaam. He lives in a comfortable house along the beach
to the north of the city with his family. His point of entry into Tanzania was through
internal promotion at his firm where he's worked for over two decades. According to
my Tanzanian contacts, Trevor has a good reputation as a progressive employer, but
he is one of the few South African managers they would categorize in these terms.
His decision to accept an international posting was shaped in part by the romantic
allure of living on the continent, in part by the lucrative dollar-denominated salary
and benefits he could attract, and in part by the independence he could exercise by
working in a branch office without having to deal with the layers of bureaucracy he
would have had to contend with in a similar position back home.

Trevor and his family kept a distance between themselves and the rest of the
South African community in Dar es Salaam, which he described as being quite insular:

TREVOR H.: That's what we find. Very South Africa–centric. And we don't,
you know, speaking of we, as a family, we don't necessarily socialize with
South Africans . . . We just stay around on the outside and dabble with
South Africans when we want to, and dabble with Brits. We'd rather get to
feel the Tanzanian life than live this sort of old funny life with the South
Africans. . . . Yeah, we kind of keep ourselves to ourselves. We live far out
of town, and we're happy with that. We live on the beach and it's actually
nice. You know, we get out at the end of the day and head back north. We're
quite comfortable with that.

Like Piet and Zoe and Martin, he relished the opportunities his children enjoyed in Tanzania:

> **TREVOR H.:** I mean, even from a South African point of view, sometimes we love it, love it, love it here as a family, and we wouldn't be heartbroken to go back either. It's . . . you have it easy here, and in South Africa you really have to work now. For the kids, for the small people, in this country it couldn't be better to bring kids up. This environment, you know, is open, lots of space, and you have the [wildlife reserves]. . . . In South Africa, it's much more like in London or wherever else you are in the world, that sort of city living.
>
> And for us, as white South Africans, you're talking about shaking up all the past and that sort of stuff. I would far rather bring up kids in this kind of environment rather than the schools down there which might or might not still have some legacy from the dark old days, and sort of the complexes and trying to get over this issue. And here it's not an issue for the kids. So if and when they choose to go back to South Africa, at least they go back with a purged mind.

He was not surprised to hear that Tanzanian authorities called the South African contingent the largest single expatriate community in Tanzania but noted that this was a very diverse group:

> **TREVOR H.:** There are probably that many South Africans, but they don't all hang out together. You'll see a few South Africans at any restaurant or at the movies or at the school—things like that. But to say, and I'm not aware, there's a place where we all hang out? Because in South Africa, you have to understand, we all come from hugely different backgrounds. From Cape Town, Durban, Pretoria—you are two different people. High-income groups, low-income groups . . . So yeah, I don't think you can say there is a place where you can say is dominated by South Africans. You could talk about some people who join the yacht club [a popular spot among South Africans based in Dar es Salaam], but then *most* people I know who join the yacht club aren't really South Africans, so I'm not sure. Perception stuff, I think, really.
>
> I mean, of course, the clever people that are attracting the South African market like the Royal Palm [Hotel] did with rugby; [it's] because they know there's a good market out there to haul in. I'm sure by putting the Spurs [a SA steak house chain] in the Sea Cliff [shopping center], they know damn well they're going to get a good South African contingent loyal to their restaurant.[14]
>
> But yeah, it's funny. There will be cliques of South Africans. Certainly there'll be cliques. You know at the school, the international school, I would say demographically that the third largest student population are the South Africans. . . . I think the Brits are probably the biggest, and I

think probably Kenyans, and then the South Africans. Which has grown. That's a big demographic shift. That hasn't always been like that.

Trevor went on to explain his experience of starting up a business in Tanzania. He said that at the outset, as far as his senior staff was concerned, he would almost "automatically" look to South Africa because he could get well-trained people willing to work for competitive wages given the poor exchange rate for South Africa's currency. More recently, he thought the South Africans had "lost their competitive advantage on the wage scale" due to the weakening dollar and stronger rand. He also extolled the virtues of his Tanzanian staff in their own right:

> TREVOR H.: Yeah. It was a challenge, it was a challenge . . . [The Tanzanian restaurant industry] is relatively young, the training inputs, the education establishment, the finances, the opportunities—it was very underdeveloped. Really, supplying people sort of at the base level, but not senior staff. So you had this problem of getting the right people. Now either you get people who are aging, to put it in a nice way, sort of forty-plus, who come from the old-style hospitality industry . . . which was driven by the state, and really have a mind-set which is sort of difficult to undo. Or you go in for the youngsters who are just coming through the colleges now. And we went that route; we went with a very open mind. We were told that Tanzanians were lazy and stupid and couldn't speak English. It was one of the key paradoxes . . . We didn't want to depend on an army of expatriate staff to run the thing. There was no sense in even doing that. So we went out there and found some good staff, absolute stars, and they've risen to the challenge. Certainly the language is an issue, but that's something that we'll, that they'll, get over . . . It's a country issue and we have to work around that. But from a skills point of view, yeah, we have to do a lot more training. But in itself, that has advantages, and we can start training according to our own style, and start contributing back into the industry. So yeah, we've been delighted with our staff, absolutely delighted. It's been good.[15]

In the end, he argued, it boiled down to the sort of attitude one could expect from the workers themselves:

> TREVOR H.: Our background is in the South African restaurant business where there isn't that level of friendliness at all. Lots of chips on all sorts of shoulders; lots of social problems there. And it manifests itself, you know, if in the service industry you're going to have a battle. You deal with an attitude issue; not with the training or anything so much, but with an attitude problem. Here [in Tanzania] you don't have the attitude problem, so it's a type of dream to work here. If they've got the right attitude, you can train them in anything, you can do what you like. If you start out with the fundamental conflict, then you can have some problems.

John S.:
"Bwana kaburu"

John S.[16] came to Tanzania to take up a senior position with a leading South African firm in the late 1990s. He remembers clearly the first time he walked into the firm's Tanzanian office and shook hands with his South African counterparts there. He described it as "a sort of 'Dr. Livingstone, I presume' moment."[17] A polished executive with well-honed public relations skills, John relished the chance to work in Tanzania's rapidly growing industrial sector: "Very few people get a chance to leave a legacy. This was a unique opportunity to promote [his company] and this magnificent country." He viewed Tanzania as "bubbling full of entrepreneurial spirit. It's been a wonderful opportunity to bring our kids here and have them experience that kind of environment."

When asked directly about the widespread antagonism directed at South African firms in Tanzania, John suggested that this was all due to "a fear of change." In his view, the arrival of South Africans in Tanzania was like when settlers first went to the United States.

> **JOHN S.:** There had to be a period of transition. . . . Early on there were some people from South Africa who came to Tanzania thinking they had the science and the cash and—"We're going to show them [Tanzanians] how to do it"—which was a really stupid way of thinking. But I am proud of the South African businesses that have come here for the most part. There have been a lot of good jobs done by these firms. Certainly more good than bad. And the rate of change has been fantastic. There has been massive positive change. And it's been a privilege to be a part of it.

John claimed he had never felt unsafe in Tanzania. Even working in an industry that had experienced its share of labor unrest, he never feared for his life:

> **JOHN S.:** Sometimes young guys will feel it necessary to challenge me once in a while with that "*kaburu*" kind of language, but it doesn't bother me. If you let that sort of thing bother you, you're in the wrong kind of business. What matters is how you treat people. Once you've taken care of that, you've got no worries . . . I often introduce myself at meetings: "My given English name is John, but otherwise I'm just known as Bwana *Kaburu*."[18] And everybody laughs, and the whole issue is put to rest.

John's social life was primarily centered on expatriates, largely, he explained, because his wife had just joined him from South Africa, but he looked forward to more and more social interaction with Tanzanians, whom he himself preferred. His kids' friends were predominantly African rather than expatriate. And the social milieu in general was so positive that he felt that he and his family could conceivably make

Tanzania their home someday. He recognized, however, that he and his fellow South Africans still had some adjustments to make:

> JOHN S.: Like it or not, you don't walk away from the past hundred years quickly. I might ask one of our workers here to do something for me, and have a difficult time getting a point across. And then I might resort to [puts on a thick South African accent and an exasperated tone]: "What I want you to do is put this in the boot of my car!" So where does that come from? It's a habit that comes from my past experience. But I'm not a racist. I am an African, and I do not accept racist behavior. I can recall going to Scotland and meeting up with a black South African friend there who was so glad to see me he threw his arms around me. He had gotten fed up with the racializing behavior [of the Scots] all around him, and was so glad to see a fellow who didn't share those sensibilities.

He also felt that some of the cultural practices of South Africans were mischaracterized as racist when they were really more about the nature of the South African work ethic:

> JOHN S.: The other thing that enters into the picture is that South Africans are hard workers . . . So we want things to happen right now. So you get these guys who get here and say that things must change *now*. And they try to get Tanzanians to work faster and respond faster. But that's not right. Again, this is not something that is unique to Tanzania. I can recall vividly standing at the bar rail in the UK trying to get the barmaid to serve me a beer, without her even glancing in my direction. I know that if I step away from that rail a hundred other people are willing to take my place, and she knows that, too. So she doesn't have any incentive to rush her work. So it's not just Tanzanians, but there are people all over the world who might not work as fast as you might want them to.[19]

In the end, John stressed, it was important to put South Africans' culpability for apartheid in a proper historical context.

> JOHN S.: We gave it [apartheid] a name, but it's all over the world. Look at the American South. You've got rednecks there who are still working out the tensions of the American Civil War. So it's all over the world. South Africans have got no monopoly on that kind of behavior.

Alain P.:
"I, for one, have always tried to stay away from that whole South Africa thing"

Alain P.[20] worked for a safari company based in northern Tanzania and had been in the country longer than just about any other South African I interviewed. His upbringing and college education took place in an area that was "pretty right wing, the whole area—very, very Afrikaans," and he found these conditions stultifying:

ALAIN P: I wanted to get out and explore things a bit for myself. Also once I started to get out a bit more in a natural environment and started to deal with people of different outlooks on the environment and life, I realized that that stereotypically Afrikaans lifestyle was not the only option. . . . And it took me a few years, up until maybe quite recently, I actually started to think, "Well, South Africa is not that bad; it's actually quite a nice country." Now going back I enjoy it again. I can see positive change there.

[My parents] were pretty much in the [political] middle and more comfortable just following the crowd, and not creating any waves or being too radical on any side. You know it was definitely not like I was irritated by how my parents treated, you know, black people. But I think it's not only the racial thing that irritated me. It was more of the whole culture, the whole rugby-playing, beer-drinking, going out on Friday night to look for fun kind of culture . . . It just was never really my thing . . . in South Africa as an Afrikaans boy when I grew up, you were frowned upon if you didn't play rugby. And you're almost born with a rugby ball in your hands. That's one thing I must say, my parents never pushed me into that.

Alain spoke at length about the challenges of getting established in business in Tanzania as a South African:

ALAIN P.: For anyone that loves the bush, East Africa is the ideal thing. . . . I think I was so ignorant coming from South Africa. And then also coming up with [names the firm he used to work for] is like the military: you're completely brainwashed. You move in a safe [corporate controlled] environment, and are very subtly introduced into Tanzania . . . It was not like a lot of South Africans, [who] are just thrown in, and they have this massive culture shock, and they have to deal with red tape in Tanzania and difficultness. It was very easy for me, and I think that's what's also making me stay. It's this gradual getting used to the culture, and really taking it in and starting to understand it.

But I've never ever had this sort of, you know—"You're South African"—thrown in my face . . . Initially [the government agency he reports to] was very reluctant to deal with me. But you know, that was more kind of verbalized a little bit. They were quite honest to say, "You're the second South African that [we] are dealing with . . . and the first guy screwed us." He's the sort of guy that's still around a little bit, but he really made it very hard for South Africans dealing with the government. But then . . . we proved that it's more of a personality thing rather than a South African thing [and we never] heard a negative word again . . . Instead now they would rather call up and ask for advice on certain things. Only now are people starting to slowly turn around, you know, to the fact that maybe I'm not so much South African anymore as I'm more Tanzanian. Back then there was a little bit of jealousy on some levels.

[The firm Alain used to work for] were very arrogant coming in. But that's just the company nature: they're very aggressive, arrogant . . . Now, twelve, thirteen years after their involvement in Tanzania, it's proven to be highly successful. But I think it took so long because a lot of people blocked them. If they had come in a little more subtle, I think it would have taken so much quicker to integrate with the whole system and prove that this can work.

Given his relatively lengthy tenure in Tanzania, I asked Alain what his perspective was on the controversy surrounding South African presence more generally. I wanted to know whether it had changed since his arrival, and whether it tended to flare up around specific issues or specific actors:

ALAIN P.: You know, I, for one, have always tried to stay away from the whole South African thing, so I've been quite unaffected. I've never really known the players on the scene. That's why they really won't really know me, even. . . . Like the whole South African *braai* [barbecue] and get-together for rugby and stuff, I don't even know about that.

I guess . . . the services and the improvement in technology in the country and making life easy. . . . On that level, I think it's good to help Tanzania develop a little bit. But I do not necessarily enjoy the players, the guys who come up to do that. Because from the South African side, the guys who were sent up here to start [names a prominent SA firm based in Dar es Salaam], I mean, they're the reprobates. [That firm] was so controversial in terms of the people who were sent to install everything. There was constant racist fights and drama like that. And I think a lot of times that is the case: that it's not a top-line management who's sent up from South Africa to come and sort things out. It's normally some racist white. And that side I don't enjoy at all. Like also the hunting companies, all the young camp managers who come up, they're a big source of irritation. And I always feel that I've worked quite hard to get rid of this racist South African image that exists, and the whole *kaburu* thing, and that you only need one or two guys to come in and do some stupid things to make it a South African issue again . . . They've only been here for two years but, man, do they do damage to the whole image thing. They're just clueless to the culture . . .

I don't think I necessarily came to Tanzania because I was really annoyed with South Africa. I didn't see that as an escape, but you know, after I've been here, I've kind of looked back and I think, yeah, maybe that's why I was so happy in Tanzania . . . And even my first two or three years, even four years of being in Tanzania, you know you always thought of South Africa as being home, and eventually one day you'd need to pack your bags and go back. Up until one day that I thought, "So what is it that I'm going to do when I go back" . . . I thought, you know, this might be a place where I want to stay for a while. I think once you make that decision then somehow Tanzania becomes home.

Conclusion

The South Africans interviewed for this study were a diverse lot. They originated from different parts of South Africa, engaged in a variety of occupational pursuits, and expressed diverse political opinions. Their reasons for coming to Tanzania in the first place were similarly varied. What they shared was the burden of their nationality and a particular racial profile as white South Africans. In Tanzania, this identified them as *makaburu,* which meant that they were associated with the racist tactics of a political regime that formally ended nearly twenty years ago.

Judging from the personal narratives provided above, the mantle of South African identity is not worn lightly. Taken collectively, this group came to Tanzania with a set of painfully ambivalent memories of life under apartheid and the early years following the 1994 elections. Some, like Piet, looked back on their service in the apartheid military and were embittered by the fact that blacks ended up taking over the government anyway. They could barely contain their irritation at having to deal with the pent-up animosities black officials in South Africa directed at them. They marked themselves as "a generation in between": they did not create apartheid—their parents did that—but they were blamed for it and they were being asked to help fix it. Like Marie, they felt defensive: back home, they felt "prejudged" and constantly had to prove that they were not "monsters" or "the enemy," that they were actually "nice people" in their own right. In Tanzania, by contrast, they were free of these social constraints.

Like Alain and Koos, they remembered how confined they felt in isolated rural settings in South Africa, or tight-knit ethnic enclaves. Like Piet, they recalled a sense of vulnerability in the face of a roiling economy, the inability to get ahead financially given the depressed value of the rand, and, for the men especially, the threat of emasculating job loss under the country's new affirmative action programs. The emotions that lay behind these memories were powerful, deeply personal, and unsettling.

The fateful decision to relocate "in Africa" rather than follow the majority of their outward-bound compatriots to Europe, North America, Australia, or New Zealand was typically carefully considered. For Martin and Zoe, there was never any question about their destination: they strongly identified as Africans and could never see themselves living the lives of expatriates in any of the neo–South African enclaves outside the continent. For others, the decision to take up residence in Africa represented an adventurous step backward in time, one that almost inevitably led to the development of neocolonial attitudes and practices. John's description of his first encounter with his South African business colleagues in Tanzania as a "Dr. Livingstone, I presume" moment offered a case in point. This characterization revealed that he saw himself and his peers as occupying isolated bastions of civilization on an otherwise backward African frontier. Similarly, Marie was initially skeptical about the professional capabilities of her Tanzanian counterparts. Before taking her job in Tanzania, her impression was that she would come and "pass on skills . . . because there *were* no skills here." After arriving, she was pleasantly surprised at how "up to date" her colleagues were. Rather than draw the conclusion that Tanzanians were her true professional peers, however, she attributed their skills to the fact that they were "part of a worldwide network." This was the only way she could make sense of the seeming contradiction.

For the most part, these individuals viewed Tanzanians much more favorably than they viewed blacks in South Africa, whom they characterized as "aggressive, angry, chip-on-the-shoulder type of people."[21] The friendly reception they received from Tanzanians was especially important to the South African parents I interviewed who considered the opportunity to raise their children in Tanzania to be a "real privilege." For Trevor this meant that "if and when [his children] choose to go back to South Africa, at least they go back with a purged mind." The need to resist racism in all its forms was thus paramount, because, as Zoe put it, "We don't think that way anymore—and I certainly don't want to expose my kids to it."

While a favorable view of Tanzanians was nearly universal, members of the South African contingent were still divided in their approach to social interaction with locals. Those who adopted Tanzania more wholeheartedly as a new home emphatically rejected the option of moving only in insular social circles with their compatriots—"If we'd wanted that sort of thing, we'd have stayed in South Africa." They actively sought to put distance between themselves and their past and had done so for a very long time. Some, like Alain, viewed themselves as being more Tanzanian than South African. From this vantage point, they greatly resented the racist actions of their (former) countrymen and women. As Alain put it, the hard work he had done to "get rid of this racist South African image" could be squandered in an instant by the culturally ignorant actions of other South Africans who followed their investments to Tanzania.

This latter group described themselves as moving in social circles where South African friends, rugby, and in some cases use of the Afrikaans language were all part of their daily routine. They joined South African "cliques" who "do everything together" and patronized hotels, bars, and restaurants—"little South Africas," or "feel at home" places—where they could insulate themselves from locals (see chapter 6). And they were actively considering and developing exit options that would allow them a safe return and smooth transition back to South Africa when the time was ripe.

In sum, the decision South Africans took to relocate to Tanzania in the 1990s and 2000s created an opportunity for reinvention, a chance to challenge the *kaburu* stereotype and establish new bilateral ties on firmer footing. Some embraced this task wholeheartedly to the point where they considered themselves more Tanzanian than South African. Others, however, recreated social patterns and reinforced stereotypes that affected not only their fellow South Africans but other white expatriates as well. In effect, whiteness itself became a hotly contested category, as the next chapter demonstrates.

6
White Spots

When anybody says South African investment,
let's call a spade a spade:
it is white investment we are talking about.
RETIRED TANZANIAN CIVIL SERVANT

It may have been the biltong that cost her her job, at least judging from the story her boss told. Lots of white patrons came into the high-end grocery outlet in Dar es Salaam where Lucy worked as a salesperson behind the butcher counter. Indeed, the store's clientele was primarily comprised of white expatriates whose salaries supported the regular purchase of high-quality meat products. The South Africans came for the biltong in particular. The spicy, vinegar-cured dried meat is a national delicacy in South Africa, one that is strongly associated with Afrikaner culture because of its use as a source of protein during the years of the great overland migrations, the Boer treks of the late nineteenth century.

There had never really been a market for biltong in Tanzania until the South Africans arrived. But due to the growing South African presence, the store where Lucy worked always kept a supply on hand. Day in and day out, South Africans came into the shop and placed their orders for biltong, *boerwors* (farmer sausages), and other types of meat prepared according to South African recipes. Many of these customers seemed to fit the cultural stereotype of the *makaburu*. Lucy found their short pants and brusque manners offensive; they provided a constant reminder of her country's rapidly changing social and political landscape.

According to Lucy's boss, her everyday encounters with South African patrons eventually became too much for Lucy to bear: she could no longer contain her distaste at having to serve South Africans *their* national dish in *her* country, and she loudly vented her frustration to co-workers. Her boss, a white "southerner" himself, remembers how shocked he was at the display of raw emotion put on by his clerk and how "frightening" it was that she felt "such hatred" against South African patrons.

He eventually felt it necessary to confront her: "I said, 'I don't *ever* want to hear you talking about anybody like that again. Because we don't know who these people are. Even if they are South Africans, how dare you, how *dare* you put a label on them and try and put them in a box!'" When Lucy defiantly told him that it was her government that had taught her to hate South Africans and that she would never be able to think otherwise, he felt he had no choice but to fire her immediately. He could not have anyone working for him who was a "racializer," who judged people solely by the color of their skin or their nationality.

As this anecdote suggests, the presence of large numbers of predominantly white South African investors in Tanzania in the late 1990s and early 2000s forced Tanzanians and South Africans to confront one another in unprecedented ways. The election of the ANC government in South Africa in 1994 led to the widespread expectation that a new era of friendship and cooperation between South Africa and Tanzania was in the offing. If Tanzanians expected to join hands with their former comrades in arms from the liberation struggles, however, they were in for a rude awakening: the South Africans who followed their investments to Tanzania were not ANC stalwarts; instead, these were the hated *makaburu,* a group of whites whose experience of *being* white and whose historical relationship with African blacks were profoundly and ineluctably shaped by apartheid.

When they first began encountering *makaburu* in their workplaces and social settings, Tanzanians responded with skepticism and hostility. The anti-*kaburu* chants and songs they once performed in schoolyards, the ideological debates about frontline solidarity at the university, Nyerere's speeches calling for vigilance in protecting the nation's borders—all of the old memories of Tanzania's involvement in the anti-apartheid struggle came flooding back. Along with them came a set of worrisome new questions: How would whites who had to be forced from power in South Africa behave in Tanzania—would they live up to, or live down, their national stereotype as racist imperialists? Did their presence mean that a new chapter of tense race relations would unfold in Tanzania?

As the cohort of white "southerners" arrived in Tanzania after the end of apartheid, a moralizing discourse distinguishing between good whites and bad whites emerged to differentiate between different groups, often along lines of nationality. Tanzanians grew increasingly alarmed throughout this period at the mounting anecdotal evidence of racist behaviors ascribed to South Africans. Informants repeatedly expressed concerns that South Africans were reproducing apartheid social relations in Tanzania. My own evidence suggests that Tanzanians were at least somewhat justified in their fears, insofar as South Africans effectively converted particular city neighborhoods and individual bars, clubs, and restaurants into de facto "white spots" where most Tanzanians no longer felt welcome.

Xenophobia and the *Makaburu*

"Thieves and bandits," "termites," "like a virus, spreading its tentacles every-where"—the response to South African presence on the streets of Tanzania was often visceral and vituperative. The *makaburu* were called "rough" and "abrasive." Their accent ("Sooth Eefrikuns") and body types ("I call them the no-necks. You see what I mean, don't you? They haven't got any necks.") were widely mocked as Tanzanians and foreign nationals alike expressed their aversion to the new arrivals. Resentment centered in particular on the *makaburu* "attitude," a superior, condescending posture that seemed to convey the message "We have come to teach Tanzanians how to run their country."[1] MM, the journalist quoted in earlier chapters, invoked each of these tropes in his own description of the "Boers":

> The South Africans, they're not very discreet people it seems to me, from what I gather. They drink and they run around and so on, make a bit of noise. And the accent is very [pauses with a sour look on his face]—you can't hide it. Tanzanian people are, maybe, more polite, more gentle and slow and . . . you know? They're not *pushy* people like these fellows [South Africans] *pushing* around. And people resent that . . . Even the dress code: these guys in their shorts—I find it revolting . . . And they swagger, walk with a swagger, and very confident, talk very self confident, etc., etc. Not necessarily arrogant but just sort of like, you know [mimes a haughty expression], "We are here. . . ." For instance, they want to bring everything from South Africa, including groceries and bottled water, rather than buy anything from here . . . Some Boers think that they are too *good,* they can't have anything from here. And that's created tremendous misunderstanding.

The generally negative response of Tanzanians toward South Africans gave other whites in the expatriate community pause, with many expressing concern that they themselves might be implicated in the anti-*makaburu* fervor of the moment. As a member of one of the old American missionary families in northern Tanzania put it, "Yeah, first it was the Zimbabweans [in the 1980s], and then it was the South Africans. We were all worried that when they started coming, Tanzanians wouldn't be able to differentiate between us and them. But the discerning Tanzanians can, I think."[2] His supposition that "discerning" Tanzanians could distinguish between his family and the "bad" whites from the south was phrased with a slight question at the end. When I repeated his statement to a Tanzanian colleague, he responded emphatically that this view was correct: "*Makaburu* are not white. No one considers them to be *wazungu* [that is, like European or North American whites]; they are *makaburu*. That's an entirely different thing altogether."[3] Another white expatriate who was born in Tanzania and remembers the original Boer settlements in the pre-independence period agreed: "That's right, they're like another tribe. One thing I've noticed is that they operate with an African concept of truth: they'll lie to your face, or tell you what they think you want to hear, rather than upset you with the truth, just like Tanzanians[!] They don't have a western, *mzungu* concept of truth."[4]

Even among South Africans there was considerable concern about the "bad apples" in their midst. As one of the leaders of the South African Business Forum (SABF) in Dar es Salaam put it,

> The key issue in the SABF is image. It's always image. My standard line is that we are the Americans of Africa. We're just like the Americans in the Middle East and other parts of the world. Anywhere we go, we are the big, bad boy, and people resent that. And frankly we South Africans are often our own worst enemy. Public relations is working below the scenes to sort of try and actively clean up our image. I think there was a time as well a couple of years ago when there was some bad South Africans trying to come over, doing whatever, bad, harmful business practices, whatever you want to call it . . . We've now got a code of conduct and say, in that instance that person will be from our point of view persona non grata. We're not going to support him . . . If that's the way you want to behave, we're having nothing to do with you. Regretfully, we had to do something to control the image.[5]

Clearly, the category of "whiteness" was thrown into graphic relief in this context in the sense that Tanzanians and expatriates alike were now much more keenly aware of, and sensitive to, the issues of white privilege and white supremacy. Tanzanians seemed to draw a sharp distinction between the people they called *makaburu* and other whites, the *wazungu,* who were constructed as being more benevolent or benign, at least in comparison to the stereotypical South African. Whites themselves, including, notably, many progressive-minded South Africans, were equally keen to distance themselves from their more overtly racist peers. In this respect, the return of the *makaburu* led to a spike in race consciousness across the board in Tanzania.

Apartheid Redux?

Much of the animosity directed at South Africans in contemporary Tanzania is easily traced to the history of the anti-apartheid struggle, as explained in previous chapters. At the same time, however, the negative national stereotype of the *makaburu* would most likely have faded with time if actions attributed to them in Tanzania had not reinforced this negative image. In the view of one critic, the problem was that they had a hard time shedding their racist attitudes from the past:

I think they have possibly imbided too much of the apartheid thing, and they have a difficult time letting go of it here in Tanzania. I ask myself, "What kind of human relations are they exporting?" . . . The leopard is having difficulty in changing its spots. In South Africa they are changing because they *have* to change. The ANC won't have it any other way. The ANC *makes* them change. A few minimal changes *had* to be done. But given half a chance, they seem to roll back to the original.[6]

Again, South Africans were often in agreement in leveling this critique at their colleagues. As one South African hunter put it, "The minute a South African crosses the Limpopo [the river forming part of South Africa's northern boundary], they feel that there's different mores that are now at play. And that irritates me; I don't like that."[7]

The behaviors Tanzanians found most problematic on the part of the *makaburu* included the use of racial slurs (*kaffirs*, "pink-feets") and other forms of derogatory address that were used when speaking or referring to Tanzanians, for example, the infantilizing of adult waiters and domestic servants as "boys" and "girls."[8] They also included the maltreatment of employees in the workplace, such as the case of the white South African mining boss who allegedly smeared wet cement on the face of one of his Tanzanian employees as punishment for a minor infraction, or the restaurant manager in Dar es Salaam who would not let her Tanzanian waiters and waitresses handle money. Given this perceived pattern of racist behavior as a background, the numerous well-publicized controversies surrounding South African–run corporations—the laying off of thousands of Tanzanian workers, the buying up of strategically important economic assets, and insensitivity expressed toward important national symbols—were readily interpreted in racial as well as nationalistic terms (see chapter 3).

A concrete example of South Africans "reverting to form" upon entering "Africa" involved two groups of South African medical researchers who were expelled from Tanzania in 2001 for testing ersatz anti-AIDS medications on Tanzanian soldiers. One of the compounds, virodene, was based on "a highly toxic industrial solvent banned in South Africa for use on humans" in 1997 (Economist Intelligence Unit 2001, 19). This "modern-day snake oil" had never even undergone animal testing prior to being used on humans in the Tanzanian trials (Schoofs 2001). The use of Tanzanian soldiers as test subjects was also a potential violation of international medical ethical standards, since soldiers cannot refuse their superiors' orders, and are thus theoretically not in a position to give informed consent as research subjects.[9] These concerns notwithstanding, sixty-four HIV-positive military and police personnel in Tanzania were subjected to different levels of virodene exposure, all to no avail since the drugs showed no verifiable effects (Schoofs 2001). When knowledge of the tests became public, the researchers who administered them were deported, leaving behind substantial debts and a swirl of controversy.[10]

Shortly after the expulsion of the virodene researchers, a second set of controversial drug tests came to light, this time involving oxihumate-K, a compound derived from burnt coal that is sometimes used as plant fertilizer (Soggot and Macfarlane 2001). Unlike virodene, oxihumate is generally considered nontoxic, but there was still no hard evidence at the time of the tests to support the claims of backers that it could help strengthen the immune system. Moreover, the fact that the South African energy utility representatives and researchers from the University of Pretoria who were responsible for these trials chose once again to administer them on Tanzanian soldiers rather than South African patients raised allegations of continuing ethical improprieties (Deane, Macfarlane, and Soggot 2001).

The analyst who reported on the virodene story for the Economist Intelligence Unit noted drily that the participation of South Africans in the bogus drug trials had neo-imperialist overtones: "Although multinational drug companies continue to test drugs in developing countries . . . these are the first known incidents of *South African* companies doing so" (Economist Intelligence Unit 2001, 19, emphasis added). For Tanzanians, the fact that their countrymen were being used as guinea pigs for medical tests that would not have been allowed in South Africa showed the *makaburu* in their true colors.

White Spots

The cornerstone of apartheid ideology and practice was the notion of separation or segregation of racial groups. In the system of grand apartheid, this meant separate "homelands" for blacks and whites; under urban apartheid, this meant separate neighborhoods; and in terms of so-called petty apartheid, this meant separate entrances and waiting rooms for different groups and whites-only access to first-class train cars, high-end restaurants, and elite schools (Christopher 1994). Given the sweeping nature of South African investments and the mounting evidence of questionable social relations they engendered, many Tanzanians grew worried that similar segregationist practices were on the rise in Tanzania:

> The only problem is this racist, tribalist, ethnicity approach, this approach of separating each group. This is not unique to South Africans . . . but they have brought it here. These things will crop out in the near future. Whoever is undermining Tanzania, this will not be forever, that much I can tell you . . . We aren't going to stand for this indefinitely. People are going to fight back. This mentality of approach where you segregate yourself, you play your own games,

set up segregated schools, this will cost them. It won't necessarily be me who will come after them, but somebody will. If you make a situation where people feel desperate in their own country, this is a recipe for a disaster.[11]

If the colonization of social enclaves and gathering places by whites, and by white South Africans in particular, was as widespread as this speaker suggests, the question of how this happened looms large, especially in a national context where the legal mechanisms that were used to justify apartheid were absent. The implication is that more subtle means of reproducing white privilege were at work in the country. At one level, the production of these "white spots" was straightforward: they came about through the personal choices individuals made to live in residential areas, frequent commercial establishments, join exclusive clubs, and send children to schools that were predominantly used and occupied by, or associated with, whites. At the same time, fundamental structuring forces and ideologies were also in play.[12] Amenities such as sewage facilities, the provision of electricity and water supply, and the maintenance of road and communications infrastructure were all historically concentrated in "European" neighborhoods in Tanzania.[13] So while it may seem that simple consumer choice was responsible for the reproduction of white enclaves, a racialized planning process also clearly channeled wealthy expatriates into some areas rather than others.

The resulting pattern of de facto segregation was quite evident in urban Tanzania in the 2000s. In Dar es Salaam, for example, residential areas and related commercial and social institutions in the Oyster Bay/Msasani peninsula areas as well as newer beachfront developments to the north of the city had been dominated by European whites for the better part of a century (Brennan and Burton 2007, 32–35). Similarly, in Arusha, the central corridor between the clock tower and Kijenge roundabouts, wealthy neighborhoods on the city's edge in Njiro and Burka, and newer peri-urban developments in the nearby countryside constituted the most sought-after neighborhoods by white residents (cf. Peligal 1999). In other parts of the country, de facto all-white "company towns" were also built near South African–managed sugar plantations in Kilombero and Moshi and mining compounds near Mwanza and Mwadui (cf. Carstens 2001; Ferguson 2005).

Coded Space: Tactics of Inclusion and Exclusion

While the protection of white privilege had been central to urban planning practice in Tanzania for decades, the arrival of new whites from the South invested existing socio-spatial relations with new meanings. In the popular imaginary, the *makaburu* were firmly associated with the practice of racial segregation under apartheid. Their mere presence thus effectively coded particular spaces as "white" even when they were not strictly segregated. (Strict segregation would be legally barred in Tanzania in any case.)

Commercial proprietors seeking to attract white clients to their establishments often deployed coded language in ads placed in newspapers and local shopping guides. A pizza parlor advertising itself as having a "European atmosphere" and a shopping center promising "secure" parking were both making race-coded appeals to prospective white clients. The South African–run Holiday Inn Hotel in Dar es Salaam (now known as the Southern Sun) made similar appeals on a series of prominent street signs in 2006. The route to the hotel from the airport was marked by boldly colored green signs indicating "Turn Left Here"; "Turn Right Here"; "Straight On." These led the traveler through Dar's dense urban landscape as though there could only be one destination. Clearly deployed to appeal to foreigners, the signs assuaged the latent fears of those who might be entering the city for the first time: "Relax," said one, "it's the Holiday Inn"; "International Standards," declared another, "with a local flavor." With a nod to the exotic colonial history of nearby Zanzibar, patrons were reassured in a print ad that they would be treated "like a sheik." These direct advertising appeals by white-spot proprietors were supplemented by special promotions featuring South African wine and beer tastings, the public broadcast of high-profile sporting events (for example, the rugby and cricket world cup matches), international film screenings, and offers to host exclusive private parties and business meetings.

Exclusionary mechanisms used to actively block entry by undesirables were similarly widespread. A classic means of creating exclusive space was the establishment of a dues-paying members-only club. Most such clubs in Tanzania—for example, the Gymkhana clubs in Arusha and Dar es Salaam, the Dar es Salaam yacht club, or the polo club outside of Arusha—once catered to the colonial elite and long predate the arrival of South Africans.[14] The influx of new "southern" members from South Africa and Zimbabwe nonetheless helped solidify their reputation as bastions of white privilege. Most of these exclusive institutions were located behind security cordons or gates barring open access and free entrance. Simple economic screens such as membership dues, inflated prices, and cover charges were also used to discourage black patronage. Informants claimed, for example, that blacks were forced to pay higher prices for drinks than whites in a bar on Zanzibar; and pubs in the heart of Arusha supposedly imposed cover charges to discourage African patronage.[15]

These tactics of attraction and repulsion were well-illustrated by two new white spots that recently emerged in urban areas of Tanzania. Neither was exclusively "white" in the sense of being strictly segregated along racial lines, nor were the whites who frequented them as patrons and workers exclusively South African. Both were nonetheless strongly associated with South African presence and were unambiguously understood to be bastions of white privilege.

Catering to White Preference

The South African–owned health club located in a gated residential complex in Dar es Salaam was known as "Fitness." The neighborhood included several commercial establishments and offices as well as long rows of bungalows with immaculately trimmed lawns. For the most part, the latter were occupied by expatriates earning substantial international salaries. To enter the compound, visitors had to pass through a security gate. Vehicles displaying residence tags were waved through, while other guests were required to sign an entry log and stipulate their destination.

The club itself offered its members a variety of exercise options: weight training equipment; stationary bicycles and rowing machines; treadmills and elliptical trainers; squash, tennis, and basketball courts; a children's playground; and a swimming pool with lap lanes. It also featured a small sports bar/pub equipped with several flat-screen televisions. These were perpetually tuned to sports events broadcast via Supersports, a South African satellite television network.

The club was managed by a number of different owners over the fifteen years since it was first built, including two South Africans, Louis and David. When Louis bought the club in the early 2000s, he was surprised when friends advised him, "Make sure you say [in your advertisements] that you are South African-owned." As he explained, his friends felt that this would enhance the club's reputation because, in their view, South Africans were known for being able to run things properly. So when he posted an ad in a local shopping guide indicating that the club was under new management, he added the statement, "Watch out for our SA technician . . . who is refurbishing the equipment!" As the manager clarified, this message was meant to establish that the club was under sound management, and to signal that the equipment would be repaired properly. "I mean this was equipment that you couldn't just get some *fundi* [Kiswahili, "local mechanic"] to come and fix for you. It had to be someone international. So we put that in the ad, so people would know." The implication here, of course, was that the club's prospective clients would themselves be "international" (read: "white"), and would both readily appreciate the complexity of maintaining sophisticated exercise equipment and share the manager's racist assumption that this task lay beyond any ordinary African's capabilities.

Louis also deliberately promoted his club as a venue for viewing rugby. Sports nationalism is intense in South Africa, and no sport was more closely identified with the nation under apartheid than rugby.[16] The sport is particularly important to Afrikaners, among whom it is jokingly referred to as "the game they play in heaven." Louis's use of rugby to draw patrons to his restaurant was thus clearly meant to attract whites rather than blacks: "There are very few places in town where you can *expect* to have rugby on. Everywhere else . . . they have football [soccer]. And football draws a real *dodgy* crowd. So, yes, we have made a very deliberate attempt to attract the rugby clientele." When South Africa met England in the finals of the 2007 Rugby World Cup competition (a match that was eventually won by South Africa), Louis promoted the event with a flyer that read in part:

SOUTH AFRICA VS ENGLAND
SATURDAY 20TH OCTOBER
Calling all South African supporters
& the English who dare to watch
18:00 BRAAI VLEIS
(Traditional South African Barbecue)
(Full Braai inclusive of Potjie, Lamb Chops,
Boerewors, Fillet Steak [*sic*], Garlic Bread, Three Salads
and doughnuts for only Tsh 8000 [approx. US $7.50]).
21:00 HAPPY HOUR
buy one get one free on all drinks
22:00 KICK OFF

Circulated through an electronic mailing list, this ad connected with its intended audience through use of the Afrikaans language, its promotion of a menu featuring traditional South African fare, including *potjie* (meat stew) and *boerewors* (farmer sausages), and its overt appeal to South African sports nationalism. By the same token, its tongue-in-cheek warning to "the English who dare to watch" served simultaneously to ward off Tanzanians who might want to socialize in the venue for their own purposes on that day.

David, the South African manager who ran the club in the mid-1990s, had made similarly explicit efforts to cater to the needs of prospective white clients, partly by privileging rugby over football. Heri T., a former Tanzanian employee who worked under David, recalled a series of incidents that left him skeptical about his boss's racial attitudes:

> **HT:** I would not go to the extent of saying that David is a racist, but I can tell you an incident which suggests that he has that side. When the club was doing very well, people would come there: at the pool, swimming. Nice view, you know? Children staying there, people lying on the mats poolside, and a lot of people in the pool. And there were black people there; some Tanzanians, some worked for [international employers in the vicinity]. And some whites also inside. David was never happy with that situation. It came out of him one day. He was not happy because, although everybody was paying . . . some of his *friends* didn't like it, you know? So, he was not happy with that at all. But he couldn't show it so openly. Now one day I saw it in him because one lady came with her kids. You know, people have dif-

ferent attitudes and different personalities. So not every *mzungu* is a racist, or not every black man is a racist, but there are people like that. This lady came with her kids: a daughter and a young boy.

RS: And she was *mzungu*?

HT: Yeah, she was *mzungu*. And the pool was full of black kids playing, you know, doing somersaults, these things. And this lady came there—I was there, I heard it—and she was like, "Shit, my kids can't go in there! I mean, my kids, they are *not* going to go there!" It was, I mean, everyone who heard those words knew that these remarks were targeted . . . that there were so many *black* kids there, and this lady didn't want her kids going there. David was very apologetic: "No, please, please, please, I am going to do something about it!" You know, he moved with the lady, and he was creating the impression that he was going to do something about it. I mean, what *are* you going to do about that? He should tell this person: "Your demands are not possible. I mean, what you want [a segregated pool] cannot happen here. Because I cannot change that. It is beyond our control." But he didn't do that. You know, he wanted to keep that client . . .

RS: Did he ever do anything then? Or was that just him trying to placate her?

HT: No, the lady left. She was furious; she was leaving. I mean, she was going towards her car. And David was escorting her, pleading with her, like: "This won't happen. You know, it's just . . ."

RS: But did he change his policies after that?

HT: He didn't. But there was some restriction. I mean when he hiked up the price, people thought like this was one of the reasons: he wants to get rid of blacks. But there were black people who are working for [international employers], who are from West Africa. Or some Tanzanians were still coming, because they were getting paid enough money [to afford the new rates].[17]

Heri's story raises a series of interesting issues. First, the woman who brought her children to the health club to swim in its pool came with a very particular set of expectations. She thought her children would be able to swim in the pool on their own, and took exception to the fact that they would have to share the space with blacks. Her expectation of being granted exclusive access revealed an unspoken sense of white privilege. Second, the club owner was clearly at pains to try and mollify his client, claiming that he would do something to make the place more comfortable for her and her children. He understood exactly what her needs were, and why she was so put out at having to share the pool. This, too, exposed a shared cultural perspective. Practically speaking, however, David had little room to maneuver in acting on that understanding. He could not simply banish black children from the pool, as that would be illegal in Tanzania. And his move to raise the entry fees, if indeed it was linked to a desire to screen out blacks, was unsuccessful, because both expatriate blacks and middle-class black Tanzanians could still comfortably afford to pay to use the club's amenities. In effect, the structural conditions favoring the implementation of old-style petty apartheid restrictions, the laws and regulations that allowed swimming pools and other social venues to be segregated by race, did not exist in Tanzania. Instead, as Heri went on to explain, if David were to be successful in attracting and satisfying his white patrons, he had to resort to other means of discouraging black patrons from using the club:

> **HT:** So during the weekends, lots of people wanted to see the Premier League [the elite European soccer league, whose games were routinely broadcast throughout Tanzania via satellite television]. These guys pay for drinks, buy food, and they watch one soccer match, or maybe more than one soccer match, and they leave. And their friends with them. There could be *two* South Africans and there is a rugby match. David would tell all these guys [the soccer fans] to *go*. You know [as if it were self-evident]: there was a rugby match! And they would say, "Look! [mimes counting patrons] One, two, three, four, five, six. We all want to watch soccer, and look what we are buying! Put soccer [on the television] please." You know how they say it like that. And David, he wouldn't want to argue with these people. And he would tell the barman, "Look, if someone has a problem with the rugby match, tell them to go! They pay, they go! Okay?" I went over to reason with the barman: "You know you're going to lose business here. You're giving a bad picture of this place. You know, this is a very bad impression. There's only two guys there who want to watch rugby." And he says, "This is David's order. You want me to go against David's order?" He said, "No!" So the guys all left. So, you can see someone through this kind of behavior. Maybe those guys [the rugby fans] were his friends, but sometimes you need to be realistic. And you just tell them: "This is my *business*." So a lot of people got the impression that David is racist.

> **RS:** But generally, the crowd was pretty mixed?

> **HT:** Yeah, it was pretty mixed. He couldn't control that, even though he may want to. Because people came with their own money. The beer, [elsewhere] it is always 300 to 250; here it is 700 [shillings]. That was the price. And they say, they don't care, they [will] pay. And if you tell them they have no right to spend their money in that place, it will give him some trouble. That's why he couldn't go to that length.

Ironically, it took the presence of middle-class blacks, that is, the sort of Tanzanians and expatriates who most directly benefited from recent structural changes in the

Tanzanian economy, to prevent a more thorough pattern of segregation from taking shape in this de facto all-white venue. It was only by dint of their higher discretionary incomes that they were able to frequent the club despite the apparent use of economic screens to discourage their presence.

Symbolic Slights to Blacks

A second incipient white spot in Tanzania occupied a plot of land carved out of an old colonial-era coffee plantation (see figure 6). Many of the white employees of the companies situated in this corporate compound lived in well-appointed homes nearby, and the entire neighborhood had round-the-clock coverage by private security companies. Entry to the compound was marked by a massive stone security gate. Its perimeter was marked by an electric fence, which was patrolled by security personnel and guard dogs following the killing a barkeeper at one of the pubs on the property during an armed robbery in 2010. The fact that locals did not always feel welcome in the vicinity was conveyed by a bit of graffiti attached to a sign near the guard post. In its original unadulterated form, the sign stated, "No Trespassing Allowed" (Kiswahili: *"Hakuna ruhusa kupita hapa"*). When I saw it in 2006, however, the first two letters of the word *"Hakuna"* had been scratched out, so its meaning was reversed to read, in effect, "Trespassing Allowed" (see figure 7). As this graffiti suggests, locals were put off by the growing white presence in the area.

The compound contained within the fenced perimeter was divided into two sections. The first was primarily devoted to office space for a suite of hunting and photographic safari companies, and the second contained a large recreational facility. The latter included squash and tennis courts, a swimming pool and sauna, weight-training equipment, stationary bicycles and treadmills, and, perhaps most notably, a full-sized rugby pitch, which doubled as the home of the Tanzanian national rugby team and was occasionally used for informal soccer and cricket matches. The recreational side of the complex also included a beauty salon, a grocery story, an ATM, two restaurants and a semi-enclosed sports bar/pub that opened onto the rugby pitch.

Because the compound was located on the outskirts of town, employees could not readily access the low-cost restaurants and other types of food vendors typically found in the city center. Consequently, they were fed a midday meal on the premises. This was a significant staff perquisite, but it had a downside in terms of what it came to represent for at least some of the Tanzanian workers, who characterized the dining facilities as being sharply segregated.

Members of the "senior" staff of the firms operating on the premises ate their meals in a large open-sided hall where they were treated to an elaborate buffet while being sheltered from the intense sun. Their sumptuous meals included a wide array of meats, vegetables, salads, and desserts. Tanzanian workers, by contrast, received much more meager fare. A typical meal for what one employee sarcastically called "Class A" Tanzanians, the "officer-officer" types who worked as clerks and bookkeepers, might consist of a chapatti and some meat stew. And "Class B" Tanzanians, the lowest-paid workers including cleaners and unskilled laborers, would receive only *ugali* and cabbage. These "junior" staff members were also served in an area that was separate from the senior staff canteen.[18] In this worker's view, the claim that the privilege to use the "senior" staff dining hall was restricted to upper-level management was belied by the fact that some of the most recently hired and least experienced staff members, a group of young white expatriates who supervised rural safari camps, also took their meals there. In the eyes of my informant, the segregated nature of the dining arrangements revealed racist intent rather than the privileges of seniority, although he readily agreed that the two were not unrelated.

I was curious to know how accurate this account was, so I asked Dominic S., a South African employee who worked on the site, if he could verify the worker's story. He explained:

> It's part truth and part fiction, as well. But there is part truth to it . . . Yeah, the "whites-only" lunch has black Tanzanians in there as well, but few and high up on the ladder. But it's true: [the menu] is just huge and amazing . . . But the next, the junior staff, it's not quite that bad. It's not just *ugali* and cabbage, you know. There's some meat and . . . I mean, I've got no interest in defending it or whatever. But what it is, is people's perceptions. Whether it's real or not, it's people's perceptions. I mean that's what counts.[19]

Perceptions of the recreational side of the complex were similarly mixed. First, with the exception of the sports pub, and, on special occasions, the sports fields, access to the exercise equipment, the pool, and ball courts was restricted to paying members.[20] Even among those who frequented the sports bar and the other restaurants, the vast majority of patrons were either *wazungu* or *makaburu*. The club accordingly acquired a reputation in town as a high-profile white spot. Indeed, my research revealed that shortly after it opened, the site was under close surveillance by Tanzanian authorities who were concerned that club managers might be illegally discriminating against Tanzanians.

In fact, the "invitation-only" club membership was not all white. Several multiracial families were included, and a number of highly placed Tanzanians, including members of Parliament, were also invited to join. According to one of the facility's managers, the carefully constructed multiracial, but class-stratified, membership profile was all part of the club's original design. Senior staff members of the different firms were asked to list friends and acquaintances who they felt would be good additions to the club. The plan was to cap enrollment to make sure that the club's facilities would not be overtaxed. An annual fee was to be assessed at roughly $40 to $50 per month per individual, or $75 per family. Ideally, according to the manager, the club would have a mixed membership but not one that provided such easy access that it would undermine the club's security:

> We're going to send out invitations and see what sort of response we get. Some people will accept our invitation, and others will reject it. It's not going to be some all-expatriate club, some sort of exclusive thing. It's not going to be like that at all . . . At the same time, we want it to be the sort of place where the members can enjoy themselves. We don't want it to be the sort of place where a woman has to worry about having her purse stolen while she sits at the pool, that sort of thing.[21]

Though he did not say as much, the subtext to this statement seemed clear enough: the risk of having a handbag snatched could only come from poor, black Tanzanians.

My research contact Dominic shed additional light on how the new club's exclusive membership list was received in his own social circle. He reported that, when membership invitations first went out, his "privileged white middle-class" friends had jokingly asked him, "Do we have to speak Afrikaans to become a member?" We discussed this public perception of the club at some length. Dominic was somewhat confounded that it was so clearly marked as a "South African" venue, especially since the majority of the capital behind the associated companies did not originate in South Africa. He silently counted out how many South Africans actually worked there and concluded that only roughly ten of some thirty expatriate employees were South African, with perhaps an additional 300 Tanzanians working for the firm. "I guess that's a lot?" he queried somewhat doubtfully.

When asked about the recruitment strategy used to attract club members, he explained:

> DS: What happened was, letters went out to everybody in the larger community that was thought to be "suitable" for membership [laughs]. And so people were invited if they wanted to join . . .
>
> RS: Did you get a letter?
>
> DS: [jokingly] I put myself down . . . [laughter]. No, all staff, all *senior* staff are included.
>
> RS: Are included automatically?
>
> DS: If they want to, yeah.

He noted that the club had several Tanzanian members, but readily acknowledged that its social makeup was quite exclusive:

DS: Yeah, there were quite a lot of Tanzanian Tanzanians [*sic*], black Tanzanians. With the lawyers, and MPs . . . But yeah, very much an elitist thing, whether they're black Tanzanians or white expatriates, or whatever . . . It is going to end up being an elitist club. There's no doubt. It's not going to be open to the world. It's a country club, and that's what it's going to stay.

Beyond the issue of membership requirements, the facility itself was symbolically marked as a white space in a number of striking ways. For example, in the hallway just off the main dining room in the most exclusive restaurant on the property, there were two large portraits. One was identified by its caption as "Sir Horace Bryan, First Governor of Tanganyika Territory, 1920," and the other showed "Lieut.-General J. C. Smuts (later Field-Marshal the Rt. Hon. J. C. Smuts, P.C.). In charge of Invading Allied Forces in Tanganyika against the Germans in 1916." Jan Smuts was an Afrikaner military officer who rose to the rank of general and eventually served two stints as prime minister of South Africa (1919–1924; 1939–1948). By a quirk of historical fate, it was Smuts who was in charge of the allied East African Army that forced the Germans out of Tanganyika in World War I.[22] Smuts's significance in East African colonial history notwithstanding, the fact that life-sized portraits of an Afrikaner general and a British colonial governor were selected for display in a restaurant in Tanzania that was founded in 2006 is curious, to say the least. It is unclear whether this was some sort of bad joke or simply a marker of cultural insensitivity on the part of the facility's managers.

A similarly provocative set of decorations adorned the walls of the smaller sports pub in the adjacent building. Located on the edge of the club's full-sized rugby pitch and equipped with the ubiquitous flat-screen televisions, the pub itself was one of the premier sites for rugby viewing in the city. This was the sort of venue Koos, the young miner whose story is told in chapter 5, would call a "feel at home" kind of place, and it served as one of the favorite social venues for South Africans who lived in the vicinity.[23]

Three autographed professional rugby jerseys, two from the South African national team, the Springboks, and one from the Australian national team, the Wallabies, were prominently displayed above the bar. Coolers were stocked with beer brands (Castle, Miller) promoted by South African Breweries. A series of photos along one wall commemorated the history of rugby in Tanzania. That this is a white history was starkly illustrated in a team photograph from 1963, which showed fourteen white men in rugby uniforms, ranging in age from perhaps twenty to thirty-five (see figure 8). The photo was accompanied by newspaper clippings detailing match results between the team from Arusha, shown in the photo, and four other teams that comprised the rest of the informal league, two from Tanganyika (Moshi and Dar es Salaam), and two from Kenya (Nairobi and Mombasa). The names of the players included in the press accounts—Van Rooyen, Pretorius, Mallinson—provided evidence of the South African families that lived in the area in the 1960s (see chapter 1).

Two other photos showed a member of one of the long-time American missionary families in action on the rugby pitch (figure 9). The first depicted him as a young man in 1975, and the second showed him as a grizzled old veteran lining up for a scrum in 2006. The gap between the photos was significant. Although rugby had been the province of white settler and missionary families in East Africa for nearly a century (see Peligal 1999), it waned in significance following the departure of the Afrikaner contingent after the 1967 Arusha Declaration. In part, this was due to the perception that rugby was a foreign game, played by whites only, and thus not worth promoting in Tanzania's public schools.[24] Only with the influx of foreign investors from South Africa and other rugby-loving nations after the adoption of neoliberal economic reforms in Tanzania was critical mass reached to revive a rugby league.

In the early 2000s, Tanzania established the Tanzanian Rugby Union, which ran a league consisting of several local rugby clubs, and fielded a national rugby side in regional competitions. Notably, the rugby union's rules stipulated that anyone who had spent just three years in Tanzania working on a residency permit was eligible to participate in league and national team competitions. Thus, approximately two-thirds of the players on the national side were white expatriates (see figure 10).[25] This situation gave rise to some unusual circumstances. For several years running in the mid 2000s, Tanzania's representative on the all-star rugby team organized by the Confederation of African Rugby was actually a South African national who worked in the Tanzanian hunting industry.[26] And at an international match against Rwanda in a subregional tournament in 2006, event organizers felt compelled to declare, "History is being made today!" As the announcer went on to explain without a trace of irony, for the first time ever the Tanzanian national rugby side was going to be captained by a Tanzanian.

Conclusion

An American woman living in Dar es Salaam in 2005 offered a revealing commentary on the re-racialized black-white social relations that took root in Tanzania after the end of apartheid. Like many of my research contacts, she was conflicted on the subject of South Africa's growing presence in Tanzania. On the one hand, she felt that the positive impact of South African investment in Tanzania was overwhelmingly obvious. In her view, South African capital had helped pave the way for a dramatic upturn in the Tanzanian economy. At the same time, it was clear that she was troubled by the emergent social relations she had seen in the wake of such investments. In an exasperated tone, she explained, "Any time you see a heavy-set foreigner standing on a street corner in Dar shaking his finger at, and berating, a Tanzanian, you know it's an Afrikaner. I just want to go up to him and tell him to *quit,* because he's spoiling it for the rest of us!"

This statement contains a number of elements that are worth examining in greater detail. First, the speaker implied that the image of a white foreigner berating a Tanzanian citizen on a street corner in Dar es Salaam was a common occurrence in the mid-2000s. The phrase "any time you see . . ." suggested that such encounters occurred often enough that they were readily recognizable. It also underscored the fact that the insensitive behaviors attributed to South Africans were not simply conducted behind closed doors in exclusive white enclaves, but were carried out in public for all to see. This was a stark reflection of how the social landscape had changed since the arrival of the *makaburu.*

The fact that she took exception with this practice and singled out Afrikaners as the primary culprits also reinforced the good whites/bad whites discourse described above. As it emerged over the past two decades, this discourse clearly staked out a moral position against undesirable behavior and worked to isolate the actions of racist whites. Such efforts to identify "bad" whites as the Other and treat them as outsiders constituted a defense mechanism among self-conscious "good" whites who worried that they, too, might be relegated to the "wrong" side of a split within the white community.

The speaker's desire to confront these circumstances—to tell the perpetrator to *"quit"*—was palpable. The reasoning behind her imagined intervention is what I find most interesting, however. The concern that boorish *makaburu* haranguing Tanzanians on street corners might *"spoil it"* for the rest of us" begs the question of what exactly would be spoiled if this behavior were to continue unchecked. Until recently in Tanzania, historical forces conspired to produce circumstances in which whites could feel especially *un*-self-consciousness about race, where the many unspoken privileges they enjoyed could go unnoticed and unchallenged, where, in effect, they could feel comfortable in their own skin. In contrast to the *makaburu,* they had never been automatically looked upon with distrust or viewed as an enemy; they were not routinely forced to *prove* that they were "nice" people and not racist. Instead, they were in a position to be judged on their own merits. All of this was at risk of being "spoiled" by the actions of newcomers who were, through their behavior, threatening to rewrite what it meant to be white in Tanzania. The stakes were high indeed.

The American woman quoted above stressed that the *makaburu* were spoiling things "for the rest of us." The use of this phrase begged the question of which "us" she meant. While she seemed to be referring to white expatriates who might be implicated in the actions of "bad whites" in Tanzania, her comment could also be understood in a broader sense: the poisoning of race relations in Tanzania has left all of "us" the poorer, Tanzanians and expatriates alike. If there was a hopeful sign in this situation, it lay in the fact that many South Africans living in Tanzania could not have agreed more with her statement.

Conclusion

In March 2010, the story about South African gemstone miners using dogs to subdue Tanzanians caught trespassing on corporate property reappeared in the Tanzanian press (see chapter 4). The article, which bore the headline, "Police nab S. African who 'fed' Tanzanians to dogs," detailed the arrest of a former Afgem/Tanzanite One employee who was allegedly part of the original security detail involved in the incident. This latest account left little to the imagination in describing how, in the original confrontation, five armed security guards detained several miners on suspicion that they were intending to steal gems from the corporation. After placing the Tanzanians in a locked freight container, the South Africans allegedly "returned with three giant dogs and stood by the door with guns as the hounds 'chewed' the screaming Tanzanians [who were] later dumped at Mirerani Police Station bleeding" (Nkwame 2010a).

The author claimed that the accused had fled the country and had been a fugitive from justice prior to his capture, an assertion that I knew from my own research to be false. In actuality, he had worked openly as one of Tanzanite One's top managers for years until leaving the firm in 2009.[1] Exactly why police waited to arrest him is open to speculation, as are the grounds they used to justify his detention. As for the newspaper account, there is no doubt that the story as reported was untrue at least as far as the accused being a "fugitive from justice" was concerned. This distortion notwithstanding, the detailed account of the "dog mauling" revived the impression that South Africans were carrying out human rights abuses in Tanzania. In effect, this notion had become a "social fact" (cf. Moore 1981; Bonilla-Silva 1990). That is, it was so widely repeated in public discourse that it hardened into a kind of truth with real material effects.

Predictably, the article provoked strong emotional reactions from readers, several of whom posted comments offering suggestions as to how justice should be pursued in the case. The entire thread, reproduced verbatim below, offers a fitting postscript to the discussion in previous chapters:

> **Comment 1:** This guy has to [be] hanged in public, anything other than that is simple spitting on the people's face. But I won't be surprised if they (CCM) left him free, they worship white people.
>
> **Comment 2:** This Inhuman act happened in our own country, kaburu is kaburu Revenge an Eye for Eye. *Fukuza makaburu kutoka katika ardhi ya Bongo.* [Kiswahili; "Drive the Boers out of Tanzania."]

Comment 3: he merits his due, in fact a very strong punishment. the same thing i remember was reported in mozambique.

Comment 4: Even if he will be hanged. It won't be worth to what he did to our dear brothers who were just looking for their daily breath in their free country.

Comment 5: Well written and interesting saga. However I don't think Tanzania can do anything to this guy, they are afraid of foreigner yet mistreat locals. We need to fight for a new and more believable independence here.

Comment 6: let there be justice. hang them high and let them have same treatment don't let them get away with it. HOPE GRAFT DOES NOT TAKE PLACE. GOD [GOOD] LUCK TO THOSE WHO WILL MELT [METE] OUT JUSTICE.

Comment 7: I am a white South African. I lived in Dar and went to school there. I just saw my friend post this link. This is completely bonkers and sickening. This guy should be given the death sentence. I hope the general Tanzanian public don't generalize that South Africans are like this, because we're not! Peace be with the Tanzanians, who live in the most beautiful country![2]

The first contributor sets the emotional tone for this exchange: the accused should be strung up and hanged for his alleged misdeeds. The magnitude of his crime warrants a "public" execution because it is ultimately an offense against *all* Tanzanians. The writer worries that CCM, Tanzania's ruling party, will instead set the man free, because "they love white people." This attempt to racialize the conflict is especially damning in the context of the politically charged debate surrounding South African presence. Letting this man go free without punishing him would be like "spitting on the people's face." It would deliver the worst kind of insult, an egregious affront to the popular will.

The second writer underscores the unthinkable nature of the crime itself. This was an "inhuman" (inhumane?) act, a savagery. The statement that this incident "happened in our own country" conveys both sadness and outrage. These are the sorts of crimes, the writer seems to suggest, that once occurred every day under apartheid, but not in Tanzania where decency and respect for humanity were woven into national consciousness by Mwalimu Nyerere. "Kaburu is kaburu": Boers will be Boers. Violence, the author implies, is in their very nature; there is nothing that could be done to change them. The phrase "Revenge an Eye for Eye" issues a command: "Take revenge," the writer urges. Seek retribution in the manner called for in the biblical Old Testament. Drive the *makaburu* out.

The third writer suggests that the inhumanity of the *makaburu* is not confined to Tanzania, but has also been experienced in Mozambique and by implication throughout the region. The fourth rehearses the old colloquialism, "Hanging's too good for 'em." This writer draws attention to the specific plight of artisanal and small-scale miners through the use of an evocative malapropism. The phrase "looking for their daily breath in their free country," simultaneously invokes the miners' hand-to-mouth existence in the search for "daily bread" and a normative expectation that they should be allowed to breathe freely in their own country.

The reason it has taken so long to bring anyone to justice in this case, suggests the fifth writer, is that the Tanzanian government is "afraid of foreigners." Officials would rather deal with the political consequences of "mistreating" locals than risk losing favor with powerful international investors. This prompts a call for a "new and *more believable* independence" (emphasis added). The implication is that the government has abandoned or undermined the moral legacy of Tanzania's original independence movement, and that citizens have lost faith in the neoliberal economic reforms. This is due in part to the depth of governmental corruption, suggests the sixth writer. S/he wishes "Go[o]d luck" to those who would be brave enough to try and "[mete] out justice."

Read in conjunction with one another, these responses by Tanzanians to the latest report on the "dog mauling" incident are telling. Twenty years after Nelson Mandela's release from prison; fifteen years, more or less, since South African investors began relocating to Tanzania; ten years since the incident in question actually occurred—all of this time has passed, and yet the commentators react as if the alleged attack took place only yesterday. Clearly the *makaburu* presence continues to feed racial, class, and national anxieties in Tanzania.

The final comment in the thread brings the perspective of a young South African to the discussion. The writer describes living in Dar es Salaam and going to school there. S/he is thus a member of the new generation of South Africans, too young perhaps to have personally experienced the apartheid system in its heyday but certainly old enough to have felt its stigma as it manifested itself in the region in 2010. The writer describes being "sickened" by the report on the dog attacks and joins the chorus of those condemning the perpetrator. Sensitive to the ongoing political ramifications of such incidents, s/he feels compelled to make a plea that Tanzanians *not* lump all South Africans together. "Don't generalize," s/he begs, because South Africans are not all like this.

The young writer's implicit claim that South African whites are not all racists resonates with the complex internal dialogue within the South African expatriate community revealed in chapter 5. That this argument had to be made at all in 2010 is testimony to the fact that the "end" of apartheid is something that is still being negotiated not just within South Africa itself, where the process has been fractious enough, but also elsewhere in the region. As the evidence presented in this book suggests, at least some of the thousands of white South Africans who invested in, and relocated to, "Africa" beyond the Limpopo are still committing "apartheid acts" in the pursuit of economic gains.

Simply invoking apartheid calls to mind specific memories for Tanzanians who belong to a certain age cohort. For the better part of three decades beginning in the early 1960s, they were deeply engaged in the southern African liberation struggles. Under the leadership of Julius Nyerere, they gave sanctuary to refugees fleeing war zones, provided safe haven for guerrilla armies, and hosted innumerable diplomatic meetings and conferences. Successful pursuit of these goals required considerable sacrifice, and they put their bodies on the line through military and national service. Nyerere's fierce and principled rejection of aid from countries supporting the white-run regimes in southern Africa meant that they were also forced at times to defer their aspirations for economic development to the liberation cause. This is simply what it meant to be a Tanzanian: looking back, this group still feels a deep sense of national pride.

Life under Nyerere's socialist regime is not universally remembered with fondness, however. For Tanzania's neoliberal economic reformers, the ujamaa period is remembered less for its embrace of "family-hood," self-reliance, and political virtue, and more as a time when economic activities were subjected to heavy-handed state control. These Tanzanians remember forced relocations and having their personal assets seized by the government; they recall the extended period of painful privation in the 1970s and 1980s when Tanzania was effectively ostracized by the west due to its adoption of socialist economic principles. The legacy of the period in their view is one of national failure and unrealized dreams. It would be best if it could be forgotten altogether in the hopes of producing a more economically productive future.

"South Africa" enters this fundamental battle over Tanzania's past, present, and future in two very different guises: as the remnant/representative of the apartheid system and as a font of investment capital and putative partner in the pursuit of new economic agendas. Which "South Africa" gets featured in the debate surrounding its presence in Tanzania depends in part on which view of history Tanzanians adopt. Those who actively "remember," that is, choose to highlight, South Africa's apartheid past, naturally tend to view its contemporary presence in a highly negative light. They express an enduring antipathy against South African whites that manifests itself in xenophobia and racial animosity. For them, certain associations automatically lock into place whenever South Africa is mentioned: "kaburu is kaburu"; white South Africans are racist imperialists. The expectation of South African wrongdoing and presumption of guilt are omnipresent.

In a less reactionary vein, the refusal to let the legacy of the anti-apartheid struggle die has simultaneously helped keep certain progressive moral precepts alive within the public sphere in Tanzania. Even in the absence of Nyerere (and perhaps *because* of his absence), many Tanzanians feel an acute obligation to uphold the norms and principles he embodied. They are watchful and vigilant: "never again," they vow, will social relations like those practiced under apartheid be reproduced on African soil, least of all in Tanzania.[3] Mwalimu's saintly, abstemious nature is frequently invoked to help discipline contemporary politicians who would otherwise seek to enrich themselves through the power of public office. Critics' insistence on "remembering from below" (Pitcher 2006) thus represents an effort to shape the moral context within which South African investors and their counterparts in the Tanzanian government must operate. This remembering shifts the burden of proof onto investors' shoulders: it is incumbent upon the South Africans themselves to demonstrate that they no longer condone apartheid attitudes and practices.

Those seeking to promote a "post-socialist" transition in Tanzania, on the other hand, actively seek to suppress memories of the past. Proponents of this position are explicitly opposed to any representation of contemporary South African investors as being responsible for, or connected to, apartheid in any way. Mimicking their partners in the ANC government, they are committed to a "color-blind" economic future. In their view, to paraphrase one informant, it does not matter if foreign investors are black or white, yellow or green; national origins and race are not the issue. The issue is, which investors are willing to come, and what can be done to make things easier for them? Their view of history (and the future) is one that has been completely "de-moral-ized," stripped of the "vocabulary" necessary "for talking and thinking about wealth, prosperity, profit and exploitation" (Ferguson 2006, 72, 75–79). Their goal is simply to forge new economic partnerships, and if this entails "mistreating" a few locals in the process, then so be it.

The "de-moral-ization" of the region's political economy has done other work as well: it has helped rehabilitate South Africa's reputation and legitimize its growing presence throughout the region. Although South African capital has long dominated the economies of its most immediate neighbors in southern Africa, its recent expansion is unprecedented in terms of both its economic scope and its geographical extent. Seizing the opportunities presented by the end of the anti-apartheid movement's economic boycott in the early 1990s, South African industrialists and service providers aggressively pushed back the frontier of capitalist investment into "risky" parts of the continent, thereby opening up new regional markets to absorb the country's surplus production. Meanwhile, waves of white migrants made redundant by affirmative action hiring practices in Cape Town, Pretoria, and Johannesburg set out on personal treks to reestablish themselves in places that offered new economic opportunities, thereby relieving social pressures within the white community back home (Marais 2011).

Arguably, these trends had their most dramatic effects in countries like Tanzania that lay beyond South Africa's historic sphere of influence. As it unfolded in the decades after the end of apartheid, the relationship between Tanzania and South Africa grew increasingly complicated. The South Africans who showed up in Tanzania in the post-apartheid era were not the South Africans most Tanzanians expected to meet. A rural woman in northern Tanzania captured the popular sense of unease in a masterful bit of understatement: "They don't look like Mandela," she said. In terms of solidarity between Tanzanians and South Africans, it clearly mattered a great deal which face the "new" South Africa presented when it arrived as an investor: was it that of an old comrade in arms representing the progressive wing of the ANC or a white corporate manager extracting super-profits from the Tanzanian economy?

South African investments in Tanzania have generated intense introspection on the part of many of my informants over cultural identity, specifically over what it means to be African, what it means to be white, and what it means to be African *and* white beyond the borders of the old bastions of white power in the southern half of the continent. Similarly, my research contacts have been forced to reconsider what it means to be Tanzanian, what it means to be South African, and what it means to be an expatriate living on the continent after the end of apartheid. Each of these questions has been enlivened in the context of economic competition. The class fractions competing for neocolonial ascendancy and control of the Tanzanian economy are themselves indelibly marked by race, ethnicity, and nationality. The growing South African presence has only served to heighten the visibility of all of these divisions.

If there is a silver lining to this story, it derives from the fact that some South Africans at least have come to embrace the opportunity to reinvent themselves in Tanzania in new, more progressive and socially responsible ways. Tanzanians can take pride in the fact that prevailing social norms and expectations in their country have had a profound influence on many of the neo-settlers from the south, who repeatedly describe the opportunity to live and work in Tanzania as a genuine privilege. They especially value the opportunity to raise their children in a setting where they can grow up to be open-minded and accepting of diversity, an opportunity that they trace directly to the political and cultural climate in Tanzania and to its citizens' national character.

These more hopeful prospects notwithstanding, de facto all-white spaces continue to take shape in many parts of Tanzania, and that remains a cause for concern. While considerably more subtle than the practices of colonial governors or the architects of apartheid, who unabashedly organized space along ascribed racial lines, the contributions South Africans have made to Tanzania's changing social landscape have nonetheless been significant. Tactics of inclusion and exclusion have marked bars, restaurants, and clubs as "white spots" for prospective white and black clients alike. New owners seeking to cater to a white clientele have not barred Tanzanians from frequenting their establishments outright, but they have promoted norms and expectations that have encouraged white patrons to make these spaces their own.

In sum, the social relations being produced in Tanzania's white spots continue to unfold. Indeed, there is a multisided battle underway to shape the post-apartheid legacy in this former frontline state. This contest pits South Africans who are interested in forging a more open and mutually beneficial relationship with "Africa" against their compatriots who are instead focused on pursuing business objectives in the region. It also pits Tanzanians who seek to uphold the moral legacies of Nyerere against those who have abandoned socialist precepts in the interests of pursuing private gain. Much will depend on the tenor of ongoing race relations within the country. Will South Africans live up to or live down their stereotyped national image? Are they bent on reproducing white privilege or renouncing it? Will Tanzanians continue to respond to the challenges posed by the expanded *makaburu* presence in the region with skepticism and mistrust? Or will they seek their own forms of reconciliation with a generation of South Africans that is itself opening up to new ways of being in the region and the world? Given the continued expansion of South African presence, these questions are likely to reverberate across Africa for years to come.

Notes

Preface

1. The original Arabic usage of this term refers to "nonbelievers" or "heathens."

2. The general problem of how to relate to occasionally unsympathetic research subjects is one that is featured in a special issue of the journal *Geoforum:* "Behind Enemy Lines: Reflections on the Practice and Production of Oppositional Research" (Thiem and Robertson 2010). On the particular topic of ethical challenges facing white researchers who study different forms of white racism in Africa, see Steyn (2001), Hughes (2010), and Hammar (2010).

Introduction

1. Nyerere was a teacher before entering politics.

2. For a selection of newspaper articles in this vein, see Okema (2005a); Kihaule (2005); Kenge (2005); Jozeni (2005); wa Kuhenga (2006b); Fox (2003); and Ulimwengu (2010). See also a series of personal memoirs and scholarly analyses devoted to the exploration of Nyerere's moral legacy: Legum and Mmari (1995); Smyth and Seftel (1998); McDonald and Sahle (2002); Mwakikagile (2006); Askew (2006); Bjerk (2008); and Chachage and Cassam (2010). For an explicit discussion of how selective such memories often are, see Ulimwengu (2009).

3. Confino (1997, 1388); Olick and Robbins (1998, 110). For a vivid illustration of this point, see Ranger's discussion of the emergence of what he calls "patriotic history" in contemporary Zimbabwe (Ranger 2004, 218–20).

4. Cohen applies this concept to a case study of Slovakia. She notes that the primary object of a given regime's attempt to promote "organized forgetting" is to "destroy [the] link to an alternative world and alternative standards for judgment" (Cohen 1999, 39). In the case of Tanzania, this would apply to the legacy of Nyerere and the political norms and principles embodied in his socialist government policies.

5. Pitcher (2006, 89); see also Pitcher (2002).

6. Olick and Robbins (1998, 126–28); cf. Askew (2006); Pred (2004).

7. See the full discussion in Pitcher (2006, 88–89, 94–98).

8. See Adedeji (1996); Daniel, Naidoo, and Naidu (2003); SARPN (2004); Daniel, Lutchman, and Naidu (2005); Adebajo et al. (2007); and Miller, Oloyede, and Saunders (2008).

9. This concept was originally developed as a central tenet of the pan-Africanist vision of Ghana's Kwame Nkrumah.

10. As one critic jokingly put it, "They should call it 'KNEE-PAD.' Get on your knees and we might throw you some crumbs" (quoted in Orakwue 2002). For favorable analyses of NEPAD, see Games (2004) and Grobbelaar (2004); for more critical perspectives, see Bond (2002); Miller (2003); Lesufi (2004); Alden and Soko (2005); and Samson (2009). Miller, Oloyede, and Saunders (2008) provide a comprehensive summary of the related debate.

11. Shivji (2006b, 169–77). Marx identified the wealth extracted through the process of "primitive accumulation" as a precursor to the development of capitalism (Marx 1976, 873–942). The latest wave of investments by South Africa and other international actors has also been likened to a "new scramble for Africa" (Southall and Melber 2009; Carmody 2011). This term derives from the late nineteenth-century "scramble" by European powers to lay claim to parts of the continent that had not yet been colonized.

12. Bond (2004); cf. Miller, Oloyede, and Saunders (2008); Samson (2009).

13. Ahwireng-Obeng and McGowan (1998); Lesufi (2004); Alden and Soko (2005); cf. Adedeji (1996); Daniel et al. (2005).

14. Apart from the South African case, the best example of this phenomenon in Africa is China. Historically, China has occupied a privileged position within Africa's "moral geography" by virtue of having actively supported the southern African liberation movements (Bailey 1975; cf. Smith 2000). When newly independent landlocked Zambia struggled to find an outlet for its copper resources that would not flow through the white-controlled territories of Angola or Rhodesia, for example, the Chinese stepped in to help construct the so-called Freedom Railway linking Zambian copper fields to Tanzanian ports on the Indian Ocean (Monson 2009; see further discussion in chapter 1). The China of the 2000s is a very different sort of political and economic actor than the China of the 1970s, however (Brautigam 2009). Whereas the original forms of Chinese assistance were at least nominally tied to development goals and the cause of national liberation, China recently adopted a much more aggressive posture toward Africa. Its support for unsavory political regimes in the Sudan and Zimbabwe signaled its primary interest in the extraction of minerals and energy resources and the expansion of markets for Chinese goods (Power and Mohan 2008). Like the South Africans, the new Chinese investors have displayed a tendency toward cultural insensitivity and racial divisiveness. In Zambia in particular, a spate of industrial accidents and the violent suppression of local resistance to Chinese management has suggested that the Chinese are no more sensitive—or welcome—than South Africans (Fitzgerald 2008; Bower 2010; Bearak 2010). The two sets of actors have mutually reinforced the significance of national capitals in contemporary African political economy, and their combined effects have helped spur a resurgent economic nationalism.

15. For evidence of South Africa's growing influence in Tanzania, see Wahome (2004); Kasumuni (2005b, 1); Maro (2005, 1); "Young Entrepreneurs Set Up Own Business Forum," *Financial Times* (2006, 1); Semberya (2006, 3); "National Empowerment Council Most Welcome" (2005, 8); Madatta (2006, 1); Mbise (7 November 2005, 16); Mbani (4 June 2004, 13); Tanzania Breweries, Ltd., executive, interview with the author (1 December 2005); Mayallah (8 August 2005); Lameck (10 February 2006, 32); Andondile (2005); "Chopper to Help Scare Away Stray Elephants," *Citizen* (4 April 2006, 7); "Capturing Big Animals Is Big Business in S. Africa," *Guardian* (14 April 2006, vii); "Seeking Medical Services Overseas Is Unnecessary," *Citizen* (31 January 2006, 8); Makawia (2000, 5); Mwamunyange (2005a, 2); and Mande (22 July 2005).

16. Afrikaners trace their ancestry back to Dutch, German, and French settlers who began arriving in South Africa in the mid-seventeenth century. The first sizable contingents of British settlers in Cape Colony arrived in the early nineteenth century. Writing in 1997, Chege estimated that there were roughly 5 million whites in South Africa; 110,000 in Zimbabwe (before the recent purge); 71,000 in Namibia; and 45,000 in Kenya, the latter including many foreign passport holders (Chege 1997, 78). There are no reliable estimates of the number of whites living in Tanzania. The 2010 CIA Factbook estimates the population of Tanzania at just over 41 million; Asians, Arabs, and Europeans combined to account for less than one percent of that total (CIA Factbook, https://www.cia.gov/library/publications/the-world-factbook/geos/tz.html; accessed 9 November 2010).

17. See chapter 5. Hughes (2010) offers an especially insightful analysis of how whites negotiated an awkward sense of belonging in contemporary Zimbabwe by literally reshaping the landscape to better reflect their own aesthetic sensibilities.

18. For discussions of whiteness within South Africa, and the ways it has been reconfigured in the post-apartheid period, see Steyn (2001, 2004, 2007); Steyn and Foster (2008); Erasmus (2005); Nuttall (2001).

19. For studies of whiteness in former settler colonies outside of South Africa, see a general discussion in Chege (1997); country-specific studies for Zimbabwe in Hughes (2010) and Hammar (2010); and country-specific studies for Kenya in McIntosh (2009), Crilly (2009) and Uusihakala (1999). This body of research complements a series of earlier ethnographies and memoirs that provide rich historical background on the social circumstances experienced by whites under white settler and colonial rule (Crapanzano 1985; Kennedy 1987; Huxley 1968; Lipscomb 1974).

20. One could argue that the "negrophobia" that surfaced in the context of xenophobic riots in South Africa in 2008 has prompted an analogous re-racialization of "blackness" in that country (Gqola 2008).

21. The country became independent as Tanganyika in 1961; in 1964, it merged with the islands of Zanzibar to become the United Republic of Tanzania.

22. For a discussion of German progress toward establishing a white settler colony prior to World War I, see Iliffe (1979, 151). For details on the cross-cutting political economic interests of the European community in Tanganyika after World War I, see Ross (1977, 522–23) and Taylor (1963, 77).

23. As Erasmus explains, the notion of "race thinking" refers to those who treat "races" as self-evident categories that are ontologically "fixed and definitive" (2005, 24). The Germans, for example, relied heavily on rigid ideologies of scientific racism in their approach to their African subjects (cf. Dubow 1995). According to this view, there was a one to one to one correspondence between biology, culture, and history/place of origin as determinants of racial identity: "Each race had a distinct skin colour, physique, mentality, character, history, and cultural difference. Like animal species, human races represented different stages in the scale of evolution" (Iliffe 1979, 149; cf. Erasmus 2005, 9–10; Goldberg 2004, 5, 213–15). A full discussion of the history of race relations in Tanzania is beyond the scope of this book. See Taylor (1963); Iliffe (1979); Nagar (1996); Peligal (1999); Aminzade (2003); Brennan et al. (2007); and Glassman (2011).

24. See Nagar (1996). The violent 1964 overthrow of the Omani caliphate on Zanzibar saw a similar sort of backlash directed against Arabs (Glassman 2011).

1. Frontline Memories

1. A scattered set of land parcels in northern South Africa, Bophuthatswana (est. 1977) was not actually a contiguous territory. Its fragmented geography illustrates the economic rationale behind the homeland system: anything of value on (or under) the land was reserved for whites; the remnants would be left for others (Butler et al. 1977).

2. Pressure on the Pretoria government took several forms. The cultural boycott sought to withhold the opportunity for cultural exchange from the ruling white minority population in the hopes that a sense of cultural isolation would cause South African citizens to pressure their own government to adopt reforms. A similar logic applied in the case of the academic and sports boycotts, which enjoined all forms of contact with South African academic institutions and sports teams (for the latter, see Limb 2008, 935–40). The economic boycott encouraged consumers not to buy South African products and called for governments, firms, and individuals to avoid doing business in South Africa or with South African firms. Pension funds and governmental agencies were similarly encouraged to divest of their existing South African holdings.

3. Frank Sinatra notoriously broke the cultural boycott with nine concerts at Sun City in 1981, for which he was paid $1.79 million. Others who bought into the "homeland" ruse, or simply chose to ignore the boycott and take advantage of the lucrative paydays on offer—an average of roughly $250,000 per tour—included Cher, Isaac Hayes, Curtis Mayfield, the Village People, the Osmonds, Tina Turner, Glen Campbell, Sha Na Na, the Beach Boys, Brook Benton, and Helen Reddy. Among the internationally prominent performers who refused to break the boycott were Roberta Flack, who turned down

$2.5 million, Ben Vereen, Gladys Knight and the Pips, the Jacksons, and Elton John. For additional details, see Beaubien (1982, 5, 13).

4. A musician who played with rock legend Bruce Springsteen, Van Zandt subsequently gained fame and notoriety as the character Silvio Dante, Tony Soprano's right-hand man in the popular television series *The Sopranos*, which ran on the HBO network from 1999 to 2007.

5. The donation to SOMAFCO reportedly totaled $220,000; SACC received $160,000; and Transafrica and ACOA were awarded $119,000 each (http://richard knight.homestead.com/bophuthatswana.html; accessed 25 June 2010).

6. Thörn (2009, 417–19); Sapire (2009, 273–74). See SADET (2008) for a compelling set of detailed case studies on the national anti-apartheid campaigns launched in England, Ireland, Sweden, the Netherlands, the United States, Canada, Australia, New Zealand, the Soviet Union, Cuba, China, India, and several other member states of the European Union.

7. Sapire (2009, 283); cf. Macmillan (2009); Morrow et al. (2004); Khadiagala (2007).

8. Nyerere (1967, 9; quoted in Chaulia 2003, 155). The OAU was the precursor to the African Union.

9. Frelimo is a shortened form of *Frente de Libertação de Moçambique*.

10. For descriptions of these facilities, see "Nation Building in the Portuguese Colonies" (1969); "South Africa's Neighbors and the Refugee Problem" (1969); Barnes (1971, 13); Houser (1989, 193); and Ishemo (2000, 87).

11. The Soweto uprising was led by South African high school students who rallied in protest of a switch in government policy that required black and colored secondary school students to use the Afrikaans language rather than English in the classroom in several key subject areas (geography, history, science, and mathematics). Some 15,000 students joined a major march and demonstration on 16 June 1976, which was disrupted when police opened fire on unarmed demonstrators. Official reports indicated that some 50,000 rounds of ammunition were fired on that day alone, and that nearly 600 deaths eventually resulted from the widespread use of deadly force by the police. Fifty school buildings were torched in ensuing riots as some 300,000 students became involved in protest and strike actions. Mass arrests were conducted over several months, and thousands of students ended up fleeing into exile (Mafeje 1978, 18–21; Ndlovu 2007b, 324–30, 349–50).

12. Solomon Mahlangu was a member of the ANC military wing, *Umkhonto we Sizwe* (MK). He became an international cause célèbre when he was sentenced to death following a shooting incident that resulted in the deaths of two white civilians in 1977. Despite the international outcry on his behalf, Mahlangu was hanged by South African security forces in 1979. The 1,000 hectare land parcel that housed SOMAFCO was seized from a Greek farmer and nationalized by the government in 1966. Tanzanians who

occupied the land prior to the establishment of SOMAFCO were summarily evicted by the Tanzanian state (Morrow et al. 2004, 16, 114). The ANC's rival for ascendancy in the anti-apartheid struggle in South Africa, the Pan Africanist Congress (PAC), established its own presence in the Tanzanian towns of Mbeya and Ruvu. The latter settlement took root on a 440-hectare plot provided by the Tanzanian government and grew in a fashion similar to SOMAFCO (South African History Online, "PAC Camps"; http://www .sahistory.org.za/pages/governance-projects/organisations/pac/origins.htm; accessed 2 June 2010).

13. Morrow et al. 2004, 3; Serote 1992, 47–48). Many in the camps never made it back to South Africa but instead died and were buried on Tanzanian soil. In 2006, a group of South African traditional healers traveled to Tanzania with the goal of ritually "relocating" the spirits of those who had died in the camps via a "cleansing ritual." This effort was conducted in full cooperation with the South African High Commission in Dar es Salaam, and was widely reported in the Tanzanian press (Kato 2006; Mkinga 2006).

14. For example, refugees associated with SWAPO, the liberation movement from Namibia, were paid 21 shillings per person per day (Houser 1989, 247).

15. The commodities produced in Mozambique included peanuts, cashews, sesame seed, beeswax and Makonde carvings ("Frelimo Consolidates Power" [1971]).

16. Various interviews by the author; Chaulia (2003, 155); "Liberation Support" (1975); see further discussion below.

17. This total is in 1974 dollars; the exchange rate was roughly $1.00 = Tsh 14.

18. "South Africa's Neighbors and the Refugee Problem" (1969).

19. "The Portuguese Territories" (1968); "Swapo Congress in Tanzania" (1970). Ralinala et al. (2004, 482); Chung (2006, 315); South African History Online, "PAC Camps"; http://www.sahistory.org.za/pages/governance-projects/organisations/pac /origins.htm, accessed 28 June 2010; SWAPO Party, "Historical Background," http:// www.swapoparty.org/swapo_historical_background.html, accessed 22 June 2010.

20. Ndlovu (2004, 454–60); Abbott et al. (1986, 9); Bailey (1975, 44–45); Houston (2008, 32–37); Sellström (2008, 454, 462); cf. Kisanga (1981, 121 n 29). See Schleicher (2008, 1123–24) and Houston (2008, 32–34) for descriptions of how the distinction between humanitarian and military support often blurred in practice.

21. "Portugal Attacks Southern Tanzania" (1972); Ishemo (2000, 82); Khadiagala (2007, 198–99); Agola (2009); Rupiah (1995, 27); retired civil servant, interview with the author (28 October 2005).

22. Testimony during South Africa's post-apartheid "Truth and Reconciliation Commission" hearings confirmed that an attack on SOMAFCO was indeed planned by Pretoria (Morrow et al. 2004, 116–17).

23. See discussion of a prospective attack by Rhodesian special forces against the Zimbabwean military encampment in Mgagao in Martin and Johnson (1981, 247).

24. This route, which connected with the "Great North Road" in Zambia, was also used to ferry fuel to Zambia via truck, a tortuous journey that was known as the "hell run" (Griffiths 1969, 214; Martin and Johnson 1981, 131).

25. The symbolic contrast between the socialist railroad and capitalist highway is described in Monson (2009, 1–4; see especially her reading of the article "The Tortoise and the Hare," *Newsweek*, 25 October 1971, 56). Americans were particularly alarmed at the significance of Chinese intervention: "As China's largest international development project and the third-largest infrastructure development project in Africa (after the Aswan and the Volta dam projects), TAZARA represented the 'great steel arm of China thrusting its way into the African interior'" (Monson 2009, 2).

26. These included Britain, the United States, West Germany, France, Japan, the World Bank and the African Development Bank, as well as the Soviet Union (Bailey 1975, 45; Monson, 2009, 23–26).

27. Bailey (1975, 46). Many of these laborers were recruited through Tanzania's National Service organization, which gave the effort clear nationalistic connotations: "The principles of liberation and freedom, the themes of brotherhood and solidarity, the exhortations to build the nation—all of these ideals were employed during the construction period to legitimize and support the projects of railway-building and villageization" (Monson 2006, 122). See further discussion of National Service below.

28. The southern African rail gauges were set at 3'6", while the East African railroads were 3'3" in width (Monson 2009, 166).

29. "Links between Tanzania and Zambia Sabotaged" (1969).

30. ZANU is the Zimbabwe African National Union; ZAPU is the Zimbabwe African People's Union; the MPLA is the Movimento Popular de Libertação de Angola; SWAPO is the Southwest African People's Organization; the ANC is the African National Congress; and the PAC is the Pan Africanist Congress of Azania.

31. Houser (1989, 247); "Swapo Congress in Tanzania" (1970). The dominant cadre within SWAPO is in fact still known as "the Tanga group" (http://www.swapoparty .org/swapo_historical_background.html; accessed 22 June 2010; wa Nyoka 5 March 2010).

32. "Father Luis Alfonso da Costa Condemns Portugal's Terrorism in Mozambique" (1972); "ILO Invites Liberation Reps" (1973); "International Meeting Focuses on 'Collaboration' with Southern African Regimes" (1979); Reddy (2008, 111); Peoples of the World against Apartheid for a Democratic South Africa (1987).

33. African National Congress, South Africa's National Liberation Movement, "Julius Nyerere on the Boycott of South Africa." http://www.anc.org.za/ancdocs/history /people/nyerere/boycottsa.html; accessed 23 June 2010 (emphasis in the original). Nyerere would eventually issue a call for a boycott against British products as well to protest ties between specific British firms and the apartheid regime ("Cigarettes Top African States' Boycott List" [1970]).

34. Tanzania made the case for breaking diplomatic ties with Britain over UDI within the OAU as well. Although the member states agreed collectively to sever ties with Britain, only nine countries eventually carried out the threat. Of these, Tanzania was the last country to resume normal diplomatic relations with Britain in 1968 (see Kisanga 1981, 100).

35. In addition to Nyerere, other Tanzanians who were prominent in the liberation struggle included his foreign minister, John Malecela; the executive director of the OAU's Liberation Committee, Brigadier Hashim Mbita; and Salim A. Salim, who served as elected chair of the OAU's Special Committee on Colonialism.

36. "UN Votes to Seat Liberation Movements" (1972).

37. FLS meetings initially included Presidents Mobutu (Zaire), Kenyatta (Kenya) and Obote (Uganda), but their participation was short-lived. Mobutu and Kenyatta both proved sympathetic to overtures by the apartheid regime and gradually withdrew from these negotiations. Obote was eventually overthrown in a coup.

38. Although Angola formally achieved its independence at roughly the same time as Mozambique, the instability of the post-independence political situation in that country mitigated against its taking a more active role in the FLS alliance (see Khadiagala 2007, 36–40).

39. See Ishemo (2000) for an extended discussion of the interrelated nature of the region's liberation struggles.

40. See Khadiagala (2007, 23, 29–30) for a detailed discussion of the Zambian position.

41. Emphasis added. This statement, which was released by Tanzania's Ministry of Foreign Affairs in February 1971, is quoted in Ndlovu (2007a, 620).

42. For a detailed analysis of the demonstration itself, see Ivaska (2005, 83–107); for its connections to the Arusha Declaration and Nyerere's new education policy, see Bienen (1969, 556–57), and Sheffield (1979, 103), respectively. For the complete text of the Arusha Declaration, see Marxists Internet Archive, http://www.marxists.org/subject /africa/nyerere/1967/arusha-declaration.htm (accessed 6 October 2010).

43. Du Toit (1998, 27–31); Spear (1997, 88). The South African Wars are also sometimes referred to as the Boer Wars or the Anglo-Boer Wars.

44. Spear (1997, 88); see also Du Toit (1998, 43, 49–50); and Iliffe (1969, 60).

45. The roughly 300 Afrikaners living in Tanganyika at this time nominally controlled between 10,000 and 15,000 hectares. See Spear (1997, 88, 115–16); and Peligal (1999, 90).

46. Spear (1997, 13, 78); see also Peligal (1999, 179).

47. A variant targeted the Portuguese: *"Chinja, chinja, chinja Mreno"* ("Slaughter, slaughter, slaughter the Portuguese").

48. NGO worker, interview with the author (26 October 2005).

49. Southern Africa Committee, http://southernafrica.homestead.com/sacpubs
.html (accessed 15 June 2010).

50. Konde (1984, 234) reports that the RTD's external service offered broadcasts
in English, Shona, Ngazija, French, Ndebele, Chowe, Umbundu, Zulu, Sotho, Makonde,
Nganja, Chuaba, Herero, Afrikaans, and Portuguese.

51. Ntetema (1999). For a full discussion of the role of music in the service of Tanzanian nationalism, see Askew (2002); for a specific discussion of the radio broadcasts
following Nyerere's death, see Askew (2006, 32–37).

52. The Mecca reference is ubiquitous; see Askew (2006, 19); "Feel at Home, Comrade Zuma" (2008); wa Nyoka (2010).

53. Othman (2005, 3); cf. Campbell (2010, 51). The reference to Mount Olympus
alludes to the fact that the university is set on a hilltop in northwestern Dar es Salaam.

54. Retired civil servant, interview with the author (28 October 2005).

55. Journalist, interview with the author (24 May 2006); see discussion in Mwakikagile (2006, 105–6).

56. University professor, interview with the author (23 March 2006); cf. Tasseni
(2006b).

57. Among the issues that may have contributed to tensions between Tanzania and
the ANC are the fact that Tanzania once gave equal recognition and support to the ANC
and its chief rival in the anti-apartheid movement, the PAC; Nyerere's support for the
Frontline States' position on merging the PAC and ANC; and the relatively even-handed
approach the Frontline States alliance took to the Mozambican, Angolan, Rhodesian,
and South African struggles. Nyerere also briefly expelled Oliver Tambo and the ANC
from Tanzania in 1970 when Tambo refused to testify in a treason trial against political
rivals who were plotting a coup against Nyerere's government (Ndlovu 2007a, 644–46,
650–57).

58. South Africa.info, "2004 National Orders Awards." http://www.southafrica
.info/about/people/nationalorders2004.htm (accessed 21 June 2010).

59. The Presidency, Republic of South Africa, "The Order of the Companions
of O. R. Tambo," http://www.thepresidency.gov.za/pebble.asp?relid=775 ; accessed 3
December 2011.

60. Shopkeeper, interview with the author (16 November 2005).

61. Newly elected South African president Jacob Zuma was similarly apologetic
during a trip to Tanzania shortly thereafter. Crush (2000, 2008); Neocosmos (2008);
Hassim et al. (2008); Dodson (2010); Oyugah and Mwambungu (2008); Kisembo and
Sadalla (2008); "South Africa's Xenophobic Attacks" (2008).

62. As Askew notes, Tanzania's national anthem, *"Mungu ibariki afrika"* (Kiswahili; "God bless Africa"), shares the same tune as the South African anthem, as do the
anthems of Zimbabwe, Zambia, and Namibia. This symbolic bond expressed through

music is seen "as a sign of their continued allegiance to each other, to Africa and to socialist brotherhood" (Askew 2006, 19 n. 8).

63. Wa Lutenango (2008). The notion that these attacks are simply an expression of xenophobia has been challenged. For a detailed and insightful analysis of the events of 2008, see Hassim et al. (2008).

2. Invasion

1. Roaming services allow cell phone users traveling outside the range of their home networks to tap into local services when making calls. Thus, a foreign tourist or business traveler could rely on local Vodacom connections to stay in touch with people abroad. The availability of such services in Tanzania is one indication of how South African capital has helped tie Tanzania into broader global economic networks.

2. Bandawe (2006); Southern African Regional Poverty Network (2004); Gibbon (1999).

3. Quoted in Moses (2002). The reference to "partnership" here is a deliberate allusion to the New Economic Partnership for African Development, or NEPAD, a regional economic development initiative strongly backed by South Africa's ANC government, which is itself quite controversial (cf. Kivamwo 2006). Mwapachu discusses Mkapa's views toward South Africans in greater detail. Somewhat remarkably, he suggests that Nyerere, too, would want Tanzanians to stop vilifying South Africans: "Yet some Tanzanians would dare insult South African investments and even use derogatory words like 'Makaburu' (Boers) to describe the investors from South Africa. Tanzanians who are concerned about their development should seriously ask who are behind such machinations and whose interests do they serve? Mwalimu Nyerere would be restless where he lies if such people would lead Tanzania" (Mwapachu 2005, 25).

4. Naidu and Lutchman 2004; Daniel et al. 2005; Rumney and Pingo 2004; cf. Toroka 2006, 12.

5. "South African Firms Seen as 'Imperialists'" (2006); see Daniel et al. (2005), Naidu and Lutchman (2004), Hudson (2007), Miller, Oloyode, and Saunders (2008), and Hall (2011) for detailed analysis of South African investment patterns throughout the region.

6. Anglo American and SAB Miller were joined by Old Mutual and Didata in relocating to London in 1999 (*Business Report* [S. Africa], http://www.busrep.co.za/index .php?fSectionId=563&fArticleId=4113952; accessed 29 May 2009).

7. Examples of such firms in Tanzania include the mining company Tanzanite One (see chapter 4), which is based in Bermuda, and the Tanganyika Plantation Company (see chapter 2), which is registered in Mauritius.

8. Indeed, much the same attitude is taken by the majority in South Africa who see the benefits of the BEE program being concentrated in the hands of a small and privileged elite (Iheduru 2004; Southall 2007).

9. Miller (2003); Lesufi (2004); Alden and Soko (2005); Samson (2009). See note 3 above.

10. South African High Commission representative, interview with the author (23 May 2006).

11. Graham (2003); Itano (2003); Games (2004); see also Stoddard (2003).

12. "Africa Offers Rich Pickings for the Brave" (2005); Stoddard (2003).

13. Advertisement appearing in *African Business,* June 1997, 8.

14. Author field notes (24 March 2006).

15. Financial consultant, interview with the author (26 August 2005).

16. Financial services executive, interview with the author (13 September 2005); cf. Rose (2005b).

17. Wakabi (2000); cf. Njau (2001); "Investors Wary of Southern Africa" (2002). See also "The Divide Widens" (1999), which details the fact that Tanzania was rated eighth in the world among preferred destinations for mining capital investment in a survey of mining executives, following only South Africa (fifth) and Ghana (seventh) among African countries.

18. Wakabi (2000); Daniel et al. (2003); Gibbon (1999); Rwambali et al. (2000); Njau (2001); Waigama (2008); author's field notes (1997–2007). The airlines partnership and electric utility management contract were subsequently dissolved (see chapter 3).

19. French (1995); Swarns (2002); cf. Bond (2004).

20. "World Business Leaders Laud Africa Growth Prospects" (2005), 1. See also Itano (2003).

21. Author field notes (7 November 2005); cf. Gibson (2003).

22. South African working in the Tanzanian restaurant industry, interview with the author (10 November 2005).

23. Author field notes (various dates, 2004).

24. Even though key assets were often "jointly" held, the real decision-making authority typically remained in the hands of the South African partner, as the case of the ill-fated joint operating agreement between Air Tanzania and South African Airways demonstrated (see chapter 3).

25. From 1990 to 2004, the UK invested in 255 projects worth Tsh 325 billion, which represented 23 percent of incoming FDI. In comparison, South Africa invested in 42 projects worth Tsh 142 billion, accounting for 10 percent of the FDI over the same period (Machumu 2001, 4; cf. Sebastian 2006, 11).

26. South Africa accounted for 23 percent of all incoming FDI in that year (Tanzanian Investment Center 2004).

27. The UAE represented 13 percent of imports; Japan, 12 percent; China, 11 percent; and India, 10 percent over the same period (Mutakyahwa 2007, 5–6).

28. Author field notes (23 March 2006).

29. Representative of the South African High Commission, interview with the author (23 May 2006).

30. SABF representative, interview with the author (10 November 2005).

31. Rupert Pardoe, quoted in Swarns (2002).

32. In Kiswahili, the term *rukhsa*, a variant of the word *ruhusa*, refers to permissions, liberties, freedoms, or licenses.

33. "Country Fact Sheet: United Republic of Tanzania," http://www.unctad.org/ (accessed 25 February 2009); cf. "Planning Minister's Speech 2006–2007" (2006).

34. The reforms included the National Investment Act (1990); Loans and Advances (1991); Banking and Financial Institutions Act (1992); Foreign Exchange (1992); Public Corporation Act (1992); Public Corporation Act Amendment (1993); Capital Market and Securities Act No. 5 (1994 and 1997 amendment); Tanzanian Investment Act (1997); Financial Laws (1997); Privatization Trust (1997); Mining Act (1998); Land Act (1999); Labor Institutions Act (2003); Employment and Labor Relations Act (2003); and Land Act Amendment (2003) (TIC 2005).

35. World Bank (2010); Redfern (2005, 8); Mwero (2005, 12); Kamndaya (2006a); Philemon (2005); Kisaka (2006b, 1). For examples of how these economic data are analyzed and repackaged for public consumption in Tanzania, see "Tanzania Tops Improvement Index" (2000), 1; Redfern (2000, 2005); Mwamunyange (2005); Kasumuni (2005a); Munaita (2006); and Gumbo (2006).

36. "Tanzania Tops Improvement Index" (2000, 1); cf. Redfern (2005, 8); Mwamunyange (2005c, 29).

37. After pledging to retain all of its employees, NBC quickly implemented a "voluntary redundancy package" to buy out existing workers (Mwakisyala 2000, 3; Rwambali 2000c, 1). See discussion in Bwire and Lazaro (2003); Orute (2004).

38. "Workers at Tanzania's Largest Bank End Strike" (2002); Mwamunyange (2003); "Union Tells NBC to Pay $3.6m Terminal Dues or Face Strike" (2005); Mosoba (2005, 1); Tarimo, (2006, 1).

39. "Moshi Sugar Plant Set Ablaze Again: Officials Suspect Arson" (2007).

40. Tanzanian executive working in a South African-owned firm, interview with the author (1 December 2005).

41. Tanzanian executive working in a South African-owned firm, interview with the author (1 December 2005).

42. Tanzanian executive working in a South African-owned firm, interview with the author (1 December 2005).

3. Fault Lines

1. For EAB, this meant aggressively pushing its venerable "Tusker" brand into the Tanzanian and South African markets, as well as Guinness Stout, for which it had local brewing and distribution rights through its parent company, the brewing and distill-

ing giant Diageo, which acquired a controlling share in EAB in 1998. SAB countered by introducing "Castle Premium Lager" and "Castle Milk Stout" into the Kenyan market (Otieno and Tagama 1999). A similar competition between SAB and a Namibian brewer is described in Mager (2010, 125–28).

2. Ashurst (2000); "Deal Ends East African 'Beer War'" (2002); Mwakisyala (27 May 2002); "Castle Brewery Closes in Kenya" (2002); cf. Kyaruzi (2000).

3. Associated Breweries, also known as Serengeti Breweries, held licensing agreements to brew and distribute the well-known Belgian brand Stella Artois and the Danish nonalcoholic product Vitamalt Plus (Super Brands East Africa, http://www.superbrands eastafrica.com/volume1/index.html; accessed 1 December 2010). The firm was acquired by Diageo/EABL in 2010 in the latest salvo in the ongoing East African beer wars.

4. "Price Tag on National Brand Names" (2006).

5. The idea that the TBL fountain had destroyed the bucolic character of the roundabout is belied by the fact that the site was already completely ringed with full-sized billboards and other commercial advertisements.

6. TBL executive, interview with the author (1 December 2005).

7. Cf. McNeil (1997, D1). The firm has recently been rebranded as "&Beyond Africa"; see And Beyond Africa, http://www.andbeyondafrica.com/ (accessed 9 June 2009).

8. And Beyond Africa; http://www.andbeyondafrica.com/ (accessed 1 December 2010).

9. Author field notes (15 September 2005).

10. South African tour operator, interview with the author (8 September 2005).

11. Author field notes (May 2004).

12. South African hunter, interview with the author (26 October 2005). The Selous Game Reserve in southern Tanzania is the largest protected area in Africa. It is prized in particular for its "wild" conditions and attracts a steady stream of hunters from the south. This characterization is ironic given the Selous's anthropogenic origins (Neumann 2001).

13. Lyimo (2005, 22); cf. Mgwabati (2006); Nestory (2005); Bwire and Lazaro (2003).

14. "IMF Warns Tanzania Over 'Too Many Economic Zones'" (2006).

15. Professor N, University of Dar es Salaam, interview with the author (23 May 2006). The COSTECH building was repainted in 2006. All of the other giant Vodacom logos were removed from buildings in Dar es Salaam in 2011 following the purchase of Vodacom by Britain's Vodaphone, whose logo is red (cf. Moholi 2011).

16. In its first decade, the firm enrolled nearly 6 million subscribers in Tanzania ("Vodacom Tanzania Seeks 150 Million to Boost Capital" [2009]).

17. Focus group data (20 October 2005).

18. Shoprite Holdings; http://www.shopriteholdings.co.za/ (accessed 13 May 2009); cf. Miller (2005, 2006, 2008); Miller, Nel and Hampwaye (2008).

19. Author field notes (19 August 2005).

20. Author field notes (22 March 2006). The hotel industry has come under similar fire; cf. Kanyabwoya (2006, 13).

21. South African hunter, interview with the author (26 October 2005).

22. Author field notes (February 2006).

23. "BoT Twin Towers Construction Costs: Revealed, Auditors Were Kept in the Dark" (2007).

24. Op. cit.

25. "BoT Twin Towers to Cost Over Sh 200 bn" (2006).

26. "BoT Twin Towers Construction Costs" (2007).

27. "Economic Reforms Must Benefit Ordinary People" (2005).

28. Kamndaya and Luhwago (2006, 7); Msombeli (2006a, 8); Madatta and Masondore (2005, 1).

29. Sebastian (2006a, 6); Joel (2005).

30. Nestory (2006, 6); cf. Lyimo (2006b, 7).

31. Nestory (2006, 6); Rutaiwa (2006, 9); cf. wa Kuhenga (2006a, 4).

32. See Lyimo (2006b, 7), and the editorial cartoon published in *The Guardian* newspaper in Dar es Salaam, 29 March 2006, 6.

33. Kamndaya and Luhwago (2006, 1, 7); "Yes, NetGroup Must Go" (2006); Mosoba and Amos (2006, 1–2); Kisaka (2006a, 1–2); Mande (2006, 5); Mosoba and Dickson (2006, 1–2).

34. Kizigha (2006a, 3). The abandonment of ATCL's IATA flight code became a major impediment to ATCL's ability to resume service as an independent airline when the partnership with SAA was dissolved in 2006 (Mosoba 2006, 10, 19; see discussion in "Why ATC-SAA Deal Failed to Take Off from Start" 2006, 9).

35. Kizigha (2006b, 3); Mosoba (2009); Kisembo (2004).

36. NGO representative, interview with author (25 November 2005).

37. Author field notes (1 March 2006).

38. Uledi Mussa, Ministry of Trade and Industry, presentation delivered to the Monthly Development Workers Learning Seminar, Hakikazi Catalyst (19 August 2005).

39. "Young Entrepreneurs Set Up Own Business Forum" (2006).

40. Op. cit., 2.

41. For analysis of this program see Iheduru (2004); Southall (2007); Freund (2007).

42. Tanzanian businesswoman, interview with the author (24 March 2006); cf. Mbogoro (2006).

43. Asian Tanzanian gem buyer, interview with the author (24 May 2007).

44. "Tanzania Breweries Set to Announce Double-digit Growth" (2009); Mushi (2008); Awett (2004); Semberya (2005, 3).

45. The "Most Respected Company" designation is determined by polling the chief executive officers of nearly 300 business firms throughout East Africa.

46. Rwambali and Edwin (2005, 2); Kitabu (2006, i); Kazingumbe (2006, 12). In that same year, another recent corporate acquisition by South Africans, DPI Simba Plastics, also won its class in the "Manufacturer of the Year" competition (Rwambali and Edwin 2005, 2).

47. Ngahemera (2006a, 5); cf. Ngahemera (2006b, 10); "Dar Sugar Firm to Spend $26 m on Factory Expansion" (2005); Temba (2006, 6). The Kilombero Sugar Company's output rose from 29,000 tons (1998) to 126,000 tons (2004) (H.E. Kavishe, Parastatal Sector Reform Commission, presentation delivered to the Monthly Development Workers Learning Seminar, Hakikazi Catalyst, 18 November 2005); Tanganyika Planting Company, a South African–managed sugar firm saw production increase from 34,900 tons in 1999 before privatization to 55,000 tons in 2002 (Nyamaume 2003).

48. Waigama (2008). Tanga Cement is a branch of Holcim SA, the South African subsidiary of the Swiss cement industry giant, Holcim, Ltd.

49. Tanzanian businesswoman, interview with the author (24 March 2006).

50. Author field notes (31 July 2005).

51. NGO representative, interview with the author (25 November 2005); cf. "Give Tanzanians the Value They Deserve—Mengi" (2005).

52. Retired civil servant, interview with the author (28 October 2005).

53. Focus group data (21 October 2005).

54. Retired civil servant, interview with the author (28 October 2005).

55. Author field notes (7 November 2005).

56. Hart (2002); Mitchell (2004); Tsing (2005); Ferguson (2006).

4. Tanzanite for Tanzanians

1. Mererani is sometimes rendered as Merelani or Merilani.

2. "Great Strides in Mining Sector Development" (2005).

3. Roe and Essex (2009, 17) report that Tanzania took in $5.94 billion in FDI between 2000 and 2009, with over $2 billion of this total attributable to the mining sector.

4. The South African–run firm Petra Diamonds acquired De Beers' stake in the Williamson mine in 2008.

5. ASM miner quoted in Mgamba (12 March 2006, 5).

6. "Bright Mining Future: Tanzania Leads the Way" (2007). See also Roe and Essex (2009).

7. Gumbo (6 July 2005, 1); "Critics Unhappy with 3 p.c. Mining Royalty Rate" (2005). Royalties for cut and polished gems have fluctuated between zero and 3 percent in recent years. The passage of a new national mining law in April 2010 significantly changed the way royalties are calculated, however. Previously, royalties were determined

as a percentage of net profits; the 2010 guidelines stipulate that they be calculated on the basis of gross earnings instead. As part of the new legislation, Tanzania will not issue new gemstone mining licenses to foreign companies. Existing agreements with foreign miners such as Tanzanite One were not affected by the new law, however (Ng'wanakilala 2010).

8. *Business Times,* 5 May 2006, 1; photo credit: Freddy Maro.

9. "Fiscal incentives provided to exploration and mining activities in the country include the exemption of import duty and Value Added Tax (VAT) on equipment and essential materials up to the first anniversary of the start of production, after which a five per cent seal applies. There are also legal provisions for depreciation allowances of 100 per cent; repatriation of capital and profit directly related to mining, and non-mandatory government participation." ("Mining Investors Happy with Legal, Fiscal Regimes" [2005], 10.) See discussion in Lange (2006).

10. Kamndaya (2006b, 3); "Review of Mining Sector Incentives Steady" (2007).

11. "Mwadui Sold" (2008).

12. TRA commissioner Harry Kitilya, cited in Jomo (14 January 2008). Cf. Curtis and Lissu (2008).

13. In 2007, Tanzania ranked 151st out of 182 countries on the UNDP's Human Development Index (see UNDP, Human Development Report Statistics, http://hdrstats .undp.org/en/countries/country_fact_sheets/cty_fs_TZA.html; accessed 26 October 2010.

14. See discussion in Kimaro (16 June 2006, 11); Lwinga (2007).

15. "Mkapa Says Investors Not Thieves" (2005).

16. The statutory taxes referred to here include payroll levy, "pay as you earn," withholding taxes, a skills development levy, import duty, and stamp duty, but exclude royalties. The costs of mine development included fees and permits for exploration and feasibility studies, legal fees, design costs, removal of overburden at the mine site, and the construction of processing plants, tailings dams, and other infrastructure (Mgamba 2007).

17. Quoted in Mgamba (2006, 5). Foreign investors were not alone in this view. A conservative Tanzanian newspaper columnist excoriated his compatriots for failing to appreciate the distinction between profit-making corporate investment ventures and development assistance: "Surely they aren't in the impression [*sic*] that the Johannes-burg firm is a branch of the World Bank, coming here as a donor organization? All the time that bureaucrats talk about privatization, the tonality they adopt and the way they evaluate results puts an analyst in the awkward position of trying to figure out if they are speaking about investors, or donors. And in a strict sense we don't notice such differences in the country, that it is [*sic*] our political culture to see 'aid' in everything that touches 'white people,' and at any rate, even if we started comprehending that investment is meant to extract a profit, we hate to hear that" (Mweta 2006, 10).

18. SAHC representative, interview with the author (23 May 2006).

19. Tanzanite Foundation, "Tanzanite Rarity," http://www.tanzanitefoundation .org/tanzanite_rarity.html (accessed 19 October 2010).

20. Most of the details in this account were taken from the Tanzanite Foundation website (http://www.tanzanitefoundation.org/, accessed 19 October 2010); see also Mmbaga (2006b) and the entry for "Tanzanite" in the International Coloured Gemstone Association's gemstone database (International Colored Gemstone Association; http:// www.gemstone.org/gem-by-gem/english/tanzanite.html; accessed 18 October 2010). Government records and contemporary newspaper accounts establish that the original tanzanite claimant was, in fact, a Goan Tanzanian prospector named Manuel D'Souza ("Hero of Tanzanite Rush Dies: Late Mr. D'Souza Made 'the Most Exciting Gemfind in a Hundred Years'" [1969, 2]; cf. "Tanzania to Tiffany's" [1969]). His original discovery was duly registered on 25 July 1967, and later upheld in a 1969 court challenge (*Gazette of the United Republic of Tanzania,* 8 December 1967, 823; 8 August 1969, 549).

21. Tanzanite One; http://www.tanzaniteone.com/ (accessed 19 October 2010).

22. In 2011, Tanzanite One was subsumed under a new corporate umbrella known as Richland Resources in deference to the firm's expanded mining portfolio, which now includes gems other than tanzanite.

23. ASM mining activist, interview with the author (25 November 2005).

24. In fact, Graphtan's original mining license explicitly included the right to mine tanzanite ("Samax Pathfinder" [1994, 347]). By 1996, when Graphtan liquidated its assets, some 6,776 tons of graphite had been produced on the site. Similar data on the firm's tanzanite output are not available, but scattered references in the trade literature make it clear that Graphtan was also mining high-quality tanzanite gems in significant quantities for the duration of its time in Mererani. See, for example, Coakley (1997).

25. Quoted in Nkwame (2004). These allegations notwithstanding, corporate documents and reports in trade journals make it quite clear that, in the case of the Afgem–Tanzanite One restructuring at least, tax benefits played a minor role in corporate decision making. Instead, the move was largely prompted by the desire to shift the firm's stock exchange listing from the rand-based Johannesburg Stock Exchange (JSE) to the dollar-based Alternative Investment Market on the London exchange. Most of the firm's business transactions were conducted in dollar currency. The strengthening of the rand against the dollar in the late 1990s meant that the firm's performance on the JSE had suffered, and investor confidence followed suit. Reincorporation allowed the firm to shift listings, improve its financial performance, and attract substantial new investment capital as a result.

26. In deference to the shared corporate history, I will at times refer to Afgem/ Tanzanite One, and at others to "the corporation" or "the firm." When I specifically mention Afgem, I am indexing the years 1996–2004; references to Tanzanite One pertain to the period 2004–2011.

27. Weldon (2001a); Mmbaga (2005); Ubwani (2006); Vegter (2006); "Tanzanite One Goes Public" (2004).

28. "Probe Grievances in the Mining Areas" (2005); Mlangila (2005); "Small Tanzanite Miners Should Be Appeased" (2006); Juma (2006).

29. Since returning from his ambassadorial stint, Mpungwe has notoriously become a fixture on the corporate boards of several South African companies with subsidiaries or large investments in Tanzania, such as Illovo Sugar (Tanzanian subsidiary, Kilombero Sugar), and Aveng Limited (LTA Construction); former Tanzanian parastatals acquired by South African firms, such as the National Bank of Commerce (SA parent: Absa Banks), Tanzanian Breweries (SAB Miller), and Air Tanzania (South African Airways); and South African firms entering the Tanzanian market as "green field" investors such as the satellite television firm Multichoice, a branch of the media giant Naspers.

30. Instead, they see themselves as competing against other colored gemstones— e.g., rubies and emeralds—and luxury goods such as Rolex watches and Louis Vuitton bags (Tanzanite One executive, interview with the author, 18 January 2006).

31. As Afgem CEO Michael Nunn put it, "We aim to double the size of the overall tanzanite market through a combination of demand and supply side initiatives, so we shouldn't make any inroads into the existing producers' market share in the long run" (quoted in Bailey 2002).

32. Tanzanite One executive, interview with the author (18 January 2006). While successful in these terms, the effort to promote tanzanite awareness in the South African market did run into at least one snag: prospective buyers were evidently smitten by the gem's beauty but complained, "It has a funny name. Can't you change the name?" (Afgem CEO Mike Nunn, quoted in Vegter, 2006).

33. "The Private Sector Agenda: 2005 Laid Solid Foundation for 2006" (2006).

34. Author field notes, 24 July 2005.

35. Toroka (2005, 2). An example of this vague usage appeared in a Nationwide Airlines magazine in 2007. The article referenced a photo of tanzanite on the magazine's cover: "It is found nowhere else in the world but in Africa. In its gleaming heart it captures the volatility of the African sky and holds the soul of the continent. Mysterious and fragile, Tanzanite represents the alchemy of Africa" (Nationwide Airlines 2007, 27).

36. Genis (2006). In theory, the Tanzanite Foundation is an independent entity representing the entire industry, and some funding has come from gemstone processors and retailers to supplement the corporation's contributions. In practice, however, the firm's managers acknowledge that the strategic plans of the firm and the foundation are carefully coordinated (South African gemstone dealer, interview with the author, 19 May 2007).

37. Campbell (2002); Global Witness (2000); Grant and Taylor (2004); Le Billon (2001, 2006, 2008); Goreux (2001); Weber-Fahr (2002).

38. Tanzanite industry observer, interview with the author (18 January 2006).

39. Only stones two carats in size or larger, with distinctive color, clarity, and a high-quality cut were certified by the firm—less than one percent of the total (Le Roux 2004).

40. Quoted in "Relations between AFGEM and Small Scale Miners Sour," *The Thailand and Chanthaburi Gem Report,* 11 February 2003, http://www.thaigem.com /press_chanthaburi_gemreport_february_2003.asp (accessed 15 June 2006). See also Kondo (2001b); gemstone dealer, interview with the author (15 May 2006).

41. Tanzanite Sales Training Manual, Tanzanite Foundation. Manuscript.

42. See a detailed discussion of the firm's corporate donations in Lange (2006). Photos of the foundation's projects are available at the websites http://www.tanzaniteone .com/ and http://www.tanzanitefoundation.com/ (accessed 19 October 2010).

43. That is, they operate as middlemen and women buying gems from miners and selling them to master dealers in Arusha.

44. While 2002 census figures place the total population of all wards in Mererani township at 47,802, informal estimates by NGO workers active in the area in 2006 suggested the actual population of Mererani was nearly three times that large, or roughly 120,000 (author field notes, 1 March 2006). Seventy-eight percent of the population was located in Mererani ward while only 18 percent of the township population lived in Naisinyai (United Republic of Tanzania 2002).

45. Author field notes (16 May 2007).

46. In 2001, the residents of Mererani turned down an offer of nearly $30,000 from the firm, arguing that this one-time donation was a clumsy attempt to "silence" small-scale miners in advance of an upcoming high-profile visit by the Minister of Energy and Mines, during which he was scheduled to hear their grievances (Muindi and Majtenyi 2001).

47. The article goes on to claim that the principal source of revenue for the Mererani village council was a miniscule daily tax (US$0.15) levied on dozens of pool tables patronized by locals in town bars and restaurants ("Mererani Reeling from Poverty Despite Abundant Gem Wealth," 2005, 1–2).

48. Author field notes (1 March 2006).

49. Gemstone dealer, interview with the author (15 May 2006).

50. ASM mining activist, interview with the author (25 November 2005). The multiplier effects of tanzanite mining are repeatedly stressed in press accounts (Matinyi 2006; Gathura 1997).

51. For a detailed account of the effects of the post 9/11 controversy in the tanzanite industry, see Schroeder (2010).

52. Quoted in Weldon (2001b). The tactic of polishing one's own reputation by contrasting it with the "dirty" dealings of brutish African miners is one that has been perfected in the diamond industry (see discussion in Le Billon 2006, 788–92). Many

184 Notes to Pages 106–113

of Herbstein's allegations against the ASM sector are nonetheless well supported. In addition to providing manpower for simple labor tasks, such as toting heavy head loads of tailings out of the mine, children known in Kiswahili as *nyoka,* or "snakes," have historically been employed by ASM miners because they can more easily pass through narrow openings to plant explosive charges, and gain access to deposits that adults are unable to reach (Chachage 2007; see LoBaido 2001; and the film, "Gem Slaves: Tanzanite's Child Labour" [Integrated Regional Information Networks 2006]). Safety conditions in the artisanal sector have also been notoriously poor. Recurrent accidents have resulted in hundreds of ASM miners being killed by suffocation, flooding or mine shaft collapse (Ihucha 2006a, 2008; Moyo 2008; "Investors Wary of Southern Africa" [2002]). By contrast, only one accidental death has occurred in the corporate mine since Afgem first began operations on the site in 2000 (author field notes, 23 June 2006). Finally, ASM miners have been implicated in cross-border smuggling operations, which they have allegedly used to avoid paying export duties and obtain premium prices. These illegal transactions are said to have cost Tanzania millions of dollars in lost revenue each year (Phillips et al. 2001; Kulindwa et al. 2000).

53. Tanzanite Foundation (2005a, 74). At 60 micrometers, the "Mark of Rarity" inscription was invisible to the naked eye. "Preferred" jewelry outlets were issued special viewing devices—mini-microscopes known as "Tanzanite Foundation Viewers"—so prospective buyers could view each stone's branded pedigree.

54. See Lange (2006, 25) for a schematic drawing of these intersecting mine shafts.

55. Naisinyai villager, interview with the author (23 May 2007).

56. Muindi and Majtenyi (2001); Kondo (2001a, 2001b); "AFGEM Employee Charged with Murder" (2003); Ihucha (2005, 2006b); "Probe Starts on the Shooting of Small Miners" (2006); Mmbaga (2006a); and Nkwame (2006). For photos depicting shooting victims, see *Arusha Times,* 10 May 2003, 1, and 17 July 2004, 1; and *Guardian,* 10 February 2006, 3.

57. "Probe Grievances in the Mining Areas" (2005).

58. Senior Tanzanite One official, interview with author (19 May 2007). For a sense of the threat posed by trespassers to corporate mine security, see the graphic description of a fatal 2006 underground shooting in Nkwame (8 April 2006).

59. ASM mining activist, interview with the author (25 November 2005).

60. Author field notes (16 May 2007).

61. Gemstone dealer, interview with the author (15 May 2006).

62. ASM mining activist, interview with the author (25 November 2005); see also Mvungi (2006, 3).

63. Pastoralist activist, interview with the author (15 May 2007).

5. Bye, the Beloved Country

1. This cartoon was reprinted in van Rooyen (2000, 42).

2. Paton also acknowledged in her letter that "black people suffer more than the whites. They do not have access to private security firms, and there are no police stations near them in the townships and rural areas. They are the victims of most of the hijackings, rapes and murders. They cannot run away like the whites, who are streaming out of this country in their thousands" (Paton 1998).

3. University of Cape Town, Development Policy Research Unit (cited in van Rooyen 2000, 27).

4. Van Rooyen calls this violence "the civil war that never happened." He labels out-migrants "refugees" and "exiles," and problematically equates them with blacks who fled violence under the apartheid regime. He suggests that the threat of violence facing white South Africans in the early 1990s was analogous to circumstances facing whites in contemporary Zimbabwe or those forced from their homes by anticolonial uprisings in the Belgian Congo, Kenya, Angola, Mozambique, and Algeria. For Afrikaners, he argues, the challenges were even greater than these other groups since they no longer had an ancestral home that they would feel comfortable returning to (van Rooyen 2000, 2, 5–9, 73; cf. Steyn 2001). For more systematic analyses of the different factors driving emigration, see Mattes and Richmond (2002); Brown et al. (2002); Adepoju (2003); and Myburgh (2004). For discussion of South Africa's affirmative action policies, see Iheduru (2004); Southall (2007); and Freund (2007).

5. SAHC representative, interview with the author (23 May 2006).

6. Dr. Abdul-Kader Shareef, quoted in Gibson (2003).

7. I have used pseudonyms and masked and/or changed incidental details contained in all of these accounts to protect the identities of the individuals involved. "Piet's" profile is based on a series of interviews with the author conducted on 26 August 2005; 7 September 2005; and 2 May 2006.

8. Ramaphosa and Sexwale are among South Africa's leading black entrepreneurs. Both were once staunch ANC partisans. See Freund (2007, 667).

9. Based on an interview with the author (26 October 2005).

10. Based on interviews with the author (4 May 2006; 19 and 23 June 2006).

11. Financial services provider, interview with the author (2 June 2006).

12. Based on a joint interview with the author (8 September 2005).

13. Based on interviews with the author (7 and 10 November 2005; 22 March 2006).

14. The Sea Cliff is a South African-run hotel and shopping complex located on Dar es Salaam's exclusive Msasani peninsula (see chapter 3).

15. All government-run schools in Tanzania conduct primary education in Kiswahili and then switch to English in secondary school. This stands in sharp contrast to the Kenyan system, which uses English as its medium of instruction throughout all grades. In this regard, Kenyan nationals have an important advantage over Tanzanians in terms of employment opportunities with international firms.

16. Interview with the author (16 January 2006).

17. The phrase, "Dr. Livingstone, I presume," is credited to Henry Morton Stanley, an early African explorer, who is supposed to have uttered it upon finally locating Dr. David Livingstone, a fellow European, on the shores of Lake Tanganyika in 1871. See Hochschild (1999, 28–30).

18. The Kiswahili term *Bwana* can be translated as "mister" or "master."

19. This was a common theme. Another research informant characterized his own behavior as follows: "Well, back home we call it 'the Durban syndrome': it can happen tomorrow. I'm not used to it. I want it *now*. The other day, when I was leaving the house, the gardener had left the hose running on the ground while he was hoeing away at some plants. I told him I wanted him to tend to the hose, and he said he would. So I drove down the driveway, watching him in the mirror. And I saw that he wasn't picking up the hose. So I drove back to him and said, 'I told you to tend to the hose.' And he said he would, and I said, 'Now!'" (financial services executive, interview with the author, 13 September 2005).

20. Based on interview with the author (16 June 2007).

21. As one informant put it, "It was actually the exact opposite of what I expected. People here [i.e., in Tanzania] are basically a very happy people. The African in South Africa is sullen, demanding; everything had to be their own way. Here, as long as you're nice to them, people are very happy. It makes me wonder who it was that was so opposed to South Africa [during the anti-apartheid struggle], like maybe the top 2 percent [of Tanzanians] were opposed, and the rest didn't really have anything to do with it" (financial services executive, interview with the author, 13 December 2005).

6. White Spots

1. Author field notes (various dates).

2. Author field notes (19 August 2005).

3. Author field notes (10 August 2005); cf. Erasmus (2005, 9).

4. Author field notes (19 August 2005).

5. SABF member, interview with author (10 November 2005).

6. Retired civil servant, interview with the author (28 October 2005).

7. South African hunter, interview with the author (26 October 2005). The Limpopo River is often cited as the boundary between "First World" South Africa and the "wilds" of Africa itself. The idea that different mores are in play beyond the nation's boundaries is effectively captured in Goodman (1999, 91–102).

8. Author field notes (various dates).

9. Whether these tests were ever cleared by Tanzanian authorities is disputed. Applications submitted on behalf of the researchers to run drug trials were denied by the National Institute for Medical Research (NIMR), which oversees all medical research in the country. Instead, the researchers proceeded with their study on the

strength of the approval of military authorities and a provisional clearance by the Ministry of Health (which stipulated that further review was nonetheless required by the NIMR). See further discussion in Schoofs (2001).

10. Arenstein and John (2001). Upon returning to South Africa, a series of investigative reports revealed that the virodene trials had been personally backed by President Thabo Mbeki, a notorious AIDS skeptic, along with a number of other high-level health ministry and ANC party officials (Schoofs 2001; "The ANC's Virodene Backers" [2002]; Myburgh 2007). Despite widespread condemnation of their professional ethics, the researchers in question continued flogging their product on line a decade later (Virodene Pharmaceutical Holdings, http://www.virodene.com/downloads/Virodene_Executive _Brouchure.pdf; accessed 12 June 2011).

11. NGO representative, interview with the author (25 November 2005).

12. Peligal explains the ideological rationale that lay behind the race-conscious planning in colonial cities: "European medical theories used in urban planning explained that tropical diseases were induced by foul air, emanations from the soil, or the odor of decomposing vegetation. Banana plants, in particular, were thought to harbor mosquitoes, which, with other vectors, would transmit diseases from immune Africans to vulnerable Europeans. To be safe, Europeans were to live apart from Africans, on hills, and in well-ventilated homes built off the ground to avoid contamination. Although the development of quinine, mosquito control and public sanitation in the early 1920s should have recast such notions, the image of African filth and the maladies of dust prevailed throughout the colonial period [as] public laws of sanitation succeeded in displacing the 'unclean'" (Peligal 1999, 102–3; see also 101–13, 177).

13. Kironde (2007, 106–7, 113–14); Brennan and Burton (2007, 31). For a discussion of racial segregation on Zanzibar under British rule, see Myers (2003); Glassman (2011). And for a broader theoretical discussion of structural racism and its impact on urban spatiality, see Pulido (2000).

14. Asians, too, operated exclusive clubs; see Nagar and Leitner (1998).

15. Both of these sites have since closed.

16. The popular film *Invictus* (2009), which is based on John Carlin's book *Playing the Enemy: Nelson Mandela and the Game that Made a Nation* (2008), captures this connection quite vividly. The film's focus is the Rugby World Cup competition, which was held in South Africa in 1995. South Africa had just emerged from the sports boycott organized by the anti-apartheid movement (see Limb 2008). In a remarkably potent symbolic gesture, newly elected President Nelson Mandela donned a Springboks jersey in a stirring public embrace of the national side, which went on to win the championship.

17. Interview with the author (1 November 2005).

18. A chapatti is an Indian flat bread typically served with soup or sauce. Chapattis were originally introduced to Tanzania by Asians but are now consumed throughout the

country. Ugali is a doughy cornmeal porridge that serves as the primary staple food in Tanzania.

19. Interview with the author (26 October 2005).

20. The club hosts pick-up soccer and cricket games intermittently when the rugby pitch is not in use. And thousands of townspeople turn out for international rugby matches whenever they are scheduled.

21. Club manager, interview with the author (7 September 2005).

22. Smuts is, in fact, a controversial figure in South African history because of his support for Britain in both WWI and WWII (Afrikaners tended to support the Germans in those wars). When Tanganyika came under British control following the end of World War I, the colonial governors even briefly considered renaming Tanganyika "Smutsland," an option, Iliffe drolly reports, that was rejected because it was deemed "inelegant" (Iliffe 1979, 247).

23. In 2011, I visited the club during its Friday night happy hour, and found two or three hundred almost exclusively white patrons drinking, dining, and socializing at the club's sports pub. Meanwhile, there were several dozen Tanzanians playing soccer on the rugby pitch, beneficiaries of the club's community outreach efforts. As darkness descended, the soccer players left and the diners carried on. The two groups did not interact.

24. See "Rugby Makes a Popular Comeback" (2006).

25. The makeup of the team was cause for comment in the Kenyan press when the Tanzanian side traveled to Nairobi for a competition in 2008. Seven different nationalities—Tanzanian, German, Dutch, British, South African, New Zealander, and American—were represented on the Tanzanian national squad, which the Kenyan press sarcastically dubbed "the rainbow team." Three other countries—Fiji, Ireland, and Canada—were also represented on the under-nineteen youth team ("Tanzania: Rugby Team to Feature Seven Different Nationalities" [2008]).

26. A regional all-star team known as the African Leopards has been selected each year since 2005. It plays exhibition matches to help promote rugby in parts of Africa where the sport is not well established.

Conclusion

1. A follow-up article noted that Tanzanite One was keeping its distance from its former employee. As far as the firm's managers were concerned, the incident took place under Afgem management and was therefore none of their concern (Nkwame 2010b).

2. The original string of comments appeared in response to Nkwame (2010a, http://dailynews.co.tz/, accessed 27 April 2010). A subsequent article by Nkwame also prompted several responses from the public, but this time readers challenged both the claim that the accused had fled the jurisdiction and the implication that he was involved in the original dog attack. One reader lamented that the author was "taking journalistic

license too far. How can our media be taken seriously?" (Nkwame 2010b, http://daily-news.co.tz/, accessed 23 November 2010).

3. The phrase "never again" is closely associated with holocaust remembrance projects. It has also been widely invoked in South Africa in the post-apartheid period. Its most famous usage in the latter context is probably the oft-quoted passage in Nelson Mandela's inaugural address: "Never, never and never again shall it be that this beautiful land will again experience the oppression of one by another. . . ." Most sources tellingly omit the remainder of the sentence, which reads, ". . . and suffer the indignity of being the skunk of the world" (Mandela 1994).

Bibliography

Abbott, Peter, Philip Botham, and Mike Chappell. 1986. *Modern African Wars: Rhodesia, 1965–80*. Oxford: Osprey Publishing.

Abdul-Aziz, Bilal. 2006. "Govt: Major Gold Miners Are Swindlers." *Guardian (Tanzania)*, 20 June, 1–2.

Adebajo, Adekeye, Adebayo Adedeji, and Chris Landsberg, eds., 2007. *South Africa in Africa: The Post-apartheid Era*. Scottsville, South Africa: University of KwaZulu-Natal Press.

Adedeji, Adebayo. 1996. "Within or Apart." In *South Africa and Africa: Within or Apart*. Ed. Adebayo Adedeji, 3–28. London: Zed Books.

Adepoju, Aderanti. 2003. "Continuity and Changing Configurations of Migration to and from the Republic of South Africa." *International Migration* 41, no. 1: 3–25.

"AFGEM Employee Charged with Murder, Victim Buried in Njiro." *Arusha Times*, 22 November 2003.

"Africa Offers Rich Pickings for the Brave." *Business Day (South Africa)*, 9 July 2005.

African National Congress, South Africa's National Liberation Movement. "Julius Nyerere on the Boycott of South Africa." http://www.anc.org.za/ancdocs/history /people/nyerere/boycottsa.html (accessed 23 June 2010).

Agola, Edwin. 2009. "Mozambican Military to Visit Nachingwea." *Sunday Observer (Tanzania)*, 22 March.

Ahwireng-Obeng, Fred, and Patrick McGowan. 1998. "Partner or Hegemon? South Africa in Africa." *Journal of Contemporary African Studies* 16, no. 1: 5–38.

Alden, Chris, and Mills Soko. 2005. "South Africa's Economic Relations with Africa: Hegemony and Its Discontents." *Journal of Modern African Studies* 43, no. 3: 367–92.

Aminzade, Ronald. 2003. "From Race to Citizenship: The Indigenization Debate in Post-socialist Tanzania." *Studies in Comparative International Development* 38, no. 1: 43–63.

"The ANC's Virodene Backers." 2002. *Mail and Guardian (South Africa)*, 5 July.

And Beyond Africa. http://www.andbeyondafrica.com/ (accessed 9 June 2009).

Andondile, Oneti. 2005. "South African Black Rhinos Find Home Away from Home in Mkomazi Game Reserve." *Citizen (Tanzania)*, 2 May, 20.

Arenstein, Justin, and Ongeri John. 2001. "Virodene Quacks Amass Huge Debt." *Mail and Guardian (South Africa)*, 14 September.

Ashurst, Mark. 2000. "Breweries Compete for Market Share in East Africa." *BBC*, 8 September.

Askew, Kelly. 2002. *Performing the Nation: Swahili Music and Cultural Politics in Tanzania*. Chicago: University of Chicago Press.

———. 2006. "Sung and Unsung: Musical Reflections on Tanzanian Postsocialisms." *Africa* 76, no. 1: 15–43.

Awett, Nicodemus. 2004. "TBL Marks Tenth Year of Brewing Success." *Arusha Times*, 17 July.

Bailey, Martin. 1975. "Tanzania and China." *African Affairs* 74, no. 294: 39–50.

Bailey, Stewart. 2002. "AFGEM and Tanzanite—Match Made in Heaven." Available at http://www.mineweb.net/events/conferences/2002/afgem/33515.htm.

Bandawe, Beatrice. 2006. "Mbeki, Kikwete Push for More Balanced Ties." *Guardian (Tanzania)*, 9 April, 1.

Barnes, Barbara. 1971. "Frelimo—September 25, 1971." *Southern Africa* 4, no. 8: 9–14.

Bearak, Barry. 2010. "Zambia Uneasily Balances Chinese Investment and Workers' Resentment." *New York Times*, 20 November.

Beaubien, Michael C. 1982. "The Cultural Boycott of South Africa." *Africa Today* 29, no. 4: 5–16.

Bienen, Henry. 1969. "An Ideology for Africa." *Foreign Affairs* 47, no. 3: 545–59.

Bilks, John. 2000. "Why Blame South Africa?" *Express (Tanzania)*, 6 July, 5.

Bjerk, Paul. 2008. "Julius Nyerere and the Establishment of Sovereignty in Tanganyika." University of Wisconsin, PhD dissertation.

Block, Robert, and Daniel Pearl. 2001. "Much-smuggled Gem Aids al-Qaida." *Wall Street Journal*, 16 November.

Bond, Patrick. 2002. "The New Partnership for Africa's Development: Social, Economic, and Environmental Contradictions." *Capitalism, Nature, Socialism* 13, no. 2: 151–80.

———. 2004. "African Development/Governance, South African Sub-imperialism and Nepad. Conference on the Agrarian Constraint and Poverty Reduction." Addis Ababa: CODESRIA.

Bonilla-Silva, Eduardo. 1999. "The Essential Social Fact of Race." *American Sociological Review* 64, no. 6: 899–906.

"BoT Twin Towers Construction Costs: Revealed, Auditors Were Kept in the Dark." *This Day (Tanzania)*, 18 July 2007.

"BoT Twin Towers to Cost over Sh 200 bn." *Sunday Citizen*, 26 March 2006, 1–2.

Bower, Eve. 2010. "Zambia Mine Shootings Raise Tensions with China." *CNN News*, 4 November.

Brautigam, Deborah. 2009. *The Dragon's Gift: The Real Story of China in Africa*. New York: Oxford University Press.

Brennan, James R. 2007. "Between Segregation and Gentrification: Africans, Indians, and the Struggle for Housing in Dar es Salaam, 1920–1950." In *Dar es Salaam: Histories from an Emerging African Metropolis*. Ed. James R. Brennan, Andrew Burton, and Yusuf Lawi, 118–35. Dar es Salaam: Mkuki na Nyota Publishers.

Brennan, James R., and Andrew Burton. 2007. "The Emerging Metropolis: A History of Dar es Salaam, circa 1862–2000." In *Dar es Salaam: Histories from an Emerging African Metropolis*. Ed. James R. Brennan, Andrew Burton, and Yusuf Lawi, 13–75. Dar es Salaam: Mkuki na Nyota Publishers.

"Bright Mining Future: Tanzania Leads the Way." 2007. *Mining Review Africa* no. 4: 12.

Brittain, Victoria. 2006. "They Had to Die: Assassination against Liberation." *Race and Class* 48, no. 1: 60–74.

Brown, Mercy, David Kaplan, and Jean-Baptiste Meyer. 2002. "The Brain Drain: An Outline of Skilled Emigration from South Africa." In *Destinations Unknown: Perspectives on the Brain Drain in South Africa*. Ed. David A. McDonald, and Jonathan Crush, 99–112. Pretoria: Africa Institute of South Africa.

Brubaker, Rogers, and Frederick Cooper. 2000. "Beyond 'Identity.'" *Theory and Society* 29, no. 1: 1–47.

Bullas, Barbara. 2003. "Is Insolence Ground for Arrest? Shame, Shame!" *Arusha Times*, 30 August.

Business Report. "Business Report (South Africa)." http://www.busrep.co.za/index .php?fSectionId=563&fArticleId=4113952 (accessed 29 May 2009).

Butler, Jeffrey, Robert I, Rotberg, and John Adams. 1977. *The Black Homelands of South Africa: The Political and Economic Development of Bophuthatswana and KwaZulu*. Berkeley: University of California.

Bwire, Nyamanoko. 2005. "Nyerere Monument to Be Built at Kijenge Roundabout." *Arusha Times*, 15 January.

Bwire, Nyamanoko, and Happy Lazaro. 2003. "Privatization Renders 600 Jobless in Arusha." *Arusha Times*, 10 May.

Campbell, Greg. 2002. *Blood Diamonds: Tracing the Deadly Path of the World's Most Precious Stone*. Boulder, CO: Westview Press.

Campbell, Horace. 2010. "Julius Nyerere: Between State-Centred and People-centred Pan-Africanism." In *Africa's Liberation: The Legacy of Nyerere*. Ed. Chambi Chachage and Annar Cassam, 44–60. Cape Town: Pambazuka Press.

"Capturing Big Animals Is Big Business in S. Africa." *Guardian (Tanzania)*, 14 April 2006, vii.

Carlin, John. 2008. *Playing the Enemy: Nelson Mandela and the Game that Made a Nation* [later released under the title *Invictus*]. New York: Penguin Press.

Carmody, Padraig. 2011. *The New Scramble for Africa*. Cambridge: Polity Press.

Carstens, Peter. 2001. *In the Company of Diamonds: De Beers, Kleinzee, and the Control of a Town*. Athens: Ohio University Press.

Cassam, Annar. 2010. "Nyerere and the Commonwealth." In *Africa's Liberation: The Legacy of Nyerere*. Ed. Chambi Chachage and Annar Cassam, 66–71. Cape Town: Pambazuka Press.

"Castle Brewery Closes in Kenya." *Daily Nation (Kenya)*, 14 May 2002.

Chachage, Chambi, and Annar Cassam, eds. 2010. *Africa's Liberation: The Legacy of Nyerere.* Cape Town: Pambazuka Press.

Chachage, Seithy L. 1995. "The Meek Shall Inherit the Earth but Not the Mining Rights: The Mining Industry and Accumulation in Tanzania." In *Liberalised Development in Tanzania.* Ed. Peter Gibbon, 37–108. Uppsala, Sweden: Nordiska Afrikainstitutet.

———. 2004. "Tanzania at 43: Why Political Pluralism Has Failed to Enhance Democracy in Africa." *East African,* 13 December.

———. 2007. "Tanzania: What Is the Human Cost of Foreign Investments?" *Citizen (Tanzania),* 6 November.

Chaulia, Sreeram Sundar. 2003. "The Politics of Refugee Hosting in Tanzania: From Open Door to Unsustainability, Insecurity, and Receding Receptivity." *Journal of Refugee Studies* 16, no. 2: 147–66.

Chege, Michael. 1997. "Africans of European Descent." *Transition,* no. 73: 74–86.

"Chopper to Help Scare Away Stray Elephants." *Citizen (Tanzania),* 4 April 2006, 7.

Christopher, A. J. 1994. *The Atlas of Apartheid.* London: Routledge.

Chung, Faye. 2006. *Re-living the Second Chimurenga: Memories from the Liberation Struggle in Zimbabwe.* Uppsala, Sweden: Nordic Afrika Institute.

CIA. "CIA Factbook: Tanzania." https://www.cia.gov/library/publications/the-world-factbook/geos/tz.html (accessed 23 August 2010).

"Cigarettes Top African States' Boycott List." *Southern Africa* 3, 1970, no. 8: 9.

Coakley, George. 1997. "The Mineral Industry of Tanzania." Available at http://minerals.usgs.gov/minerals/pubs/country/1997/9238097.pdf (accessed 16 August 2007).

Cohen, Shari J. 1999. *Politics without a Past: The Absence of History in Postcommunist Nationalism.* Durham, NC: Duke University Press.

Confino, Alon. 1997. "Collective Memory and Cultural History: Problems of Method." *American Historical Review* 102, no. 5: 1386–1403.

"Country Fact Sheet: United Republic of Tanzania." http://www.unctad.org/ (accessed 25 February 2009).

Crapanzano, Vincent. 1985. *Waiting: The Whites of South Africa.* New York: Random House.

Crilly, Rob. 2009. "Thomas Cholmondeley Convicted of Manslaughter over Kenya Ranch Killing." *The Times (Kenya),* 8 May.

"Critics Unhappy with 3 p.c. Mining Royalty Rate." *Daily News (Tanzania),* 8 August 2005, 10.

Crush, Jonathan. 2000. "The Dark Side of Democracy: Migration, Xenophobia, and Human Rights in South Africa." *International Migration* 38, no. 6: 103–33.

———. 2008. *The Perfect Storm: Xenophobia in Contemporary South Africa.* Cape Town: Southern African Migration Project.

Curtis, Mark, and Tundu Lissu. 2008. *A Golden Opportunity? How Tanzania Is Failing to Benefit from Gold Mining,* 2nd ed. Dar es Salaam: Christian Council of Tanzania.

Daniel, John, Jessica Lutchman, and Sanusha Naidu. 2005. "South Africa and Nigeria: Two Unequal Centres in a Periphery." In *State of the Nation: South Africa 2004–2005.* Ed. John Daniel, Roger Southall, and Jessica Lutchman. Cape Town, South Africa: HSRC Press.

Daniel, John, Varusha Naidoo, and Sanusha Naidu. 2003. "The South Africans Have Arrived: Post-apartheid Corporate Expansion into Africa." In *State of the Nation: South Africa 2003–2004.* Ed. John Daniel, Adam Habib, and Roger Southall, 368–90. Cape Town: HSRC Press.

"Dar Sugar Firm to Spend $26 m on Factory Expansion." *East African,* 10 October 2005, 23.

Davis, Stephen R. 2009. "The African National Congress, Its Radio, Its Allies, and Exile." *Journal of Southern African Studies* 35, no. 2: 349–73.

"Deal Ends East African 'Beer War.'" *BBC.* 14 May 2002.

Deane, Nawaal, David Macfarlane, and Mungo Soggot. 2001. "Coal-fired AIDS Muti Tested on Soldiers." *Mail and Guardian (South Africa),* 28 September.

"The Divide Widens." 1999. *Mining Journal,* 22 October, 1.

Dodson, Belinda. 2010. "Locating Xenophobia: Debate, Discourse, and Everyday Experience in Cape Town, South Africa." *Africa Today* 56, no. 3: 3–22.

Du Toit, Brian. 1998. *The Boers in East Africa: Ethnicity and Identity.* Westport, CT: Bergin and Garvey.

Dubow, Saul. 1995. *Scientific Racism in Modern South Africa.* Cambridge: Cambridge University Press.

Duncan, Michael. 2005. "Prepare for Risk of Investing in Africa." *Business Day (South Africa),* 4 August.

"Economic Reforms Must Benefit Ordinary People." *Guardian (Tanzania),* 25 May 2005.

Economist Intelligence Unit. 2001. "South African Researchers Test AIDS Drugs in Tanzania." In *Country Report, Tanzania/Comoros,* 18–19. London: Economist Intelligence Unit.

Edwin, Wilfred. 2005. "Tanzania to Get Millennium Challenge Cash." *East African,* 21 November, 6.

Erasmus, Zimitri. 2005. "Race and Identity in the Nation." In *State of the Nation: South Africa 2004–2005.* Ed. John Daniel, Roger Southall, and Jessica Lutchman, 9–33. Cape Town: HSRC Press.

"Father Luis Alfonso da Costa Condemns Portugal's Terrorism in Mozambique." *Southern Africa,* 1972, no. 18.

"Feel at Home, Comrade Zuma." *Daily News (Tanzania),* 4 September 2008.

Feierman, Steven. 1990. *Peasant Intellectuals: Anthropology and History in Tanzania.* Madison: University of Wisconsin Press.

Ferguson, James. 2005. "Seeing Like an Oil Company: Space, Security, and Global Capital in Neoliberal Africa." *American Anthropologist* 107, no. 3: 377–82.

———. 2006. "De-moralizing Economies: African Socialism, Scientific Capitalism, and the Moral Politics of Structural Adjustment." In *Global Shadows: Africa and the New World Order,* by James Ferguson, 69–88. Durham: Duke University Press.

Fisher, Eleanor. 2007. "Occupying the Margins: Labour Integration and Social Exclusion in Artisanal Mining in Tanzania." *Development and Change* 38, no. 4: 735–60.

Fitzgerald, Mary. 2008. "Zambia Becomes Shorthand for What Can Go Wrong." *Irish Times,* 25 August.

Fleshmen, Michael. 1980. "Mozambique and Zambia: Solidarity at High Costs." *Southern Africa* 13, no. 3: 4.

Fox, John. 2003. "Liberalisation: Mwalimu Nyerere Must Be Turning in His Grave." *Arusha Times,* 5 July.

"Frelimo Consolidates Power." *Southern Africa* 6, 1971, no. 10: 17.

French, Howard. 1995. "Out of South Africa, Progress." *New York Times,* 6 July.

Freund, Bill. 2007. "South Africa: The End of Apartheid and the Emergence of the 'BEE Elite.'" *Review of African Political Economy* 34, no. 114: 661–78.

Games, Dianna. 2004. "The Experience of South African Firms Doing Business in Africa: A Preliminary Survey and Analysis." Johannesburg, South Africa: South African Institute of International Affairs.

Gathura, Gatonye. 1997. "Arusha: Hosting the Region's Hopes and Aspirations." *East African,* 20 October, 1–12.

Gazette of the United Republic of Tanzania. 8 December 1967, 823; 8 August 1969, 549. Dar es Salaam: Government Printer.

Genis, Robert. 2006. "The Tanzanite Foundation: An Interview with Sarah Cort." Available at http://www.aigsthailand.com/aigsgems_research.php?art_id=00193 (accessed 11 April 2007).

Ghanadan, Rebecca. 2009. "Connected Geographies and Struggles over Access: Electricity Commercialization in Tanzania." In *Electric Capitalism: Recolonizing Africa on the Power Grid.* Ed. David A. Mcdonald, 400–436. Capetown: HSRC Press.

Gibbon, Peter. 1999. "Privatisation and Foreign Direct Investment in Mainland Tanzania, 1992–98." *CDR Working Paper Subseries,* March. Denmark: Center for Development Research.

Gibson, Erika. 2003. "SA at Home in Dar es Salaam." http://www.News24.com.

"Give Tanzanians the Value They Deserve—Mengi." *Guardian (Tanzania),* 18 January 2005.

Glassman, Jonathon. 2011. *War of Words, War of Stones.* Bloomington: Indiana University Press.

Global Witness. 2000. *Conflict Diamonds: Possibilities for the Identification, Certification, and Control of Diamonds.* London: Global Witness.

Goldberg, David Theo. 2004. "The End(s) of Race." *Postcolonial Studies* 7, no. 2: 211–30.

Goodman, David. 1999. *Fault Lines: Journeys into the New South Africa.* Berkeley: University of California Press.

Goreux, Louis. 2001. *Conflict Diamonds.* World Bank: Washington DC.

Gqola, Pumla. 2008. "Brutal Inheritances: Echoes, Negrophobia, and Masculinist Violence." In *Go Home or Die Here: Violence, Xenophobia, and the Reinvention of Difference in South Africa.* Ed. Shireen Hassim, Tawana Kupe, and Eric Worby, 209–24. Johannesburg: University of Witwatersrand Press.

Graham, Stuart. 2003. "South African Businesses Reap Rewards in 'Risky' Africa." *Agence France Presse,* 13 September.

Grant, Andrew, and Ian Taylor. 2004. "Global Governance and Conflict Diamonds: The Kimberley Process and the Quest for Clean Gems." *Round Table* 93, no. 375: 385–401.

"Great Strides in Mining Sector Development." *Daily News (Tanzania),* 1 August 2005, 11.

Green, Judi. 2005. "Courage and Humour." *Moneyweb,* 1 April.

Griffiths, Ieuan. 1969. "The TAZAMA Oil Pipeline." *Geography* 54, no. 2: 214–17.

Grobbelaar, Neuma. 2004. "'Every Continent Needs an America': The Experience of South African Firms Doing Business in Mozambique." Johannesburg, South Africa: South African Institute of International Affairs.

Gumbo, Parege. 2005. "Three Percent Gold Royalty Accepted International Practice." *Financial Times (Tanzania),* 6 July, 1, 3.

———. 2006. "Investors' Confidence in Tanzania Ranks Top Again." *Financial Times (Tanzania),* 1 February, 5.

Hall, Sarah. 2011. "Land Grabbing in Southern Africa: The Many Faces of the Investor Rush." *Review of African Political Economy* 38, no. 128: 193–214.

Hammar, Amanda. 2010. "Ambivalent Mobilities: Zimbabwean Commercial Farmers in Mozambique." *Journal of Southern African Studies* 36, no. 2: 395–416.

Hart, Gillian. 2002. *Disabling Globalization: Places of Power in Post-apartheid South Africa.* Berkeley: University of California Press.

Hassim, Shireen, Tawana Kupe, and Eric Worby, eds. 2008. *Go Home or Die Here: Violence, Xenophobia, and the Reinvention of Difference in South Africa.* Johannesburg: Witwatersrand University Press.

"Hero of Tanzanite Rush Dies: Late Mr. D'Souza Made 'the Most Exciting Gemfind in a Hundred Years.'" *Northern News (Tanzania),* 29 August 1969, 2.

Hochschild, Adam. 1999. *King Leopold's Ghost: A Story of Greed, Terror, and Heroism in Colonial Africa.* Boston: Houghton Mifflin.

Houser, George M. 1989. *No One Can Stop the Rain: Glimpses of Africa's Liberation Struggle.* New York: Pilgrim Press.

Houston, Gregory. 2008. Introduction to *The Road to Democracy in South Africa*, vol. 3, part 1. SADET, 1–39. Pretoria: Unisa Press.

Howe, Herbert. 1998. "Private Security Forces and African Stability: The Case of Executive Outcomes." *Journal of Modern African Studies* 36, no. 2: 307–31.

Hudson, Judi. 2007. "South Africa's Economic Expansion into Africa: Neo-colonialism or Development?" In *South Africa in Africa: The Post-Apartheid Era*. Ed. Adekeye Adebajo, Adebayo Adedeji, and Chris Landsberg, 128–49. Scottsville, South Africa: University of KwaZulu-Natal Press.

Hughes, David McDermott. 2010. *Whiteness in Zimbabwe: Race, Landscape, and the Problem of Belonging*. New York, New York: Palgrave Macmillan.

Huxley, Elspeth. 1968. *White Man's Country: Lord Delamere and the Making of Kenya*. New York: Praeger Publishers.

Iheduru, Okechukwu. 2004. "Black Economic Power and Nation-Building in Post-apartheid Africa." *Journal of Modern African Studies* 42, no. 1: 1–30.

Ihucha, Adam. 2005. "Tanzanite Miners in Bitter Row over Boundaries." *Financial Times (Tanzania)*, 5 October, 16.

———. 2006a. "The Mererani 100 Remembered." *Guardian (Tanzania)*, 29 April, 3.

———. 2006b. "Tanzanite Miners Shot in Underground Row." *Guardian (Tanzania)*, 9 February, 2.

———. 2008. "Mererani Disaster: Mining Suspended as Scores Missing." *Guardian (Tanzania)*, 31 March.

Iliffe, John. 1969. *Tanganyika under German Rule*. Cambridge: Cambridge University Press.

———. 1979. *A Modern History of Tanganyika*. Cambridge: Cambridge University Press.

"ILO Invites Liberation Reps." *Southern Africa* 6, 1973, no. 7: 42.

"IMF Warns Tanzania over 'Too Many Economic Zones.'" *East African*, 5 May 2006, 6.

Integrated Regional Information Networks. 2006. "Gem Slaves: Tanzanite's Child Labour." Documentary film.

International Colored Gemstone Association. "Gem by Gem: Tanzanite." http://www.gemstone.org/gem-by-gem/english/tanzanite.html (accessed 18 October 2010).

"International Meeting Focuses on 'Collaboration' with Southern African Regimes." *Southern Africa* 4, 1979, no. 4: 18.

"Investors Wary of Southern Africa." *BBC*, 4 February 2002.

Invictus. 2009. Film. Directed by Clint Eastwood. Warner Brothers, USA.

Ishemo, Shubi L. 2000. "'A Symbol that Cannot Be Substituted': The Role of Mwalimu J. K. Nyerere in the Liberation of Southern Africa." *Review of African Political Economy* 27, no. 83: 85–94.

Itano, Nicole. 2003. "South African Companies Fill a Void." *New York Times*, 4 November.

Ivaska, Andrew. 2005. "Of Students, 'Nizers,' and a Struggle over Youth: Tanzania's 1966 National Service Crisis." *Africa Today* 51, no. 3: 83–107.

Joel, Lawi. 2005. "What's Happening with Tanesco?" *Guardian (Tanzania),* 19 November, 7.

Jomo, Frank 2008. "Under-declaration of Profits by Mining Companies Costs Tanzania US$207 Million." *Mineweb,* 14 January.

Jozeni, Ani. 2005. "Caring Government: Could Kikwete Confirm Himself Worthy Emulator of Nyerere?" *Guardian (Tanzania),* 22 October, 7.

Juma, Mussa. 2006. "Foreigners at Mererani Told to Stop Harassment." *Citizen (Tanzania),* 23 February, 6.

Kamndaya, Samuel. 2006a. "Government Urged to Speed Up Reforms." *Citizen (Tanzania),* 15 February, 22.

———. 2006b. "Miners Pay Only Sh2.4 Billion Tax in 20 Years." *Citizen (Tanzania),* 18 May, 3.

———. 2006c. "Return on Investment Is What Counts Says South African Expert." *Citizen (Tanzania),* 26 May, 6.

Kamndaya, Samuel, and Rodgers Luhwago. 2006. "Keep Off Power Deal, Govt Warns Tanesco." *Citizen (Tanzania),* 21 March,1–7.

Kanyabwoya, Damas. 2006. "Agriculture: Four Decades of Talks and More Talks." *Citizen (Tanzania),* 13 April, 13.

Kasumuni, Ludger. 2005a. "Investors in Research Prefer Tanzania—UNDP Eeport." *Guardian (Tanzania),* 30 September, 1.

———. 2005b. "Mkapa Calls for SA-Style Poll Guidelines." *Guardian (Tanzania),* 20 July, 1.

Kato, Levina. 2006. "Healers to Lay to Rest 'Spirits' of SA Fighters." *Citizen (Tanzania),* 24 March, 1–2.

Kavishe, H. E. 2005. "Tanzania's Parastatal Sector Reform Commission." Monthly Development Learning Seminar. Hakikazi Catalyst, Arusha, Tanzania.

Kazingumbe, Mohamed. 2006. "Why TBL Enjoys Consecutive Award Winning." *Business Times (Tanzania),* 26 May, 12.

Kelley, Kevin. 2000. "US May Stop Rich Nations from Acting on Africa Debt Relief." *East African,* 17 July, 4.

Kenge, Abduel. 2005. "Parties Told to Uphold Mwalimu's Legacy." *Daily News (Tanzania),* 15 October, 3.

Kennedy, Dane. 1987. *Islands of White: Settler Society and Culture in Kenya and Southern Rhodesia, 1890–1939.* Durham, NC: Duke University Press.

Khadiagala, Gilbert M. 2007. *Allies in Adversity: The Frontline States in Southern African Security, 1975–1993.* New York: University Press of America.

Kihaule, Emmanuel. 2005. "Mwalimu's Legacy Disgraced—Dons." *Guardian (Tanzania),* 15 October, 1.

Kimaro, Robert. 2005. "Poverty Reduction: Greatest Challenge of the Fourth Phase Government." *Guardian (Tanzania),* 11 August, 6.

Kimaro, Sadikiel N. 2006. "Reorienting Our Approach to the Mining Sector." *Guardian (Tanzania),* 16 June, 11.

Kironde, J. M. Lusugga. 2007. "Race, Class, and Housing in Dar es Salaam: The Colonial Impact on Land Use Structure, 1891–1961." In *Dar es Salaam: Histories from an Emerging African Metropolis.* Ed. James R. Brennan, Andrew Burton, and Yusuf Lawi, 97–117. Dar es Salaam, Tanzania: Mkuki na Nyota Publishers.

Kisaka, Joyce. 2006a. "Net Group Contract Will Not Be Renewed." *Sunday Citizen,* 21 May, 1–2.

———. 2006b. "TIC Ready for Single Investment License." *Citizen (Tanzania),* 29 January, 1–2.

Kisanga, E. J. 1981. "Tanzania and the Organization of African Unity (OAU)." In *Foreign Policy of Tanzania 1961–1981: A Reader.* Ed. K. Mathews and S. S. Mushi, 97–122. Dar es Salaam: Tanzania Publishing House.

Kisembo, Patrick. 2004. "ATCL Workers Accuse SAA Management of Sabotage." *Family Mirror (Tanzania),* 25 May, 1.

Kisembo, Patrick, and Mwinyi Sadalla. 2008. "Xenophobia Not Cause of Tanzanians Deaths." *Guardian (Tanzania),* 18 September.

Kitabu, Gerald. 2006. "TBL Overall Winner of President's Manufacturer's Award 2006." *Guardian (Tanzania),* 11 May, 1.

Kivamwo, Simon. 2006. "NEPAD Another Imperialist Manoeuvre." *Sunday Observer (Tanzania),* 22 January, 1, 3.

Kizigha, Charles. 2006a. "ATCL, SAA 'Divorce' Now Formal." *Daily News (Tanzania),* 12 June, 3.

———. 2006b. "Controversy Surrounds Lease of ATCL Plane." *Daily News (Tanzania),* 30 January, 3.

———. 2006c. "SAA 'Golden Handshake' for ATCL?" *Daily News (Tanzania),* 16 January, 3.

Knight, Richard. 2002. "Bophuthatswana." http://richardknight.homestead.com /bophuthatswana.html (accessed 25 June 2010).

Konde, Hadji. 1984. *Press Freedom in Tanzania.* Arusha, Tanzania: Eastern Africa Publications, Ltd.

Kondlo, Kwandiwe. 2008. "'In the Twilight of the Azanian Revolution': The Exile History of the Pan Africanist Congress of Azania (South Africa): (1960–1990)." University of Johannesburg, PhD dissertation.

Kondo, Hamza. 2001a. "Merelani Mining Conflict Results in Death." *Colored Stone,* May/June.

———. 2001b. "Tensions Boil Over at Tanzanite Mines." *Colored Stone,* May/June.

Kulindwa, Kassim, Oswald Mashindano, Fanuel Schechambo, and Hussein Sosovele. 2000. *Macroeconomic Reforms and Sustainable Development in Tanzania: The Case of Mining.* Dar es Salaam: University of Dar es Salaam.

Kyaruzi, Ibrahim. 2000. "TBL to Produce 'Castle Milk Stout' Locally." *Business Times (Tanzania),* 8 December.

Lameck, David. 2006. "Young Tennis Players for SA Training." *Citizen (Tanzania),* 10 February, 32.

Lange, Siri. 2006. *Benefit Streams from Mining in Tanzania: Cases Studies from Geita and Mererani.* Bergen: Chr. Michelsen Institute.

Lazaro, Happy. 2003. "Mererani Tops Charts of Criminal Cases." *Arusha Times,* 16 August.

Le Billon, Philippe. 2001. "Angola's Political Economy of War: The Role of Oil and Diamonds 1975–2000." *African Affairs* 100, no. 398: 55–80.

———. 2006. "Fatal Transactions: Conflict Diamonds and the (Anti)terrorist Consumer." *Antipode* 38, no. 4: 778–801.

———. 2008. "Diamond Wars? Conflict Diamonds and Geographies of Resource Wars." *Annals of the Association of American Geographers* 98, no. 2: 345–72.

Le Roux, Helen. 2004. "Laser Inscriptions Included on Stones." *Engineering News,* 5 March.

Legum, Colin, and Geoffrey Mmari, eds. 1995. *Mwalimu: The Influence of Nyerere.* Oxford, England: James Currey.

Lesufi, Ishmael. 2004. "South Africa and the Rest of the Continent: Towards a Critique of the Political Economy of NEPAD." *Current Sociology* 52, no. 5.

"Liberation Support." *Southern Africa* 8, 1975, no. 2: 28.

Limb, Peter. 2008. "The Anti-apartheid Movements in Australia and Aotearoa/New Zealand." In *The Road to Democracy in South Africa,* vol. 3, *International Solidarity, Part 2.* South African Democracy Education Trust (SADET), 906–82. Pretoria: Unisa Press.

"Links between Tanzania and Zambia Sabotaged." *London Observer,* 28 December 1969.

Lipscomb, J. F. 1974. *White Africans.* Westport, CT: Greenwood Press.

Lissoni, Arianna. 2009. "Transformations in the ANC External Mission and Umkhonto we Sizwe, c. 1960–1969." *Journal of Southern African Studies* 35, no. 2: 287–301.

LoBaido, Anthony C. 2001. "Africa's New Bloodstained Gems: Children Dig for Tanzanite, Coltan in Dangerous Mines." http://www.worldnetdaily.com/news/article.asp?ARTICLE_ID=25484.

Luhwago, Rodgers. 2005. "Mkapa Refutes Claims on Foreign Investors." *Citizen (Tanzania),* 30 November, 1–2.

Lwinga, Imani. 2007. "Tanzania Yet to Use Its Mineral Riches to Drive Economy." *Sunday Observer (Tanzania),* 5 August.

Lyimo, Karl. 2005. "Tanzania Must Rethink Costs of Doing Business." *Citizen (Tanzania)*, 17 November, 22.

——. 2006a. "That Gold Ghost Still Resurfaces." *Citizen (Tanzania)*, 11 May, 15.

——. 2006b. "We Aspire for Guinness Record Running Economy on Torchcells." *Citizen (Tanzania)*, 18 June, 17.

Machumu, Bakari. 2001. "UK Largest Investor in Tanzania." *Business Times (Tanzania)*, 5 October, 4.

Macmillan, Hugh. 2009. "The African National Congress of South Africa in Zambia: The Culture of Exile and the Changing Relationship with Home, 1964–1990." *Journal of Southern African Studies* 35, no. 2: 303–29.

Madatta, Anthony. 2005. "Mining Taxes Similar the World Over—Dar." *Business Times (Tanzania)*, 21 October, 1–2.

——. 2006. "Dar Call Echoes SA Lobby Proposals." *Business Times (Tanzania)*, 4 April, 1–2.

Madatta, Anthony, and Engtraud Masondore. 2005. "Dar Industries Strangulated: Power Load Shedding." *Business Times (Tanzania)*, 4 November, 1–2.

Mafeje, Archie. 1978. "Soweto and Its Aftermath." *Review of African Political Economy* 5, no. 11, 17–30.

Mager, Anne. 2010. *Beer, Sociability, and Masculinity in South Africa.* Bloomington: Indiana University Press.

Makawia, Cathlex. 2000. "South Africa to Help Fight Dynamite Fishing." *Guardian (Tanzania)*, 19 July, 5.

Mande, Mike. 2005. "South African Ship Hunts Poachers in Dar's Waters." *East African*, 22 July.

——. 2006. "Tanesco Contract: SA Firm Fights Back." *East African*, 29 May, 5.

Mande, Mike, and Edwin Wilfred. 2008. "Dar Seeks Auditors over BoT Scam." *East African*, 31 March.

Mandela, Nelson. 1994. "Inaugural Address, May 10, 1994." http://www.wsu.edu/~wldciv/world_civ_reader/world_civ_reader_2/mandela.html (accessed 2 December 2010).

Marais, Hein. 2011. *South Africa Pushed to the Limit: The Political Economy of Change.* London: Zed Books.

Mariwa, Sharon. 2006. "WB Cancels Dar Debt." *Business Times (Tanzania)*, 7 April, 1.

Maro, Freddy. 2005. "Learn from SA Farmers—Mkapa." *Sunday Observer (Tanzania)*, 25 September, 1.

Marsh, Dave. 1985. *Sun City: Artists United against Apartheid.* New York: Penguin Books.

Martin, David. 2001. "A Voice from the Dark Past." *Southern African News Features.* December.

Martin, David, and Phyllis Johnson. 1981. *The Struggle for Zimbabwe*. London: Faber and Faber.

Marx, Karl. 1976. *Capital,* vol. 1. London: Penguin Books.

Marxists Internet Archive. "Arusha Declaration." Available at http://www.marxists.org/subject/africa/nyerere/1967/arusha-declaration.htm (accessed 6 October 2010).

Masayanyika, Charles. 2006. "Man Jailed 18 Months for Injuring Dog." *Guardian (Tanzania),* 4 May, 2.

Masoy, Joseph. 2000. "Award TBL for the Most Absurd Piece of Advertising in Africa." *Arusha Times,* 1 July, 6.

Matinyi, Masyaga. 2006. "Arusha: City Propelled by Tanzanite Money." *This Day (Tanzania),* 2 March, 21.

Mattes, Robert, and Wayne Richmond. 2002. "The Brain Drain: What Do Skilled South Africans think?" In *Destinations Unknown: Perspectives on the Brain Drain in Southern Africa.* Ed. David A. McDonald and Jonathan Crush, 17–46. Pretoria: Africa Institute of South Africa.

Mayallah, Elisha. 2005. "Tourism Development: Lesson from South Africa." *Daily News (Tanzania),* 8 August, 6.

Mbani, Mnaku. 2004. "S. African Education Group Comes to Tanzania in Strength." *Business Times (Tanzania),* 4 June, 13.

Mbise, Amana. 2005. "The Best in the Region?" *Citizen (Tanzania),* 7 November.

Mbogoro, Damas. 2006. "Having Country's Economy Managed by Nationals." *Business Times (Tanzania),* 21 April, 5.

McDonald, David A., and Eunice Sahle, eds. 2002. *The Legacies of Julius Nyerere: Influences on Development Discourse and Practice in Africa.* Trenton, New Jersey: Africa World Press.

McIntosh, Janet. 2009. "Seeing Themselves Being Seen: The Cholmondeley Case and White Kenyan Nationalism." Paper presented at the annual meeting of the African Studies Association. New Orleans.

McNeil, Donald G., Jr. 1997. "Packaging Luxury with Wildlife." *New York Times,* 25 June, D1, D4

"Mererani Reeling from Poverty Despite Abundant Gem Wealth: Main Source of Village Income Is Pool Table Fee." *Arusha Times,* 12 November 2005, 1–2.

Mgamba, Richard. 2006. "Questions Haunt Tanzania's 'Thriving' Mining Sector." *Sunday Citizen,* 12 March, 5.

———. 2007. "Miners Speak Out." *Citizen (Tanzania),* 16 November.

Mgwabati, Faraja. 2006. "Govt Asked to Favour Locals." *Daily News (Tanzania),* 2 May, 5.

Mhawi, Joe. 2004. "Kigoda Riled by Economic Reform Critics." *Business Times (Tanzania),* 28 May, 1.

Miller, Darlene. 2003. "Nepad and SA Multinational Corporations in Africa: Whose 'African Renaissance'?" Occasional paper. Woodstock, South Africa: International Labour Research and Information Group.

———. 2005. "White Managers and the African Renaissance: A 'Retail Renaissance' or a New Colonial Encounter at South African Companies in Foreign, African Countries?" *Codesria Eleventh General Assembly.*

———. 2006. "'Spaces of resistance': African workers at Shoprite in Maputo and Lusaka." *Africa Development* 31, no. 1: 27–49.

———. 2008. "'Retail Renaissance' or Company Rhetoric: The Failed Partnership of a South African Corporation and Local Suppliers in Zambia." *Labour, Capital, and Society* 41, no. 1: 34–55.

Miller, Darlene, Etienne Nel, and Godfrey Hampwaye. 2008. "Malls in Zambia: Racialised Retail Expansion and South African Foreign Investors in Zambia." *African Sociological Review* 12, no. 1: 35–54.

Miller, Darlene, Olojide Oloyede, and Richard Saunders. 2008. "South African Corporations and Post-apartheid Expansion in Africa: Creating a New Regional Space." *African Sociological Review* 12, no. 1: 1–19.

Mines and Communities. 2001. "Buried Alive? The Bulyanhulu Accusations." http://www.minesandcommunities.org/article.php?a=430 (accessed 3 December 2010).

"Mining Investors Happy with Legal, Fiscal Regimes." *Daily News (Tanzania),* 3 August 2005, 10.

Minter, William. 1994. *Apartheid's Contras: An Inquiry into the Roots of War in Angola and Mozambique.* London: Zed Books.

Mitchell, Katharyne. 2004. *Crossing the Neoliberal Line: Pacific Rim Migration and the Metropolis.* Philadelphia: Temple University Press.

"Mkapa Says Investors Not Thieves." *Daily News (Tanzania),* 17 August 2005, 9.

Mkinga, Joyce. 2006. "Souls of S. Africans Buried in Tanzania Set for 'Relocation.'" *Guardian (Tanzania),* 24 March, 1–2.

Mlangila, Alfred. 2005. "Vital Lessons to Learn from Resentment of Foreign Investors." *Citizen (Tanzania),* 25 July, 6.

Mmbaga, Charles. 2005. "Mining Firm Acquires Modern Grading System." *Daily News (Tanzania),* 8 October, no. 30, 2.

———. 2006a. "Four Miners Wounded in Mirerani." *Daily News (Tanzania),* 9 February, 3.

———. 2006b. "The Mystery of Tanzanite Discoverers." *Daily News (Tanzania),* 26 March.

Moholi, Ayanda. 2011. "Vodacom Rebrands to Red." *Financial Mail (South Africa),* 5 April.

Molloy, Judith. 1971. "Political Communication in Lushoto District, Tanzania." University of Kent at Canterbury, PhD dissertation.

Monson, Jamie. 2006. "Defending the People's Railway in the Era of Liberalization: TAZARA in Southern Tanzania." *Africa* 76, no. 1: 113–30.

———. 2009. *Africa's Freedom Railway: How a Chinese Development Project Changed Lives and Livelihoods in Tanzania.* Bloomington: Indiana University Press.

Moore, Sally Falk. 1986. *Social Facts and Fabrications: "Customary" Law on Kilimanjaro, 1880–1980.* Cambridge: Cambridge University Press.

Morrow, Sean, Brown Maaba, and Loyiso Pulumani. 2004. *Education in Exile: SOMAFCO, the ANC School in Tanzania, 1978–1992.* Cape Town: HSRC Press.

Moses, John. 2002. "Tanzanians Concerned about SA 'Colonisation.'" *African Eye News Service,* 28 October, 1.

"Moshi Sugar Plant Set Ablaze Again: Officials Suspect Arson." *Arusha Times,* 7 April 2007.

Mosia, Lebona, Charles Riddle, and Jim Zaffiro. 1994. "From Revolutionary to Regime Radio: Three Decades of Nationalist Broadcasting in Southern Africa." *African Media Review* 8, no. 1: 1–24.

Mosoba, Tom. 2005. "Stand-off at NBC Paralyses Services." *Citizen (Tanzania),* 25 October, 1–2.

———. 2006. "Was ATC-SAA Deal Doomed from Start?" *Citizen (Tanzania),* 15 March, 1, 10, 19.

———. 2009. "ATC Pull-Out from SAA Not as Easy as Many Think." *Citizen (Tanzania),* 16 March, 10, 19.

Mosoba, Tom, and Dickson Amos. 2006. "Tanesco in Dire Financial Straits, Says Net Group Chief." *Citizen (Tanzania),* 24 May, 1–2.

Moyo, Omar. 2008. "Govt Closes Down All Mirelani Mining Operations after Tragedy." *This Day (Tanzania),* 31 March.

Msombeli, Limbe. 2006a. "Power Supply Paradox Must Be Solved." *Citizen (Tanzania),* 27 February, 8.

———. 2006b. "Twin Towers Project Not Man-Centred." *Citizen (Tanzania),* 5 April, 13.

Muindi, Mattias, and Cathy Majtenyi. 2001. "Miners Accuse Company of Setting Monopoly." Africa News, 4. http://web.peacelink.it/afrinews/63_issue/p4.html.

Munaita, Peter. 2006. "Dar Signs Guidelines on Investment." *East African,* 27 March.

Munyaga, Mboneko. 2006. "Indeed Mining Benefits No One." *Daily News (Tanzania),* 22 April, 3.

Mushi, Theo. 2008. "PSRC: Did It Achieve Its Mission?" *Guardian (Tanzania),* 23 January.

Mutakyahwa, Ruta. 2007. "A Market Research Report on Business Opportunities in Tanzania for South African SMEs." Dar es Salaam: South African International Business Linkages Programme.

Mvungi, Asraji. 2006. "Small Tanzanite Miners Want Govt to Publish Probe Team Findings." *Guardian (Tanzania),* 11 April, 3.

"Mwadui Sold: De Beers Still Owe Tanzanians Outstanding Remittances and Taxes." *This Day (Tanzania),* 11 September 2008.

Mwakikagile, Godfrey. 2006. *Life in Tanganyika in the Fifties.* Johannesburg, South Africa: Continental Press.

Mwakisyala, James. 2000. "ABSA Pledges to Retain NBC Bank Workers." *East African,* 10 April, 3.

———. 2002. "Tanzania Says Beer Share Swap Is Not Yet Legal." *East African,* 27 May.

Mwamunyange, Joseph. 2003. "International Financing Corporation (IFC) Directors to Discuss National Bank of Commerce (NBC)." *East African,* 11 August.

———. 2005a. "Tanzania Calls for Joint Efforts to Combat Cross-border Crime in SADC and EAC." *East African,* 22 August.

———. 2005b. "Tanzania Imposes Destination Inspection Fees on Gold, Gems." *East African,* 3 October, 27.

———. 2005c. "Tanzania Leads East Africa in 117-Country Global Survey Ratings." *East African,* 3 October, 29.

Mwapachu, Juma. 2005. *Confronting New Realities: Reflections on Tanzania's Radical Transformation.* Dar es Salaam, Tanzania: E & D Limited.

Mwase, Ngila. 1987. "Zambia, the TAZARA and the Alternative Outlets to the Sea." *Transport Review* 7, no. 3: 191–206.

Mwero, Emmanuel. 2005. "Investment in Tanzania: A Silver Chalice, or a Poisoned Cup?" *The Observer (Tanzania),* 25 September, 12.

Mweta, Nimi. 2006. "Completing Privatisation and Saving Failing Privatised Firms." *Financial Times (Tanzania),* 15 February, 10.

Myburgh, Andrew. 2004. "Explaining Emigration from South Africa." *South African Journal of Economics* 72, no. 1: 122–48.

Myburgh, James. 2007. "The Virodene Affair." *Politicsweb,* 17–21 September.

Myers, Garth. 2003. "Designing Power: Forms and Purposes of Colonial Model Neighborhoods in British Africa." *Habitat International* 27: 193–204.

Mytton, Graham. 1983. *Mass Communication in Africa.* London: Edward Arnold.

Nagar, Richa. 1996. "The South Asian Diaspora in Tanzania: A History Retold." *Comparative Studies of South Asia, Africa, and the Middle East* 16, no. 2: 62–79.

Nagar, Richa, and Helga Leitner. 1998. "Contesting Social Relations in Communal Places: Identity Politics among Asian Communities in Dar es Salaam." In *Cities of Difference.* Ed. Ruth Fincher and Jane M. Jacobs, 226–51. New York: Guilford Press.

Naidu, Sanusha, and Jessica Lutchman. 2004. "Understanding South Africa's Engagement in the Region: Has the Leopard Changed Its Spots?" *Stability, Poverty Reduction, and South African Trade and Investment in Southern Africa.* Ed. SARPN, 12–15. Pretoria: HSRC.

"Nation Building in the Portuguese Colonies." *Southern Africa* 2, 1969, no. 1: 7–10.

"National Empowerment Council Most Welcome." 2005. *Citizen (Tanzania)*, 17 November, 8.

Nationwide Airlines. 2007. "The Alchemy of Africa." *Altitude: Nationwide Airlines In-flight Magazine*, January, 27.

Ndebele, Nhlanhla, and Noor Nieftagodien. 2004. "The Morogoro Conference: A Moment for Self-Reflection." In *The Road to Democracy in South Africa*, vol. 1, *1960–1970*. Ed. SADET, 573–99. Pretoria: Unisa Press.

Ndlovu, Sifiso M. 2004. "The ANC in Exile, 1960–1970." In *The Road to Democracy in South Africa*, vol. 1, *1960–1970*. Ed. SADET, 411–78. Pretoria: Unisa Press.

———. 2007a. "The ANC's Diplomacy and International Relations." In *The Road to Democracy in South Africa*, vol. 2, *1970–1980*. Ed. SADET, 615–67. Pretoria: Unisa Press.

———. 2007b. "The Soweto Uprising, Part 1, Soweto." In *The Road to Democracy in South Africa*, vol. 2, *1970–1980*. Ed. SADET, 317–50. Pretoria: Unisa Press.

Neocosmos, Michael. 2008. *From "Foreign Natives" to "Native Foreigners": Explaining Xenophobia in Post-apartheid South Africa*. Dakar: CODESRIA.

Nestory, Rutashubanyuma. 2005. "Can President Mkapa Be a Judge of His Own Cause? (2)," *Citizen (Tanzania)*, 27 November, 30.

———. 2006. "Lessons from NetGroup Solutions." *Sunday Citizen*, 4 June, 6.

Neumann, Roderick P. 2001. "Africa's 'Last Wilderness': Reordering Space for Political and Economic Control in Colonial Tanzania." *Africa* 71, no. 4: 641–65.

Ngahemera, Shermarx. 2006a. "Kilombero Sugarcane Farmers' Output Up." *Daily News (Tanzania)*, 29 May, 5.

———. 2006b. "Sugar Industry Has a Bright Future." *Daily News (Tanzania)*, 9 June, 10.

Ng'wanakilala, Fumbuka. 2010. "Tanzania Increases Royalties in New Mining Law." *Reuters*, 24 April.

Niblock, Timothy. 1981. "Tanzanian Foreign Policy: An Analysis." In *Foreign policy of Tanzania 1961–1981: A Reader*. Ed. K. Mathews, and S. S. Mushi, 24–33. Dar es Salaam: Tanzania Publishing House.

Njau, Adrian. 2001. "SA Imports Elbow out Tanzanian Goods." *Business Times (Tanzania)*, 7 December, 1.

Nkwame, Valentine Marc. 2000. "Residents Express Anger about Beer Bottle Statue." *Arusha Times*, 1 July, 1–2.

———. 2004. "Local Miners Detest 'Small-Scale Miners' Label." *Arusha Times*, 19 June.

———. 2006. "One Dies in Mirerani Underground Shooting." *Daily News (Tanzania)*, 8 April, 2.

———. 2010a. "Police Nab S. African Who 'Fed' Tanzanians to Dogs." *Daily News (Tanzania)*, 31 March.

———. 2010b. "Tanzanite-One Disowns Rounding South African." *Daily News (Tanzania)*, 1 April.

Ntetema, Vicky. 1999. "Nyerere: A Personal Recollection." *BBC,* 14 October.

Nuttall, Sarah. 2001. "Subjectivities of Whiteness." *African Studies Review* 44, no. 2: 115–40.

Nyamaume, Simba. 2003. "TPC Privatization Boosts Sugar Production." *Arusha Times,* 5 April.

Nyerere, Julius. 1967. *Tanzania Policy on Foreign Affairs.* Dar es Salaam: Ministry of Information and Tourism.

———. 1970. "Address by the President of the United Republic of Tanzania, Mwalimu Julius K. Nyerere, at the General Assembly of the United Nations on Thursday, October 15, 1970." Reprinted in *Southern Africa 3, 1970,* no. 9: 3–6.

———. 1978. *Crusade for Liberation.* Oxford: Oxford University Press.

Ohayo, James. 1999. "Calling South Africans Rotten Eggs a Classic Case of Sour Grapes." *East African,* 6 May, 27.

Okema, Michael. 2005a. "Despite Failed Policies, Nyerere Was a Leader Who Cared." *East African,* 10 October, 19.

———. 2005a. "Nico and the Limits of Economic Nationalism." *East African,* 17 January.

Olick, Jeffrey and Joyce Robbins. 1998. "Social Memory Studies: From 'Collective Memory' to the Historical Sociology of Mnemonic Practices." *Annual Review of Sociology* 24, no. 1: 105–40.

Orakwue, Stella. 2002. "NEPAD or Knee-pad? (Not in Black or White)." *New African* (May).

Orute, Vincent Obiro. 2004. "How Privatization Has Thrown Workers Out of Job." *Arusha Times,* 11 December.

Othman, Haroub. 2005. "An Intellectual in Power (Part 1)." *Guardian (Tanzania),* 25 October, 3.

Otieno, Barrack, and Herald Tagama. 1999. "Battle of the Brewing Bruisers." *New African* (January).

Oyugah, Noela, and Lina Mwambungu. 2008. "Tanzania: 164 People Back at Home after Attacks." *Citizen (Tanzania),* 24 June.

Palloti, Arrigo. 2009. "Post-colonial Nation-building and Southern African Liberation: Tanzania and the Break of Diplomatic Relations with the United Kingdom, 1965–1968." *African Historical Review* 41, no. 2: 60–84.

Parry, Yohannes. 2000. "Tanzania's Golden Age?" *African Business* (October).

Paton, Alan. 1976. *Cry, the Beloved Country.* New York: Charles Scribner's Sons.

Paton, Anne. 1998. "Why I'm Fleeing South Africa." *London Sunday Times,* 29 November.

Patterson, Sala. 2004. "Radio Tanzania Dar es Salaam: State Control, Broadcasting, and National Development." School of Oriental and African Studies, University of London, MSc. thesis.

Peligal, Rona. 1999. "Spatial Planning and Social Fluidity: The Shifting Boundaries of Ethnicity, Gender, and Class in Arusha, Tanzania, 1920–1967." Columbia University, PhD dissertation.

Peoples of the World against Apartheid for a Democratic South Africa. 1987. "Report and Declaration of the International Conference convened by the African National Congress in Arusha." Tanzania, 1–4 December. http://www.anc.org.za/ancdocs /history/solidarity/conferences/arusha_report.html (accessed 22 June 2010).

Philemon, Lusekelo. 2005. "Tanzania Too Costly to Start Business, Says SIDA Rep." *Guardian (Tanzania)*, 26 September, i.

Phillips, Lucie C., Haji Semboja, G. P. Shukla, Rogers Sezinga, Wilson Mutagwaba, Ben Mchwampaka, Goodwill Wanga, Godius Kahyarara, and Peter C. Keller. 2001. *Tanzania's Precious Minerals Boom: Issues in Mining and Marketing.* Washington, DC: USAID.

Pitcher, Anne. 2002. *Transforming Mozambique: The Politics of Privatization, 1975–2000.* Cambridge: Cambridge University Press.

———. 2006. "Forgetting from Above and Memory from Below: Strategies of Legitimation and Struggle in Postsocialist Mozambique." *Africa* 76, no. 1: 88–112.

Pitcher, Anne, and Kelly Askew. 2006. "African Socialisms and Postsocialisms." *Africa* 76, no. 1: 1–14.

"Planning Minister's Speech. 2006–2007." *Citizen (Tanzania)*, 16 June 2006, 1–7.

"Portugal Attacks Southern Tanzania: Two Planes Shot Down." *Southern Africa* 5, 1972, no. 6: 37.

"The Portuguese Territories." *Southern Africa* 1, 1968, no. 5: 8.

Power, Marcus, and Giles Mohan. 2008. "Good Friends and Good Partners: The 'New' Face of China-African Cooperation." *Review of African Political Economy* 35, no. 115: 5–6.

Pred, Allan. 2004. *The Past Is Not Dead: Facts, Fictions, and Enduring Racial Stereotypes.* Minneapolis: University of Minnesota Press.

The Presidency, Republic of South Africa. "The Order of the Companions of O. R. Tambo." http://www.thepresidency.gov.za/pebble.asp?relid=775 (accessed 3 December 2011).

"Price Tag on National Brand Names." *Arusha Times*, 8 April 2006, 5.

"The Private Sector Agenda: 2005 Laid Solid Foundation for 2006." *Citizen (Tanzania)*, 12 January 2006, 13.

"Probe Grievances in the Mining Areas." *Sunday Citizen*, 24 July 2005, 6.

"Probe Starts on the Shooting of Small Miners: The Two Contesting Firms Have Opened Court Cases against Each Other." *Citizen (Tanzania)*, 22 February 2006, 6.

Pulido, Laura. 2000. "Rethinking Environmental Racism: White Privilege and Urban Development in Southern California." *Annals of the Association of American Geographers* 90, no. 1: 12–40.

Ralinala, R.M., J. Sithole, Gregory Houston, and Bernard Magubane. 2004. "The Wankie and Sipolilo Campaigns." In *The Road to Democracy in South Africa,* vol. 1, *1960–1970.* Cape Town: Zebra Press. 479–540.

Ranger, Terence. 2004. "Nationalist Historiography, Patriotic History and the History of the Nation: The Struggle Over the Past in Zimbabwe." *Journal of Southern African Studies* 30, no. 2: 215–34.

Reddy, Enugu. 2008. "The United Nations and the Struggle for Liberation in South Africa." In *The Road to Democracy in South Africa,* vol. 3, part 1. Ed. SADET, 41–139. Pretoria: Unisa Press.

Redfern, Paul. 2000. "Multinationals Have an 'Obligation' to the Poor." *East African,* 3 July, 5.

———. 2005. "Doing Business: East Africa Praised for Flexibility, Speed, and Legal Protection." *East African,* 19 September, 8.

Reed, T. V. 2005. *The Art of Protest: Culture and Activism from the Civil Rights Movement to the Streets of Seattle.* Minneapolis: University of Minnesota Press.

"Relations between AFGEM and Small-Scale Miners Sour." *The Thailand and Chanthaburi Gem Report,* February 2003. http://www.thaigem.com/press_chanthaburi _gemreport_february_2003.asp (accessed 15 June 2006).

Reno, William. 1997. "African Weak States and Commercial Alliances." *African Affairs* 96, no. 383: 165–86.

"Review of Mining Sector Incentives Steady." *This Day (Tanzania),* 9 May 2007.

Rioba, Ayub. 2006. "God Gave Us the Mine and Gave Investors the Brain." *Citizen (Tanzania),* 12 April, 12.

Robertson, Don. 1999. "Rail Corridor Opens Africa to Freight." *Business Times (South Africa),* 22 August.

Roe, Alan, and Mark Essex. 2009. *Mining in Tanzania—What Future Can We Expect? The Challenge of Mineral Wealth: Using Resource Endowments to Foster Sustainable Development.* London: International Council on Mining and Metals.

Roodt, Monty. 2008. "The Impact of Regional Integration Initiatives and Investment in a Southern African Cross-border Region: The Maputo Development Corridor." *African Sociological Review* 12, no. 1: 88–102.

Rose, Rob. 2005a. "Filling the Vacuum of Risk Ratings." *Business Day (South Africa),* 22 August.

———. 2005b. "Profitability Abounds in Africa." *Business Day (South Africa),* 14 April.

Ross, Alistair. 1977. "The Capricorn Africa Society and European Reactions to African Nationalism in Tanganyika, 1940–60." *African Affairs* 76, no. 305: 519–35.

"Rugby Makes a Popular Comeback." *Arusha Times,* 20 August 2006, 16.

Rumney, Reg, and Michelle Pingo. 2004. "Mapping South Africa's Trade and Investment in the Region." In *Stability, Poverty Reduction, and South African Trade and Investment in Southern Africa.* Ed. SARPN, 16–23. Pretoria: HSRC.

Rupiah, Martin. 1995. "Demobilisation and Integration: Operation Merger and the Zimbabwe National Defence Forces, 1980–1987." *African Security Review* 4, no. 2: 52–64.

Rutaiwa, Francis. 2006. "Indeed, Dubious Contracts Need Renegotiating." *Citizen (Tanzania),* 29 April, 9.

Rutter, Karen. 2004. "Africa Blue." *Good Taste.*

Rwambali, Faustine. 2000a. "Illovo Sugar Group May Pull Out of Tanzania." *East African,* 26 June, 1, 36.

———. 2000b. "NBC and Workers Union Row Ends." *East African,* 24 July, 4.

———. 2000c. "NBC to Declare Redundancies." *East African,* 22 May, 1, 2.

———. 2000d. "State Lays Off All 3,000 Kilombero Sugar Workers." *East African,* 3 July, 1, 3.

———. 2000e. "Tanzanian PS Summoned Over Bank Sale." *East African,* 6 March, 1.

Rwambali, Faustine, and Wilfred Edwin. 2005. "Kenya Airways Steals EABL's Thunder in Sixth Edition of Awards." *East African,* 21 November, 2, 3.

Rwambali, Faustine, James Mwakisyala, and Alfred Ngotezi. 2000. "SA Investors in Tanzania: Is the Honeymoon Over?" *East African,* 5 June, 1–2.

Sachedina, Hassan, and Pippa Trench. 2009. "Cattle and Crops, Tourism and Tanzanite: Poverty, Land-Use Change and Conservation in Simanjiro District, Tanzania." In *Staying Maasai? Livelihoods, Conservation, and Development in East African Rangelands.* Ed. Katherine Homewood, Patti Kristjanson, and Pippa Trench, 263–98. New York: Springer.

SADET (South African Democracy Education Trust). 2004. *The Road to Democracy in South Africa,* vol. 1, *1960–1970.* Pretoria: Unisa Press.

———. 2007. *The Road to Democracy in South Africa,* vol. 2, *1970–1980.* Pretoria: Unisa Press.

———. 2008. *The Road to Democracy in South Africa,* vol. 3, *International Solidarity.* Pretoria: Unisa Press.

Sahnoun, Mohamed. 2010. "Nyerere, the Organisation of African Unity and Liberation." In *Africa's Liberation: The Legacy of Nyerere.* Ed. Chambi Chachage and Annar Cassam, 61–65. Oxford: Fahamu Books.

"Samax Pathfinder." 1994. *The Mining Journal,* 11 November, 347.

Samson, Melanie. 2009. "(Sub)imperial South Africa? Reframing the Debate." *Review of African Political Economy,* no. 119, 93–103.

Sanchez, Diana. 2008. "Transnational Telecommunications Capital Expanding from South Africa into Africa: A Case Study of Ericsson." *African Sociological Review* 12, no. 1: 103–21.

Sapire, Hilary. 2009. "Liberation Movements, Exile, and International Solidarity: An Introduction." *Journal of Southern African Studies* 35, no. 2: 271–86.

Saramba, Peter. 2004. "Mererani Miners Establish Safety, Peace Committee." *Arusha Times,* 27 March.

Saunders, Mark. 2000. "Tanzania Breweries, Did You Get the Message?" *Arusha Times,* 1 July, 6.

Schleicher, Hans-Georg. 2008. "The German Democratic Republic and the South African Liberation Struggle." In *The Road to Democracy in South Africa,* vol. 3, *International Solidarity, Part 2.* Ed. SADET, 1069–1153. Pretoria: Unisa Press.

Schoofs, Mark. 2001. "Tanzanian Military Helped Company Skirt Drug Regulations to Test Virodene." *Wall Street Journal,* 19 July.

Schroeder, Richard. 2010. "Tanzanite as Conflict Gem: Certifying a Secure Commodity Chain in Tanzania." *Geoforum* 41, no. 1: 56–65.

Sebastian, Constantine. 2006a. "Tanesco Tariffs Shoot Up as Country Mull [*sic*] Alternatives." *Citizen (Tanzania),* 21 March, 6–7.

———. 2006b. "UK, Not South Africa, Is Major Investor in Tanzania." *Citizen (Tanzania),* 2 February, 11.

"Seeking Medical Services Overseas Is Unnecessary." *Citizen (Tanzania),* 31 January 2006, 8.

Sellströmm, Tor. 2008. "Sweden and the Nordic Countries: Official Solidarity." In *The Road to Democracy in South Africa,* vol. 3, *International Solidarity, Part 1.* Ed. SADET, 421–531. Pretoria: Unisa Press.

Semberya, Daniel. 2005. "TBL Performance Tremendous." *Business Times (Tanzania),* 11 November, 3.

———. 2006. "Link Up with Foreign Investors Ole'Naiko." *Business Times (Tanzania),* 5 May, 3.

Serote, Pethhu. 1992. "Solomon Mahlangu Freedom College: A Unique South African Educational Experience in Tanzania." *Transformation* 20: 47–60.

Sheffield, James. 1979. "Basic Education for the Rural Poor: The Tanzanian Case." *Journal of Developing Areas* 14, no. 1: 99–110.

Shekighenda, Lydia. 2007. "House Team Stunned by Mining Losses." *Guardian (Tanzania),* 7 February.

Shivji, Issa. 2006a. "Lawyers in Neoliberalism." *Pambazuka News,* 24 August, no. 266.

———. 2006b. *Let the People Speak: Tanzania Down the Road to Neoliberalism.* Dakar, Senegal: CODESRIA .

Shoprite Holdings. http://www.shopriteholdings.co.za/ (accessed 13 May 2009).

Shubin, Vladimir, and Marina Traikova. 2008. "There Is No Threat from the Eastern Bloc." In *The Road to Democracy in South Africa,* vol. 3, *International Solidarity, Part 2.* Ed. SADET, 985–1066. Pretoria: Unisa Press.

Sibanda, Eliakim. 2005. *The Zimbabwe African People's Union: A Political History of Insurgency in Southern Rhodesia.* Trenton, NJ: Africa World Press.

Simonson, Serena. 2000. "Signs of the Times." *Arusha Times,* 17 June, 7.

"Small Tanzanite Miners Should Be Appeased." 2006. *Daily News (Tanzania)*, 12 April, 3.

Smith, David. 2000. *Moral Geographies: Ethics in a World of Difference*. Edinburgh: Edinburgh University Press.

Smyth, Annie, and Adam Seftel, eds. 1998. *Tanzania: The Story of Julius Nyerere through the Pages of* Drum. Dar es Salaam//Kampala: Mkuki na Nyota Publishers//Fountain Publishers Ltd.

Soggot, Mungo, and David Macfarlane. 2001. "HIV/AIDS Fertiliser Hits the Fan." *Mail and Guardian (South Africa)*, 5 October.

South Africa.info. "2004 National Orders Awards." http://www.southafrica.info/about /people/nationalorders2004.htm (accessed 21 June 2010).

"South African Firms Seen as 'Imperialists.'" *International Herald Tribune*, 9 October 2006.

South African History Online. "PAC Camps." http://www.sahistory.org.za/pages /governence-projects/organisations/pac/origins.htm (accessed 2 June 2010).

"South Africa's Neighbors and the Refugee Problem." *Southern Africa* 2, 1969, no. 1: 2–3.

"South Africa's Xenophobic Attacks: We Are Very Sorry, Says Zuma." *Daily News (Tanzania)*, 5 September 2008.

Southall, Roger. 2007. "Ten Propositions about Black Economic Empowerment in South Africa." *Review of African Political Economy* 34, no. 111: 67–84.

Southall, Roger, and Henning Melber, eds. 2009. *A New Scramble for Africa? Imperialism, Investment, and Development*. Scottsville, South Africa: University of Kwazulu Natal Press.

Southern Africa Committee. "Southern Africa." http://southernafrica.homestead.com/ sacpubs.html (accessed 15 June 2010).

Southern African Regional Poverty Network (SARPN). 2004. *Stability, Poverty Reduction, and South African Trade and Investment in Southern Africa*. Pretoria: Human Sciences Research Council.

Spear, Thomas. 1997. *Mountain Farmers: Moral Economics of Land and Agricultural Development in Arusha and Meru*. Oxford: James Currey.

Stauffer, Thomas. 2002. "U.S. Clears Tanzanite of a Terrorist Connection." *Arizona Daily Star*, 10 February.

Steyn, Melissa. 2001. *"Whiteness Just Isn't What It Used to Be": White Identity in a Changing South Africa*. Albany: SUNY Press.

———. 2004. "Rehabilitating a Whiteness Disgraced: Afrikaner *White Talk* in Post-apartheid South Africa." *Communication Quarterly* 52, no. 2: 143–69.

———. 2007. "As the Postcolonial Moment Deepens: A Response to Green, Sonn, and Matsebula." *South African Journal of Psychology* 37, no. 3: 420–24.

Steyn, Melissa, and Daniel Conway. 2010. "Intersecting Whiteness, Interdisciplinary Debates." *Ethnicities* 10, no. 3: 283–91.

Steyn, Melissa, and Dan Foster. 2008. "Repertoires for Talking White: Resistant Whiteness in Post-apartheid South Africa." *Ethnic and Racial Studies* 31, no. 1: 25–51.

Stoddard, Ed. 2003. "SA Investors Banking on Africa." *South Africa Republic,* 30 December.

Superbrands East Africa. http://www.superbrandseastafrica.com/volume1/index.html
(accessed 1 December 2010).

"Swapo Congress in Tanzania." *Southern Africa* 3, 1970, no. 3: 18.

SWAPO Party. "Historical Background." http://www.swapoparty.org/swapo
_historical_background.html (accessed 22 June 2010).

Swarns, Rachel L. 2002. "Awe and Unease as South Africa Stretches Out." *New York
Times,* 17 February.

"Tanzania Breweries Set to Announce Double-Digit Growth." *Business Monitor International,* March, 2009.

"Tanzania: Rugby Team to Feature Seven Different Nationalities." *The Nation* [Nairobi],
19 June, 2008.

"Tanzania to Tiffany's." *Life Magazine,* 9 May, 1969.

"Tanzania Tops Improvement Index." *The Express (Tanzania),* 6 July 2000, 1.

Tanzanian Investment Centre. 2004. *Benchmarking Tanzania's Foreign Direct Investment.* Dar es Salaam: Tanzanian Investment Centre.

Tanzanite Foundation. 2005a. "Is She Really Who She Says She Is?" (advertisement).
Modern Jeweller. June: 74.

———. 2005b. "Tanzanite Foundation Is Formally Introduced to the Gemstone Industry." Press release. http://www.tanzanitefoundation.org/PressReleases
/TucsonTradePressRelease.pdf.2005 (accessed 10 December 2006).

———. 2006. "Tanzanite Foundation Champions an Ethical Gemstone." Press release.
http://www.tanzanitefoundation.org/PressReleases/Dec2006_TF_Release.pdf (accessed 20 June 2008).

———. "Tanzanite rarity." http://www.tanzanitefoundation.com/tanzanite_rarity.html
(accessed 28 August 2006).

Tanzanite One. 2004. "Tanzanite: A Rare Beginning." 2004 annual report. http://www
.tanzaniteone.com/ (accessed 21 October 2010).

———. "Tanzanite Foundation." http://www.tanzaniteone.com/tanzanite_tanzanite
_foundation.htm (accessed 22 October 2010).

———. "Tanzanite One history." http://www.tanzaniteone.com/ (accessed 23 September
2005).

"Tanzanite One Goes Public." *Colored Stone,* September/October, 2004, 17.

Tarimo, Judica. 2006. "NBC Workers Stage Nationwide Strike." *Guardian (Tanzania),* 16
June, 1, 3.

Tasseni, Mike. 2006a. "Angela Davis 1973 Visit and Forgotten Issues on the African
Revolution." *Citizen (Tanzania),* 15 February, 16.

———. 2006b. "Justinian Rweyemamu and Walter Rodney: Contrasting Images of the Early UDSM." *Citizen (Tanzania)*, 15 February, 12–13.

Taylor, P. Clagett. 1963. *The Political Development of Tanganyika.* Stanford: Stanford University Press.

Temba, Peter. 2006. "TPC Predicts Record Sugar Production This Year." *Daily News,* 28 June, 6.

Thiem, Claudia, and Morgan Robertson. 2010. "Behind Enemy Lines: Reflections on the Practice and Production of Oppositional Research." *Geoforum* 41, no. 1: 5–6.

Thörn, Hakan. 2006. *Anti-apartheid and the Emergence of a Global Civil Society.* New York: Palgrave Macmillan.

———. 2009. "The Meaning(s) of Solidarity: Narratives of Anti-apartheid Activism, 1946–1960." *Journal of Southern African Studies* 35, no. 2: 417–36.

Toroka, Eric. 2005. "Controversy over 'Tanzanite' Origins in SA." *Business Times (Tanzania),* 2 December, 2.

———. 2006. "Dar Exports to SA Increase 31-fold." *Business Times (Tanzania),* 19 May 12.

Tripp, Aili. 1997. *Changing the Rules: The Politics of Liberalization and the Urban Informal Economy in Tanzania.* Berkeley: University of California Press.

Tsing, Anna Lowenhaupt. 2005. *Friction: An Ethnography of Global Connection.* Princeton: Princeton University Press.

Turana, Johnstone ole. 2009. "EABL's Cup Not Exactly Frothing Over as Adetu Team Steps In." *East African,* 7 September.

Ubwani, Zephania. 2006. "Machine to Grade and Sort Gemstones Is Commissioned." *Citizen (Tanzania),* 2 February, 13.

Ulimwengu, Jenerali. 2009. "Julius Nyerere: This Adulation Has a Reason." *East African,* 19 October.

———. 2010. "Smuggled in by the Opposition, Nyerere Has Become the Ghost at CCM's Banquet." *East African,* 1 November.

"UN Votes to Seat Liberation Movements." *Southern Africa* 5, 1972, no. 10: 12.

UNCTAD (United Nations Conference on Trade and Development). 2005. *Case Study on Outward Foreign Direct Investment by South African Enterprises.* Geneva: United Nations Conference on Trade and Development.

———. 2009. "World Investment Reports, Inward FDI Flows by Host Region and Economy, 1970–2008." http://www.unctad.org/Templates/Page .asp?intItemID=3277&lang=1.

UNDP. "Human Development Report Statistics." http://hdrstats.undp.org/en/countries /country_fact_sheets/cty_fs_TZA.html (accessed 26 October 2010).

"Union Tells NBC to Pay $3.6m Terminal Dues or Face Strike." *East African,* 3 October 2005, 5.

United Republic of Tanzania. 2002. Population and Housing Census 2002. Dar es Sa-
    laam: National Bureau of Statistics, United Republic of Tanzania.
Uusihakala, Katja. 1999. "From Impulsive Adventure to Postcolonial Commitment:
    Making White Identity in Contemporary Kenya." European Journal of Cultural
    Studies 2, no. 1: 27–45.
Van Rooyen, Johann. 2000. The New Great Trek: The Story of South Africa's White Exo-
    dus. Pretoria: Unisa Press.
Vegter, Ivo. 2006. "The Million-Rand Tanzanite Myth." Maverick 1, no. 6: 54–60.
Venter, Irma. 2004. "Tanzanite Prices Surge in 2003." MiningWeekly, 13 February
Virodene Pharmaceutical Holdings. "Virodene Executive Brouchure [sic]." http://www
    .virodene.com/downloads/Virodene_Executive_Brouchure.pdf (accessed 15 July
    2009).
"Vodacom Tanzania Seeks 150 Million to Boost Capital." Reuters, 23 July 2009.
Wa Kuhenga, Makwaia. 2006a. "Net Group Solution's Exit Good Riddance." Daily News
    (Tanzania), 26 May, 4.
———. 2006b. "On Principles and the Search for Social Justice for All." Citizen (Tanza-
    nia), 10 April, 9.
Wa Lutengano, Lute. 2000. "Beer Is Our Lord Nelson at Trafalgar Square." Arusha
    Times, 17 June, 5.
———. 2008. "I Sadly Sing the Nkosi Sikelel." Arusha Times, 24 May.
Wa Nyoka, Kiangiosekazi. 2010. "Tanga and the SWAPO Politics." Daily News (Tanza-
    nia), 5 March.
Wahome, Muna. 2004. "NMG in Joint Magazines Venture with SA's Media24." East
    African, 2 August.
Waigama, Samwel. 2008. "Privatization Process and Asset Evaluation: A Case Study of
    Tanzania." Royal Institute of Technology, Stockholm, Sweden. PhD dissertation.
Wakabi, Wairagala. 2000. "SA Companies Targeting East African Markets." East Afri-
    can, 28 February, 21.
Weber-Fahr, Monica. 2002. Treasure or Trouble? Mining in Developing Countries. Wash-
    ington, DC: World Bank.
Weldon, Robert. 2001a. "Tanzanite Takes a Hit." Gems and Pearls/News, July.
———. 2001b. "Tanzanite/Terrorist Debate Continues." Professional Jeweler, 29 Novem-
    ber.
Weldon, Robert, and Peggy Jo Donahue. 2002. "Sept. 11 Suit Filed against Tanzanite
    Dealer and TAMIDA." Professional Jeweler, 15 February.
"Why ATC-SAA Deal Failed to Take Off from Start." Citizen (Tanzania), 18 March
    2006, 9.
Wilson, Jennifer. 2001. "Nedlac Acts as Campaign Midwife." Independent Online. http://
    www.iol.co.za/html/features/proudlysa/page4.php (accessed 13 May 2009).
"Workers at Tanzania's Largest Bank End Strike." 2002. Namibian, 27 June.

World Bank. "Doing Business: Measuring Business Regulations." Available at http://www.doingbusiness.org/ (accessed 27 November 2010).

"World Business Leaders Laud Africa Growth Prospects." 2005. *Business Times (Tanzania)*, 22 July, 1.

"Yes, NetGroup Must Go." 2006. *Daily News (Tanzania)*, 25 May, 4.

"Young Entrepreneurs Set Up Own Business Forum." 2006. *Financial Times (Tanzania)*, 3 May, 1, 3.

Zachariah, Tony. 2005. "Traveling and Visa Blues." *Sunday News (Tanzania)*, 18 September, 3.

Index

ix–x, 9, *16*, 26, 37, 38, 107, 122, 130, 134, 136, 137, 138, 141, 143–44, 145, 148, 149–51, 153, 157, 158, 160, 161; stereotypes of, ix, 45, 68, 114, 136, 139, 140, 141, 142, 159, 161, 164, 186n19; and the stigma of apartheid, x, xi, 7, 114–15, 118, 119, 122, 128, 134–36, 137, 138, 160, 161–62, 189n3; as whites, 7, 79, 97–98

southerners, 8, 68, 119, 140, 141

Southwest Africa. *See* Namibia

Southwest African People's Organization (SWAPO), 19, 170n14, 171nn30–31. *See also* Namibia

Soweto, 12, 169n11

Spurs, 46, 131

standards: product and service, 53, 60, 62, 122, 128; South Africa as source of improved, 67–68, 70–71, 75, 86, 147

Steers, 26

sugar industry: Kilombero Sugar Company, 57, 81, 146, 179n47, 182n29; South African investment in, 50, 179n47; Tanganyika Plantation Company, 57, 81, 146, 174n7, 179n47; worker resistance in, 57, 81

Sun City: anti-apartheid anthem, 10–11, 13, 38; as focal point of anti-apartheid cultural boycott, 10–11; resort complex in Bophuthatswana, 10, 168n3

symbolic violence, 64–66, 69, 73, 74–75, 86–87, 112, 144, 177n5, 182n32, 182n35

Tambo, Oliver, 19, 28, 36, 173n57. *See also* Order of the Companions of O. R. Tambo

Tanzania: and bilateral ties with post-apartheid South Africa, 1, 30, 31–38, 49, 84–85, 139, 162–63; under colonialism, 8; as development backwater, 47, 88, 122; foreign direct investment (FDI) in, 2,

6, 52, 179n3; as heavily indebted poor country (HIPC), 56; as leader of liberation movement diplomacy, 2, 19–24, 161, 172n34; as model of socially progressive race relations, 120, 128, 138; neoliberal economic reforms in, 2, 54–61; as opponent to apartheid, xi, 2 (*see also* liberation struggle); as preferred outlet for South African capital, 2, 50, 175n17; as sanctuary for political exiles and civilians displaced by liberation wars, 2, 11–13, 27, 28, 33, 40, 60, 161, 169nn10–11; as staging area for liberation movement armies, 2, 13–16, 18, 161, 170n20

Tanzania Breweries Limited (TBL). *See* brewing industry

Tanzania Electric Supply Company (TANESCO), 50, 73–75, 175n18; as site of resistance, 56, 58

Tanzania Investment Centre (TIC), 52, 55, 59, 76

Tanzania Zambia Mafuta (TAZAMA), 17, 18

Tanzania Zambia Railway Authority (TAZARA), *15*, 17–18, 171nn25–27. *See also* Freedom Railway

Tanzanian nationalism, 3–4, 24–28, 33–34, 65, 75–76, 161; economic nationalism, 63–64, 71, 72, 74–75, 78–80, 82–83, 93, 95, 98–101, 108, 166n14; and nation building, 8, 11, 24; and national identity, 30, 98; nationalist songs and chants, 25, 26, 27, 34, 36–37, 141, 172n47, 173n51; newspapers and, 26–27; and patriotic duty toward the liberation struggle, 11, 13, 41; and product branding, 64, 66–67, 71, 101–102, 112, 121; radio broadcasts and, 27

tanzanite: branding of, 101–102, 105–106, 183n39, 184n53; as conflict gem,

104–105, 183nn51–52; discovery and naming of, xiii, 98, 181n20; economic impact of, 98, 102–104, 112; geology of, 93, 98, 181n24; and mine violence, 106–12; mined by artisanal and small scale miners, 99, 100, 101, 103, 105–106, 107–108, 111–12, 184n5; as national symbol, 98, 101

Tanzanite Foundation, 101, 182n36; and Corporate Social Responsibility, 102–104, 105–106, 111, 112, 183n42, 183n46. *See also* tanzanite

Tanzanite One, 94, 99–103, 106–108, 111–12, 158, 174n7, 182n30, 188n1; and corporate tax payments, 95, 99, 100–101, 181n25. *See also* tanzanite

taxation, 44, 56, 68–69, 75, 86, 95, 99, 180n9, 180n16, 183n47, 184n52; off-shore havens from, 42, 69

television, 6, 50, 148, 151, 155, 182n29

Transafrica, 11, 169n5

tourism industry: hunting safaris, 68, 136, 177n12; photographic safaris, 6, 40, 50, 66, 67–68, 109, 112, 116, 121, 126, 152, 156, 174n1

ubaguzi, 34. *See also* apartheid; segregation

Uganda, *16*, 55, 56, 79, 81, 84, 172n37

ujamaa, 2, 110, 161. *See also* Arusha Declaration; socialism

United Kingdom (UK), 21, 52, 115, 134, 175n25. *See also* Britain

United Nations, 20, 23, 30

University of Dar es Salaam, 173n53; as bastion of liberation movements in exile, 28, 31, 34, 38, 141, 173n56, 177n15; and counter-revolutionary political elite, 24–25, 172n42

Van Zandt, Steven, 10, 169n4. *See also* Sun City

visas: travel restrictions after apartheid, 33, 34–35; travel restrictions during apartheid, 21

Vodacom, 26, 40, 50, 69, 88, 174n1, 177nn15–16

white Africans: future of, xv, 185n4; populations of, 6–7, 167nn16–17. *See also* Kenya; South Africa; Zimbabwe

white businesses, 5, 38, 140, 180n17

white privilege: challenges to, 7–8; under colonialism, 5, 8; in South Africa, 3; in Tanzania, 122–23, 146, 150, 157, 164

white spots, xi, 124–25, 129, 131, 138–139, 140, 157, 163; and expatriate social life in Tanzania, ix–x, 188n23; Msasani peninsula as, 46, 146, 185n14; rugby club as, 90–92. *See also* Arusha; Dar es Salaam

whiteness, 139, 143; in Africa, 6–9, 163, 167n19; as field of study, 6–7; good whites/bad whites discourse, 8–9, 68, 124, 128, 135–36, 141, 142–43, 156–57, 159; invisibility of, 7; in South Africa, 7, 115, 167n18

xenophobia, 35; against African foreigners in South Africa, 33, 35–37, 167n20, 173n61, 174n63; against white South Africans in Tanzania, 4, 141, 142, 161

Zaire, *15*, 23, 172n37. *See also* Congo (Democratic Republic of)

Zambia, 2, 11, 14, *15*, *16*, 17–19, 21–23, 33, 129, 166n14, 171n24, 171n29, 172n40, 173n62

Zimbabwe, 2, 11, 35, 115, 129, 165n3, 166n14, 173n62; liberation struggle in,